DATE DUE

**Three (3) week loans are subject
to recall after one week**

OCT 2 9 1993		
OCT − 6 1994		

The
Nature
of
Argument

THE
NATURE
OF
ARGUMENT

Karel Lambert · William Ulrich

Department of Philosophy
University of California, Irvine

Macmillan Publishing Co., Inc.
New York
Collier Macmillan Publishers
London

Copyright © 1980, Macmillan Publishing Co., Inc.

Printed in the United States of America

All rights reserved. No part of this book may be reproduced or
transmitted in any form or by any means, electronic or
mechanical, including photocopying, recording, or any
information storage and retrieval system, without permission in
writing from the Publisher.

Macmillan Publishing Co., Inc.
866 Third Avenue, New York, New York 10022

Collier Macmillan Canada, Ltd.

Library of Congress Cataloging in Publication Data

Lambert, Karel (date)
The nature of argument.

Includes index.
1. Reasoning.   I. Ulrich, William, joint author.
II. Title.
BC177.L27   160   79-600
ISBN 0-02-367280-3

Printing: 1 2 3 4 5 6 7 8   Year: 0 1 2 3 4 5 6

To
Mrs. Justine Lambert
Mrs. Ruth Ulrich

"Voters are basically lazy, basically uninterested in making an *effort* to understand what we're talking about. . . ," Gavin wrote. "Reason requires a high degree of discipline, of concentration; impression is easier. Reason pushes the viewer back, it assaults him, it demands that he agree or disagree; impression can envelop him, invite him in, without making an intellectual demand. . . . When we argue with him we demand that he make the effort of replying. We seek to engage his intellect, and for most people this is the most difficult work of all. The emotions are more easily roused, closer to the surface, more malleable. . . ."

Joe McGinnis, *The Selling of the President* (New York: Trident Press, 1968)

Preface

Logic is used both to *evaluate* arguments and to *clarify* them. In most contemporary textbooks the former purpose dominates. Hardly more than lip service is paid to the goal of clarification. For example, one normally finds a great deal of attention paid to the development of formal techniques for assessing arguments, but only the most cursory consideration is given to the development of an orderly method for spotting arguments in the first place. Even less attention is given to the explanation of many claims underlying the evaluation procedures. For example, the formal system used to express and evaluate arguments in colloquial discourse is often called "a language," but the sense in which this is so is seldom explained. Consider another example. Logic, in most texts, is characterized as the study of reasoning or arguments— or something of that order. But the connection between valid arguments and legitimate grounds for belief usually goes unexplained and often even unstated. The student, in other words, is assumed already to understand the motivation underlying logic, or it is hoped that such understanding will develop in an osmotic way during the course of learning the evaluation procedures.

We think the emphasis on the goal of evaluation at the expense of clarification has three bad pedagogical consequences. First, and foremost, is the acquisition of procedures and techniques that have only the most limited use, if any use at all, in the future endeavors of most students. Second, the student is thereby led to regard logic as a kind of game if he sees any clear motivation behind it at all, and he misses the truly valuable contribution of logic to the grounding of beliefs and action. Third, as we and our colleagues at the University of California, Irvine, have discovered over the years, even philosophy majors shunted through the traditional program in logic typically have only the most confused perception of what an argument is and how it functions. Nor, of course, do they have any clear idea of the clarificatory benefits claimed to issue from the acquisition of formal skills.

The present text, arising from deep dissatisfaction with traditional courses, seeks to redress this imbalance. Our goal is to concentrate on the most important ideas and applications of logic, thereby providing the student with a genuinely helpful understanding of everyday arguments, and hence an enduring appreciation of the serious role of logic. There are three chapters and two appendices. Chapter 1 is devoted to discussion of some of the basic ideas of logic, for example, the character of arguments, their importance, and some of their most important properties and uses. This discussion is explicitly motivated by consideration of the justification of belief by (deductive) inference. It is explained, for example, how arguments can record inferences and how one's ability to justify a belief by (deductive) inference relates to various properties of the recording argument. Chapter 2, the principal chapter of the book, is concerned with the identification and clarification of arguments. We introduce (for the first time, as far as we know) a step-by-step procedure for identifying an argument in everyday discourse, extracting it, and then para-phrasing it into the formal idiom. To *identify* an argument is to extract it from its colloquial context and rephrase it in a way that makes clear the separation of premises (whether explicit or suppressed) from conclusion (explicit or suppressed) and removes irrelevant material. We call this process paraphrase into "gross standard form." Thus, to identify an argument is to paraphrase it into gross standard form. Our discussion of how to use the "contextual features" of an argument's colloquial phrasing to accomplish paraphrase into gross standard form, while not pretending to be exhaustive, gives stu-dents a firm grasp of relevant phenomena of ordinary language upon which the profitable application of formal techniques depends. To *clarify* an argu-ment is to paraphrase it from gross standard form into the formal idiom. Unlike most texts, the present book's treatment of this process is painstaking because we feel that a thorough understanding of paraphrase is essential for understanding the nature and purpose of a formal language and the related notions of logical form and logical validity. This understanding, in turn, is required for understanding what is really involved in evaluation. Moreover, practical skill in paraphrasing is crucial for using logic to clarify the logical structure of arguments confronted outside the artificial environment of the classroom.

In Chapter 3 our account of paraphrase is used to motivate a truth defini-tion for the formal language. Our main evaluation procedure, which is based on this truth definition, is informal and almost entirely semantical in charac-ter. The student is not required to memorize formulas or rules of proof; there are none. In this respect, the book is quite nonmathematical. On the other hand, the semantical material is current and rigorous. For those who wish to use mechanical evaluation procedures, however, Appendix II provides one that may be substituted for our preferred method.

The approach in this text is well suited to an elementary course drawing its enrollment from the entire college spectrum, from the sciences, premedicine and prelaw programs as well as the humanities, for example, and not merely from philosophy and its cognate areas. Our choice and treatment of topics reflect our belief that it is much more important to provide the student with an understanding of what an argument is, how to spot one and clarify it and, to some extent, evaluate it using informal reasoning than it is to overload him with a vast array of evaluation techniques of little future use. We have found during numerous trials that our approach is highly successful in accomplishing our two major goals: to provide nonphilosophy majors with some widely applicable and useful clarificational procedures and an equally useful informal evaluation method, and to provide philosophy majors with fundamental background tools to be used in further study in philosophy. To accomplish these goals, we have chosen to turn our attention away from other topics we believe to be less crucial. Such topics include the construction of arguments, such as derivations or proofs, informal fallacies, and induction. For example, we have relegated our brief discussion of induction to Appendix I. In spite of this, much of what we say about the identification and clarification of deductive arguments applies equally well to inductive arguments. Second, our discussion of the so-called "informal fallacies" is very brief because we feel, for reasons given in Chapter 1, Section 3, that the study of informal fallacies is of highly questionable utility. Finally, we have omitted natural deduction altogether. Our reasons for this decision are as follows: First, we have found that our main goals can be achieved without devoting the requisite large amount of time to natural deduction. Second, many other books cover this area; there is no need for yet another. Finally, and most important, we feel that proof theory in general is not the *best* topic for a first course in logic. This is because students already possess considerable reasoning skills when they come into a course. They do not need to master elaborate methods of proof to reason; often such systems succeed only in confusing them and undermining the native reasoning ability they brought with them into the course. On the other hand, they know very little about the identification and clarification of arguments. By relying on their native reasoning ability, and concentrating instead on the more difficult and ultimately more important topics of identification and clarification, we have found our elementary courses to be more successful in the long run.

Earlier versions of the present text have been used for five years by us, our departmental colleagues, visiting colleagues at the University of California, Irvine, and colleagues at other colleges and universities. The present text, then, is the outcome of much experience and discussion. We have been gratified by the response of students at our university, who continue to enroll in the elementary logic course in large numbers, and by the responses of colleagues, many of whom were initially quite sceptical of our approach. They have sustained us in our belief that our admittedly nonmainstream approach is the best one, and well worth the effort to develop it at the elementary level.

Several specific acknowledgments are in order. We are grateful to Rudolf Carnap's heirs for permission to reprint the excerpt—the present Prescript—from Professor Rudolf Carnap's informal address given at Harvard University in 1936. To Professor Kit Fine, Ms. Gael Janofsky, and M. Pabst Battin we are indebted for both stylistic and substantive textual suggestions. To Professors Robert L. Martin, Betty Safford, and Edgar Morscher, all of whom used the present text in draft, we are indebted for many important suggestions and for their encouragement. But our greatest obligation is to Professor Charles Young, whose enthusiasm, numerous substantive suggestions, and critical support for our pedagogical point of view has sustained us during the past five years; to him, for his kind and thoroughly generous supply of time, effort, and good ideas, we are extremely grateful.

K. L.
W. U.

Contents

CHAPTER
3

APPENDIX
I

APPENDIX
II

APPENDIX
III

PRESCRIPT
"Logic" by Rudolf Carnap

When we reflect upon the behavior of men, whether of individuals or of groups, we see that they are dominated more by their passions than by their reason. Especially when surveying contemporary society, one could almost despair of the role of logic as a factor determining human behavior. Nevertheless, to see clearly on the matter, it is essential that we obtain an adequate conception of the province of logic. By doing so we will be able to distinguish between thinking which is irrational or illogical and thinking which is reasonable or logical, and thus win a richer understanding of the ways in which logical and illogical thought may influence the activities of men.

The cardinal point about which we must become clear is that logic is not concerned with human behavior in the same sense that physiology, psychology, and social sciences are concerned with it. These sciences formulate laws or universal statements which have as their subject matter human activities as processes in time. Logic, on the contrary, is concerned with *relations* between factual sentences (or thoughts). If logic ever discusses the truth of factual sentences it does so only *conditionally*, somewhat as follows: *if* such-and-such a sentence is true, *then* such-and-such another sentence is true. Logic itself does not decide whether the first sentence *is* true, but surrenders that question to one or the other of the empirical sciences. Consequently, since the rules of logic refer simply to various *relations* between sentences (or thoughts), we can distinguish between thinking which is in accordance with these rules and thinking which violates them. The former we shall call *logical thinking*, the latter *illogical*. On the other hand, although logic itself is not concerned with facts, a process of thought, whether it be logical or illogical, is an actual fact. And it is a question of greatest importance, both for the individual and for society, whether our thinking is logical or not.

Contemporary logical theory is too vast and technical to be summarized here. It is, however, possible to view at least a part of this theory as defining the conditions of logical thought. And in what follows, I wish to consider [some] requirements which thinking must satisfy in order to be logical or reasonable. . . .

1. The *condition of clarity* may be formulated as follows. We must become clear as to what is the subject of our talking and thinking. Although this requirement may seem trivial, in practice it is often not observed. The most serious and frequent breaches of this rule occur whenever sentences are uttered which are taken to assert something, although in fact nothing is asserted, whether truly or falsely. Such self-deceptions have their source, for the most part, in the structure of our common-day language. For our common language is well adapted for obtaining the gross agreements necessary in practical affairs; but when employed in theoretical pursuits to formulate and communicate knowledge, it is very often not merely inadequate but even seriously misleading.

A little reflection will therefore show that we must distinguish between two main functions which expressions may have. Certain expressions in our language assert something, and are therefore either true or false. Such expressions exercise a *cognitive function* and have a cognitive meaning. On the other hand, certain expressions express the emotions, fancies, images, or wishes of the speaker, and under proper conditions evoke emotions, wishes, or resolutions in the hearer. Such expressions will be said to exercise an *expressive function,* and it is possible to subdivide them further into expressions with pictorial, emotional, and volitional functions. An expression may exercise these different expressive functions simultaneously; and it often is the case that a sentence with cognitive meaning may also possess one or more of the expressive functions. It is of prime importance to note that not all expressions of our language possess a cognitive meaning, so that we must distinguish between those which do and those whose function is solely expressive.

This distinction is frequently concealed by the fact that sentences with solely expressive functions sometimes have the grammatical form of statements which are either true or false. Hence we are led to believe, quite mistakenly, that such sentences do have cognitive meaning. When a lyric poet sings of the melancholy forest or the friendly gleam of moonlight, his utterances take the form of factual statements. However, everyone realizes that the poem is not to be taken as a factual description of the forest or the moon; for it is tacitly understood that the lyric poem is simply expressive of a mood, exactly as music is. . . .

The consequences of the indicated confusion are much more serious when it occurs in discussions concerning individual or political conduct. When I say to some one "Come here!" it is evident that my words exercise a volitional function, and express my desire in order to evoke a certain response in my hearer. My utterance is not an assertion, and any debate about its truth or falsity would clearly be irrelevant. If a theoretical discussion were to arise concerning it, the debate would be significant only if it were to deal with such questions as whether the person addressed will obey me or what the consequences of his decision will be.

But although the matter is obvious for this simple case, the situation is not so readily apprehended when sentences expressing a command have the grammatical form of assertions. Frequent illustrations of this are found in politics, with serious practical consequences. For example, suppose that the following creed is promulgated in a certain country: "There is only one race of superior men, say the race of Hottentots, and this race alone is worthy of ruling other races. Members of these other races are inferior, so that all civil rights are to be denied them so long as they inhabit the country." This pronouncement certainly has the appearance of an assertion. Some of those who dissent from it, taking the grammatical form at face value, may regard it as a genuine assertion and may therefore propound a doctrine in opposition to it. In fact, however, the pronouncement has no cognitive meaning and exercises merely a volitional function. The true nature of the doctrine (or better, pseudo-doctrine) is made clear if we state the pronouncement in the imperative form, to reveal its exclusively volitional function. It then reads as follows: "Members of the race of Hottentots! Unite and battle to dominate the other races! And you, members of other races! Submit to the yoke or fly from this land!" It is now obvious that the political creed is a command, concerning which it is not significant to raise questions of truth or falsity. It is, of course, true that it is possible to raise cognitively significant issues in connection with such a command. But these will involve questions such as whether and to what degree the command will be executed, and what the consequences will be of obeying it or not. It is also possible to debate the factual statements about races, which are usually connected with the command; these are clearly scientific issues belonging to anthropology, and must be critically investigated by specialists in this field. It is, however, of great practical importance for understanding the effective appeal of political war-cries like the above to note that they take the form of misleading pseudo-assertions. This is to be explained by the fact that many men respond less readily to what are obviously commands than to such assertions or pseudo-assertions, especially when the latter are accompanied by powerful emotional appeals.

2. The *condition of consistency*, that our ideas agree with one another, is the second requirement for logical thinking. Logic is not competent to decide whether a judgment of ours having factual content is either true or false.

However, logic is competent to determine whether our assertions or supposi-
tions are consistent with one another. The task of logic may also be viewed as
making evident the consequences of a given assumption, irrespective of its
truth or falsity. For logic as the study of valid consequences is identical with
logic as the inquiry into conditions of consistency, and the insight that one
sentence follows from another is the same as the insight that the contradictory
of the first is incompatible with the other. If, for example, I assume that iron
does not float on water and that my latch-key is made of iron, the supposition
that my latch-key will float on water is incompatible with my original assumptions. In order to avoid contradicting my own premises, I must therefore
assume that my key will sink. Logic itself does not affirm this last assumption;
it simply renders explicit what is implicitly contained in the two premises
previously assumed.

It will be clear, therefore, that the requirements of logic are much weaker
than those of the empirical sciences. The latter demand of us that we accept
certain assertions and reject others. Logic, however, does not prescribe what
factual assertions we are to accept or reject; it simply demands that we do
not at the same time accept and also reject an assertion. This demand is
made in our own name, so to speak, by recalling to us our own intent and
pointing out that to accept a given assertion would contravene some resolutions previously made. . . .

These points may become clearer in the context of a more concrete illustration. In order to build a bridge, the engineer must take into account certain
laws of nature, partly formulated as general laws of mechanics and partly as
specific laws of the materials to be employed. With the help of these laws he
can calculate that a bridge with a specified structure is capable of carrying
such-and-such a load. Now these laws are supplied to the engineer by the
empirical sciences, in particular by physics. Mathematics and logic, on the
other hand, enable him to deduce the strength of the bridge from the physical
laws and the initial data concerning the details of its structure. The logico-
mathematical instrument is thus essential for every type of rational, planned
activity. This is true not only in constructing machines but also in organizing
human associations and activities, for instance, in the field of economics for
planning both individual enterprises and large-scale social undertakings.
Without this instrument, it is clear that civilization as we know it today
would not be possible. . . .

The conditions which logic sets for rational thinking [some of] which we
have now surveyed, are not to be understood as possessing some absolute
metaphysical validity or as resting on the will of God. The requirements made
by logic are based on the simple fact that unless they are satisfied, thought
and knowledge cannot perform their function as instruments for arriving at
successful decisions in practical matters. Now since our actual thinking frequently violates the requirements of logic, it follows that illogical thought is

an important factor in determining human behavior. Indeed, certain anti-rationalistic tendencies of our day preach the view that reason should be esteemed less, and that men ought to assign a smaller role to rational thought in practical life. Furthermore, the confusions in practice and doctrine which are to be found in society, science, and art are asserted to be consequences of overvaluating the intellect. In fact, however, it is not of much importance whether men think much or little; it is of far greater consequence, *if* they think at all, whether their thinking is logical or not. And advocates of irrationalism are most successful in strengthening men in their biases and prejudices, confirming mankind in its errors instead of disciplining men's thoughts to aim at objectivity.

Logic must often play the role of the critic, especially in our own day. Its task is to serve as a spiritual hygiene, cautioning men against the disease of intellectual confusion. It has the ungrateful duty, whenever it finds symptoms of this disease, to pronounce the unwelcome diagnosis. But in what manner, it may be asked, shall we conduct the therapeutic treatment? The logician by himself has no remedy to offer, and must turn to psychologists and social scientists for aid; for it is obvious that the mere discovery and acknowledgment of errors have no significant influence upon the thoughts and actions of men. Logic can point out the anomalies, but it is psychology which must find curative methods for them.

Logicians sometimes imagine that they can effect practical changes by their critical analyses; [but this view] is based on our desires, in utter disregard of facts clear to every observer of individual and social behavior. The laws of human conduct in observing and violating the requirements of logical thinking must be discovered by psychology and the social sciences. These are the disciplines which must locate the irrational sources of both rational and illogical thought. This theoretical problem once solved, it then becomes the practical task of education, conceived in the broadest sense, to apply suitable methods for healing the indicated anomalous behavior. Indeed, a far better aim of education and a more effective program for it is the establishment of prophylactic methods for eliminating the source of illogical types of thought. Logic itself, however, must remain content with the more modest task of pointing them out.

CHAPTER

1

Arguments—What They Are, Why They Are Important, and How They Are Used

1.
ARGUMENTS AND ARGUMENT DESCRIPTIONS

We begin with an example.

(1) *We'd better not invite McMurraghue to the party; he'll try to start an argument with Austin Smith-Jones and that will ruin the entire evening.*

The word 'argument' here refers to a dispute anticipated between two people who are presumed not to be on the best of terms. This sense of the word 'argument' is to be contrasted with that occurring in the following sentences:

(2) *The Surgeon General's argument for the conclusion that smoking causes cancer is based on careful statistical research.*
(3) *In* The Origin of Species, *Darwin's argument involved the claim that the variety of life forms could be explained by his principle of natural selection.*
(4) *The most frequently heard argument in favor of amnesty for war resisters seems to presuppose that their actions were morally permissible because they did what they thought was right.*

> *Some opponents of amnesty challenge this presupposition by arguing that what the resisters* thought *is irrelevant to the question of whether or not their actions were, in fact, morally permissible.*

In (2) to (4) the word 'argument' refers not to a type of social behavior, as in (1), but to something that can represent reasoning processes. An example of the relevant sort of reasoning process involves Roscoe Frostbite, the noted violinist, explorer, and pharmacologist, who happens to believe that any cause of cancer is a public health menace. Having heard about the Surgeon General's report on smoking, he has also come to believe that smoking causes cancer. Now, he may reason from these two beliefs to the conclusion that smoking is a public health menace. A colloquial way of describing Roscoe's reasoning is to say that he *argued* from what he originally believed to a new belief. In this sense of the word 'argue', no behavior of the sort described by the phrase "starting an argument" is suggested. It may well be that no one would disagree with Roscoe about this matter; indeed, he need not even have told anyone about his bit of reasoning.

In this book we shall use the word 'argument' in the second of the senses described above: that is, to designate something that can represent reasoning processes. Roscoe's argument, for example, consists of the premises from which he argued (in this case, the original beliefs that his new belief was "premised upon") and the conclusion he drew from these premises. In the most central case, the conclusion of an argument is what one attempts to establish by one's reasoning, and whatever one cites in support of the conclusion are the premises.

If a piece of reasoning is intended to *establish* the conclusion, given the truth of the premises, then whether or not it succeeds in doing so, it is said to be *deductive reasoning* and the argument that represents this reasoning is a *deductive argument*. Further, for ease of exposition we shall stipulate that any argument that does in fact establish the truth of its conclusion, given the truth of the premises, is deductive. Roscoe's reasoning was deductive because he took his conclusion to be decisively established by the truth of his premises. If a piece of reasoning is not deductive, but nevertheless is intended to provide some evidence for the conclusion, then it is said to be *inductive reasoning,* and the argument that represents it is an *inductive argument*. In this book we shall be concerned only with deductive arguments. A more extensive discussion of the difference between deduction and induction is found in Appendix I.

Arguments may or may not be expressed in language, written or spoken. Here is a written expression of Roscoe's argument:

A (1) *Anything that causes cancer is a public health menace.*
(2) *Smoking causes cancer.*
(3) *Therefore, smoking is a public health menace.*

Sentences (1) and (2) express the premises of his argument and (3) expresses the conclusion. Roscoe's coming to believe the conclusion [what (3) expresses] on the basis of the premises [what (1) and (2) express] is the result of his having *inferred* the conclusion from the premises. This mental transition is marked in the written expression of the argument by the word 'therefore' before the sentence expressing the conclusion. In this case, Roscoe's inference took him from two previously held beliefs to a new belief, and indeed that is the most common type of inference, but, as we shall see in Section 6, not all inferences result in new beliefs.

The three sentences listed in the preceding paragraph constitute one of *many* possible written expressions of Roscoe's argument, but written expressions of arguments must not be confused with arguments themselves. The expression of an argument is a linguistic entity; it consists of marks on a piece of paper or sound waves in the air. An argument is not a linguistic entity. The distinction between arguments and their expressions is already implicit in our discussion so far, for we said that Roscoe may have argued that smoking is a public health menace even if he did not say anything or write anything down. In such a case there would have been an argument, but it would not have had any written or spoken expression.

To see more clearly the distinction between arguments and their written expressions consider, first, the obvious distinction between a name and what it designates. As an example, no one would confuse the name 'Paris' with the city of Paris. 'Paris' is composed of five letters, whereas Paris is composed of buildings, streets, and parks. Paris is a city, but 'Paris' is not. Now consider the sentence 'Paris is a city.' Just as one wants to avoid confusing the linguistic entity, 'Paris' with the nonlinguistic entity, Paris, so should one avoid confusing the *sentence* 'Paris is a city' with what this sentence expresses. What a declarative sentence expresses is an abstract thing called a *proposition*. That propositions are abstract can be seen from the following consideration. The sentences

(1) Paris is a city.
(2) Paris est une ville.

are quite different. Someone who spoke only English would be able to understand the first, but not the second, whereas the opposite would be true of a French speaker. Nevertheless, both persons can perfectly well believe *that* Paris is a city even though the French speaker could not express his belief in English. In such a case it is correct to say that the two people have the same belief because *what* they both believe is the same—they both believe the common proposition expressed by (1) and (2). This proposition may be thought of as the common "content" of the French and English sentences.

Arguments consist of propositions. For example, argument **A** consists of the propositions expressed by the premise sentences, (1) and (2), and the conclusion sentence, (3). It is precisely because arguments are composed of propositions rather than sentences that it is possible for one and the same argument to have many different written expressions. Roscoe's argument, for example, could easily be expressed in French. In that case the English and French expressions would be quite different—would involve entirely different sentences—but the arguments would be the same. For this reason, a French speaker may properly be said to give the *same* argument as Roscoe, provided that he inferred the same conclusion from the same premises as Roscoe.

The various written expressions of an argument, whether they belong to different languages or are different formulations within the same language, can be employed to talk about the argument itself just because the sentences comprising the written expressions express the propositions comprising the argument. A qualification is in order here: Some written expressions of arguments are more *revealing* than others. This is because, as we shall see in Chapter 2, it is possible for written expressions of arguments to be "incomplete," that is, one or more sentences may be left out, or be "inflated," that is' they may contain some irrelevant sentences. If a written expression of an argument contains *exactly* those sentences expressing its premises and conclusion, we shall say that it is an *argument description*. The written expression of Roscoe's argument presented earlier is an example of an argument description.

Arguments and their descriptions are related in two important ways. First, because the sentences comprising an argument description express exactly those propositions that comprise the argument, the description tells us which propositions belong to the argument. Second, the argument description imposes a certain structure on the argument it expresses. An argument is not *merely* a collection of propositions. Just as the same collection of bricks can be used to make entirely different buildings if they are put together in different patterns, so can different arguments be composed of the same propositions if those propositions are related to one another in different ways. Thus, when we think of an argument as a collection of propositions, it is to be understood that a certain structure is present. We shall be occupied with the structure of arguments in great detail below, but one structural feature should be mentioned immediately. In *any* argument, one of the constituent propositions is the conclusion and all the others are the premises. So, employing the spatial metaphor suggested by argument descriptions, an argument is to be thought of as a *pattern* of propositions mirroring the pattern of sentences in its description such that, at the very *least*, the premises are distinguished from the conclusion. The premises and conclusion may have internal structure or they may themselves be composed of more simple propositions. So the pattern in question may be rather intricate.

Consider the following argument description:

B (1) *Anything that causes cancer is a public health menace.*
(2) *Smoking is a public health menace.*
(3) *Therefore, smoking causes cancer.*

Arguments **A** and **B** are different, although they contain the same propositions, because they have different structures, as may readily be discerned by looking at their argument descriptions. In particular, the proposition expressed by (2) is a premise of **B,** whereas it is the conclusion of **A**. The premises and conclusions of **A** and **B** are different, so they have different structures and therefore are different arguments. A person who reasoned to the conclusion of **A** from its premises would be reasoning in a different way from a person who reasoned to the conclusion **B** from its premises. (Intuitively, a person who reasoned in the first way would be reasoning correctly, whereas someone who reasoned in the second way would not. Since arguments are meant to represent reasoning processes, different arguments must represent these different reasoning processes.)

The *order* in which the premise sentences occur in an argument description does not impose any structure on the corresponding argument. For example, argument **A** is the very same argument as

A' (1) *Smoking causes cancer.*
(2) *Anything that causes cancer is a public health menace.*
(3) *Therefore, smoking is a public health menace.*

A and **A'** are the same arguments because they have the same premises and the same conclusion.

Propositions, as well as arguments, have structure. One of our goals in Chapter 2 will be to expose the internal structure of the premises and conclusions of arguments, for, as we shall see in Section 2 of the present chapter, the most important property of arguments depends upon the internal structure of the premises and conclusion.

We have chosen arguments instead of disputes for study because we are not interested in debating techniques but in the development of a sensitivity for detecting, and to some degree evaluating, some of the connections between a person's beliefs and his reasons for holding them. Arguments in our sense are intimately associated with rationality. One of the main differences between rational and irrational people is the degree of their concern with providing good arguments for their beliefs and demanding good arguments from those who seek to persuade them to adopt new beliefs or give up old ones. An irrational person may not care to justify his beliefs or may be unable to recognize the difference between good and bad arguments. Of course, there is more to rationality than being concerned with good arguments to support one's beliefs. Rationality itself is a matter of degree—no one is perfectly rational. Nevertheless, if one develops a sensitivity for what makes arguments good or bad, he can learn to reason correctly much more of the time.

1.1 Exercises

In answering the following questions, you may find it helpful to refer to the summary of concepts and definitions introduced in this chapter (p. 45). Starred exercises are answered in Appendix III.

1. Briefly explain the difference between deductive reasoning and inductive reasoning.
2. Explain the difference between arguments (in the sense of that word used in the book) and disputes. Make use of sentences (1) to (4) on p. 3 in your explanation. Are arguments sometimes related to disputes? If so, how?
★3. Suppose that a French speaker were heard to say "Le monde est rond" and an English speaker were heard to say "The world is round." Is the fact that they uttered sentences in different languages good evidence that French propositions are different from English ones? That French beliefs are different from English ones?
4. Exactly what is an argument? What is the difference between an argument and its written expressions? What is an argument description? How can two different argument descriptions express the same argument? Of the argument descriptions below, which ones express the same argument? Defend your answers. (Do not be concerned with the question of which, if any, of the following are *good* arguments.)

a. (1) All philosophers are wise.   b. (1) Socrates is a philosopher.
   (2) Socrates is wise.   (2) Socrates is wise.
   (3) Therefore, Socrates is a   (3) Therefore, all philosophers
       philosopher.   are wise.

c. (1) Socrates is wise.
   (2) All philosophers are wise.
   (3) Therefore, Socrates is a philosopher.

d. (1) Socrates is wise.
   (2) Socrates is a philosopher.
   (3) Therefore, all philosophers are wise.

e. (1) All philosophers are wise.
   (2) Socrates is a philosopher.
   (3) Therefore, Socrates is wise.

f. (1) Socrates is a philosopher.
   (2) All philosophers are wise.
   (3) Therefore, Socrates is wise.

5. Suppose Jones argued from the propositions that he already believes that Socrates is a philosopher and that all philosophers are wise to a new proposition that Socrates is wise. Which of the argument descriptions in Exercise 4 express Jones's argument? What are the premises and conclusion of his argument?

Difficult

6. Do the members of the following pairs of sentences express the same proposition or different ones? Why? Defend your answer.
  ★a. If Tom is tall, then Dick is short.
  ★b. If Dick is short, then Tom is tall.
   c. Tom is a bachelor.
   d. Tom is an unmarried adult male.

2.
TWO IMPORTANT PROPERTIES OF ARGUMENTS: VALIDITY AND SOUNDNESS

Although one sometimes hears utterances such as "That's a valid proposal" or "His reasons for refusing to turn over the requested documents are really quite invalid," it would be unwise to use these terms so loosely here. Strictly speaking, validity is a property of arguments, not of single propositions or collections of propositions that are not arguments. Similarly, one sometimes hears utterances such as "His argument was entirely false; it simply does not follow from the fact that astronauts go to the moon that they are well traveled." Strictly speaking, truth and falsity are not properties of arguments; rather they are properties of propositions alone. It is, however, both useful and legitimate to extend the terms 'valid (invalid)' and 'true (false)' to apply to argument descriptions and sentences, respectively. We may call an argument description valid (invalid) just in case the argument expressed is valid (invalid), and a sentence may be said to be true (false) just in case the proposition it expresses is true (false).

Intuitively, a valid argument is one that represents correct deductive reasoning. If a person were to infer the conclusion of a deductive argument from its premises, then his inference would be *correct* just in case that argument is *valid*. We shall explore the connections among arguments, inferences, and beliefs in the next section. Here we shall undertake to explain an important fact about validity. In Section 1 it was remarked that argument descriptions reveal two things about the arguments they express: They show what propositions belong to the argument, and then they show which of these comprise the premises and which the conclusion. The distinction between premise and conclusion is a structural feature of an argument imposed automatically by the separation of premise and conclusion sentences in its argument description. An additional structural feature imposed upon arguments by the sentence structure of their descriptions is the internal structure of the premises and conclusion, that is, the relations among the propositions that comprise the (perhaps complex) premises and conclusion of the argument. This internal structure is called the *logical form* of the argument in question. As we shall shortly see, *logical validity* and *logical invalidity* are features of arguments that depend only upon their logical form. Consequently, whether or not an argument is logically valid is independent of what its constituent propositions actually are. The particular propositions comprising an argument give it its (perhaps

10

unique) content, but it is the way in which these propositions are related that determines its logical validity or invalidity. Logical validity or invalidity, then, are purely *formal* properties of arguments; they depend on the form of an argument rather than on its content. The logical form of an argument is *discerned* by examining the structure of its written description, in a manner to be described next.

Consider, first, the following argument descriptions:

A (1) *Boston is a city and Boston is in the United States.*
    (2) *Therefore, Boston is in the United States.*

B (1) *Penang is a city and Penang is in Sri Lanka.*
    (2) *Therefore, Penang is in Sri Lanka.*

C (1) *Boston is a city or Boston is in the United States.*
    (2) *Therefore, Boston is in the United States.*

D (1) *Penang is a city or Penang is in Sri Lanka.*
    (2) *Therefore, Penang is in Sri Lanka.*

Although they are extremely simple, it is intuitively obvious that the arguments expressed by **A** and **B** represent correct reasoning, whereas those expressed by **C** and **D** do not. If one inferred the conclusion of **A**[1] from its premise, he would be reasoning correctly because it is not possible for his inference to take him from a true premise to a false conclusion. It could not be the case *both* that Boston is a city *and* Boston is in the United States without its also being the case that Boston is in the United States. In point of fact, the premise of **A** is true, so its conclusion is also true.

Although both its premise and conclusion are false, argument **B** also represents correct reasoning. Someone who believed, for whatever reason, that Penang is a city and that it is in Sri Lanka, would be making two errors about geography, but there is a distinction between such errors of *fact* and errors of *reasoning*. Even though someone who believed the premise of **B** would be misinformed about Asian geography, he could not be blamed for his reasoning if he went on to infer the conclusion of **B** from that mistaken premise. This is because the conclusion he drew would be true if the premise were true. Correct reasoning consists in reasoning from premises, be they true or false, to conclusions that stand in the sort of relationship that the conclusion of **B** bears to its premise. It is important to note that we can see that this relation-

---

[1] Because of the intimate connection between an argument description and the argument it expresses (where the context makes it clear which is intended) we shall use boldface uppercase letters such as '**A**', '**B**', and so on, to designate *either*.

ship holds between the premise and conclusion of **B** even though most of us do not know what or where Penang is. Thus we can sometimes recognize when inferences would be correct independently of whether or not they proceed from true premises. If there were no distinction in general between errors of reasoning and errors of fact, it would be impossible to use inference to discover new facts. For, before one could know that his inference was correct, he would have to know whether or not his conclusion was true. If this were so, the inference would be useless.

Contrast arguments **A** and **B** with argument **C**. Both the premise and the conclusion of **C** happen to be true. So one who believed them would be making no error of fact. Yet, if he inferred the conclusion of **C** from its premise, thinking that premise thereby to establish the truth of his conclusion, he would be making an error in reasoning. After all, it could be true that Boston is a city *or* Boston is in the United States without it also being true that Boston is in the United States. This would be the case if, for example, Boston were a city in Sri Lanka. Thus the relationship between premise and conclusion that **A** and **B** exemplify is missing in argument **C**.

The same is true of **D**. Its premise and conclusion both happen to be false, so anyone who believed either of them would be making an error of fact. Moreover, someone who believed the premise and then came to believe the conclusion as a result of inferring it from his first belief would be making an error in reasoning as well. Not only is Penang not a city (it is an island) nor is it in Sri Lanka (it is in Malaysia), but even if it were *either* a city *or* in Sri Lanka, that would not establish that it is in Sri Lanka. For, consistent with the truth of the premise, it could be a city in the United States.

Having exercised some of our intuitions about correct and incorrect reasoning by means of arguments **A** to **D**, we are now in a position to make four observations about argument descriptions **A** to **D**. Let us call any sentence in **A** to **D** that does not contain either the word 'and' or 'or' a "simple sentence." Examples are 'Boston is a city', 'Penang is in Sri Lanka', and so on. 'Penang is a city and Penang is in Sri Lanka' is not a simple sentence because it contains the word 'and'. Inspection of the four argument descriptions shows the following:

1. The *only* things **A** and **B**—the descriptions of valid arguments—have in common are the occurrences of 'and' and a certain pattern of simple sentences.
2. The *only* things **C** and **D**—the descriptions of invalid arguments—have in common are the occurrences of 'or' and a certain pattern of simple sentences.

3. The *only* difference between **A** and **C** is that 'and' occurs in **A** where 'or' occurs in **C**. .
4. The *only* difference between **B** and **D** is that 'and' occurs in **B** where 'or' occurs in **D**.

All that the valid arguments share is the occurrence of 'and' together with a certain pattern of simple sentences in their argument descriptions, whereas the only respect in which they differ from the invalid arguments is that 'and' occurs in their descriptions where 'or' occurs in the invalid ones. It seems clear, therefore, that *all* that matters for the logical validity or invalidity of *these* arguments is the choice of the words 'or' or 'and' together with the pattern of simple sentences in their argument descriptions.

That is, the structure of argument descriptions **A** to **D** determines a certain structure in the arguments themselves: The way the simple sentences in the argument descriptions are related by 'and' and 'or' determines the way the propositions expressed by those simple sentences are related. This structure, imposed on an argument by the structure of its argument description, is what we mean by its *logical form*. Because the logical form of an argument is imposed on by its argument description, we also speak of the logical form of the argument description and the sentences comprising it.

The logical form of an argument description or a sentence is just the form it imposes on the associated argument or proposition, respectively. To display the logical form of arguments such as **A** to **D**, begin with a stock of uppercase letters, '*A*', '*B*', '*C*', '*D*' (with subscripts, if more are needed), then apply this rule: Replace each *simple* sentence in the argument description with one of these letters, the same sentence with the same letter throughout the argument description. The form of argument **A**, for example, is

A' (1) *A and B.*
.   (2) *Therefore, B.*

where '*A*' replaces 'Boston is a city' and '*B*' replaces 'Boston is in the United States'. The logical form of argument **B** is

B' (1) *A and D.*
      (2) *Therefore, D.*

In *this* case, '*A*' replaces 'Penang is a city' and '*D*' replaces 'Penang is in Sri Lanka'. '*A*' replaces different sentences in the two different argument descriptions, but this does not violate the rule because it says only that the same letter must replace the same sentence throughout a given argument description.

Now **A** and **B** have the *same* logical form because **A'** and **B'** display the same choice of 'and' and the same pattern of simple sentences; they differ only in the choice of letters representing the simple sentences. Do not confuse argument *forms* with argument *descriptions*. The sentences expressing an argument comprise its argument description. An argument form is what you get when you replace the nonlogical phrases in an argument description with the symbols 'A', 'B', and so on. These symbols are only placeholders: They show where nonlogical phrases may be inserted in the argument form to produce an argument description. The point can be put this way: Argument forms, such as **A'** and **B'**, do not *say* anything; they do not express arguments. But when nonlogical phrases from the appropriate grammatical categories (sentences in this case) are put into those places, argument descriptions such as **A** and **B,** which do say something, result.

Let us confine ourselves to form **A'**, since both arguments **A** and **B** share it. The reason arguments **A** and **B** are valid is that there is no replacement of the simple sentences in their argument descriptions, in conformity with the pattern displayed by **A'**, which results in an argument description expressing an argument with true premises and false conclusion. The logical form of the arguments prohibits this. For, suppose there were some such replacement. Then 'B' would have to be replaced by a sentence that expresses a false proposition. Given that 'B' is replaced by such a sentence, then 'A and B' will be false, no matter what replaces 'A'. This is because *any* sentence of the form 'A and B' will be false if either (or both) of the simple sentences comprising it is false. Thus there is *no* replacement of 'A' and 'B' with sentences resulting in an argument description expressing an argument with a true premise and a false conclusion.

We may display the common logical form of **C** and **D** as follows:

C' (1) *A or B.*
        (2) *Therefore, B.*

where 'A' replaces 'Boston is a city', in **C,** and 'Penang is a city', in **D,** while 'B' replaces 'Boston is in the United States' and 'Penang is in Sri Lanka', respectively. **C** and **D** are not valid because there are consistent replacements for 'A' and 'B' in the preceding argument form that result in an argument description with a true premise and a false conclusion. For example, replace 'A' with 'Boston is a city' and 'B' with 'Boston is in Sri Lanka'. The result is

  C″   (1) *Boston is a city or Boston is in Sri Lanka.*
        (2) *Therefore, Boston is in Sri Lanka.*

which has a true premise and a false conclusion. (1) is true because Boston is a city; this is sufficient for the truth of 'Boston is a city or Boston is in Sri Lanka'. But (2), obviously, is false because Boston is not in Sri Lanka.

Arguments **C** and **D** are both invalid because their logical form does not prohibit their premises' being true and their conclusions' being false. Although in the case of **C** the conclusion *is* true, its truth is not guaranteed by the logical form of the argument (given that the premise is true), as **C″** shows.

We now sketch an account of validity for *all* arguments but shall defer a full discussion until Chapter 3. The basic idea is this: The words of our language, or any natural language, can be divided into two classes, the *logical phrases* and the *nonlogical,* or descriptive, *phrases.* The first class includes, in addition to '. . . and ____' and '. . . or ____', such phrases as '. . . unless ____', 'if . . . , then ____', 'it is not the case that ____', and '. . . if and only if ____'. An important subclass of the logical phrases, called *quantifiers,* include 'all . . .' and 'some . . .'. Examples of descriptive phrases are *names,* such as 'Boston', and *predicates,* such as '. . . is a city' or '. . . is east of ____'.

Descriptive phrases are used to construct simple sentences such as 'Penang is in Sri Lanka' or 'Boston is in the United States' which express propositions that might be used truly or falsely to describe the world. We shall call any sentence containing *only* descriptive phrases a *simple sentence.* The logical phrases, excluding quantifiers, are called *propositional connectives* because they are used to construct new descriptive sentences by connecting other (perhaps simple) sentences. The result of connecting the appropriate number of sentences, depending on the connective, is a *complex sentence* expressing a complex proposition. These logical phrases are called "propositional" connectives rather than "sentential" connectives to emphasize that the propositions expressed by the simple sentences thus connected may themselves be said to be "connected" to form a complex proposition. If a given sentence occurs within the context of a complex sentence, we say that it is *embedded* in that context (complex sentence). Similarly, we may say of the proposition expressed by that sentence that it is embedded in the complex proposition expressed by the complex sentence. For example, given the two simple sentences 'Penang is in Sri Lanka' and 'Boston is in the United States', we can construct complex sentences such as 'If Penang is in Sri Lanka, then Boston is in the United States', and 'Penang

is in Sri Lanka if and only if Boston is in the United States'. The difference between the propositions expressed by these complex sentences is
that the embedded propositions expressed by the constituent simple
sentences are differently related.

One can ascertain the relations among the propositions that go into
making up the premises and conclusion of an argument by looking for
the occurrences of propositional connectives and quantifiers in the written argument description. In nonquantificational arguments (such as **A**
to **D**) it is *simply* the occurrences of propositional connectives together
with the *pattern* of simple sentences in an argument description that
determines the logical form of the argument, but in the more complex
quantificational arguments it is this structure (if any) together with the
internal structure of the various quantified and nonquantified sentences
in the argument description that determines the argument's logical
form. If we suppose the logical form of an argument **A** to be revealed, we
may define validity as follows:

> **A** *is* valid *if and only if there is no consistent replacement of nonlogical
> phrases (names, predicates, or simple sentences) in its argument descrip-
> tion (s), the same replacement for the same nonlogical phrase throughout
> a given argument description, that results in an argument description
> (expressing an argument) with true premises and a false conclusion.*

As remarked above, this is only a rough preliminary definition, but it
will serve our purposes adequately until a more precise definition can be
offered in Chapter 3. The important point is that in both the nonquantificational and quantificational cases, validity depends on the impossi-
bility of replacing the descriptive phrases, be they names, predicates, or
simple sentences, in an argument description in a way that results in an
argument description with true premises and a false conclusion.

We shall briefly illustrate some quantificational argument forms. Recall Roscoe Frostbite's argument in Section 1:

E   (1) *Anything that causes cancer is a public health menace.*
   (2) *Smoking causes cancer.*
   (3) *Therefore, smoking is a public health menace.*

In Section 1 we said that, intuitively, this argument represented correct
reasoning. Now we can see that it is valid. This time we shall use the
uppercase letters '*F*', '*G*', and '*H*', with or without subscripts, to represent the nonlogical phrases in argument description **E**, but in this case
the nonlogical phrases are predicates instead of simple sentences (this is
the reason we have chosen a different set of letters to represent them).

Replace 'causes cancer' with 'F', 'a public health menace' with 'G', and 'smoking' with 'H'. Then a crude representation (a more precise one will be possible only after we develop some of the technical concepts of Chapter 2) of **E**'s logical form is

E' (1) *Anything that (is/does) F is G.*
      (2) *H (is/does) F.*
      (3) *Therefore, H (is/does) G.*

There is no consistent replacement of the nonlogical phrases in **E** in accordance with argument form **E'** which results in an argument description with true premises and false conclusion. The reader should verify this for himself by trying to find such a replacement. Contrast **E** with

F (1) *Anything that causes cancer is a public health menace.*
    (2) *Smoking is a public health menace.*
    (3) *Therefore, smoking causes cancer.*

In Section 1 we said that this argument represents an instance of incorrect reasoning. We can now see that it is invalid by finding a replacement for its nonlogical phrases in accordance with argument form

F' (1) *Anything that (is/does) F is G.*
     (2) *H (is/does) G.*
     (3) *Therefore, H (is/does) F.*

which results in an argument description **F"** with true premises and a false conclusion. Let 'F' and 'G' be replaced with the same predicates they have themselves replaced in (1), but let 'H' be replaced with 'putting arsenic in the water supply'. The result is

F" (1) *Anything that causes cancer is a public health menace.*
      (2) *Putting arsenic in the water supply is a public health menace.*
      (3) *Therefore, putting arsenic in the water supply causes cancer.*

which has true premises but, as far as anyone knows, a false conclusion. Because **F"** has true premises and a false conclusion, it is invalid. And, because it has the same logical form as argument **F**, the latter argument is invalid also, even though it happens to have true premises and a true conclusion.

Recall arguments **C** and **D** and argument **C"**, which showed the first two to be invalid. Argument **C"** had true premises and a false conclu-

sion, so it was obviously invalid. Because it had the same logical form as
C and **D,** it follows that they are also invalid. Argument **C″** is said to be
a *counterexample* to arguments **C** and **D.** Similarly, **F″** is a counterexample to **F.** In general, a *counterexample* to an argument is another argument of the same logical form as the first, but one that has true premises
and a false conclusion.

Two important consequences should be noted. First, all arguments
with the same logical form must be the same with respect to logical
validity and invalidity. This is because the same possibilities of replacing the nonlogical phrases in their argument descriptions exist for all of
them. Second, it follows from the definitions of *validity* and *counterexample* that an argument is valid if and only if it has no counterexample. This does not mean that an argument is valid if we are
merely unable to *think* of a counterexample because an argument could
be invalid yet sufficiently complex so that no one has been able to find a
counterexample to it. In Chapter 3 we shall introduce techniques that
make finding counterexamples to invalid arguments quite easy, and in
Appendix II we shall discuss techniques that make this process mechanical. Of course, even without these techniques, finding a counterexample to an argument is *sufficient* to show the argument invalid.

If an argument has a counterexample (i.e., it is invalid), then it is said
to be *fallacious* and, by extension, the inference that it represents may
also be said to be a fallacious inference. Conversely, any inference represented by a valid argument may be said to be a valid inference. Arguments, if they are fallacious, are so because their logical form does not
rule out the existence of counterexamples. The logical form of an invalid
argument is called a *formal fallacy* and any argument that has the form of
a formal fallacy is said to *exemplify* or be *an instance* of that fallacy. Thus
argument forms **C′** and **F′** are formal fallacies and the arguments that
exemplify them—**C, D,** and **F,** respectively—are fallacious.

The second important property of arguments that we shall discuss is
soundness.

*An argument is sound if and only if (1) it is valid, and (2) all its premises
are true. An inference is sound just in case the argument representing it is
sound.*

It is important not to confuse soundness with validity. If an argument or
inference is sound, then it is valid. But the converse does not hold; an
argument or inference can be valid yet unsound because valid arguments sometimes have false premises, whereas sound arguments, by
definition, do not. Of the two notions, validity best corresponds with
the intuitive notion of a "good argument." A "good argument" is one

that might represent a correct inference and, as we have noted, a person can reason correctly even if he is given false premises to work with. Argument **B,** at the beginning of this section, was such an example.

If an argument is sound, then it is valid and the premises are all true. It follows that the conclusion is true also. For, if an argument is valid, there is no replacement of the nonlogical phrases in its argument description which results in an argument description with true premises and a false conclusion. Consequently, the argument description that results from replacement of all the nonlogical phrases in the original argument description with *themselves* does not have true premises and a false conclusion. Hence, if that original description has true premises, it does not have a false conclusion. So it has a true conclusion. Arguments **A** and **E** are examples of sound arguments because they are valid and their premises are true.

Note that the definition of soundness does not imply that any argument with true premises and a true conclusion is sound. The argument

G (1) *The sky is blue.*
     (2) *Grass is green.*
     (3) *Therefore, tigers are carnivorous.*

has true premises and a true conclusion, but it is not sound because it is not valid. One can replace the simple sentences in its premises and conclusion to yield a counterexample, as follows:

G' (1) *Snow is white.*
     (2) *Oceans are salty.*
     (3) *Therefore, water is magnetic.*

In this case the counterexample consisted simply of replacing each simple sentence in the argument description with another simple sentence in accordance with the following argument form:

G" (1) *A.*
     (2) *B.*
     (3) *Therefore, C.*

A final word is in order about logical form. One and the same argument may have *many different forms* depending on the number of ways it is possible to replace the various sentences in its description, both simple and complex, with '*A*', '*B*', '*C*', and so on. The argument is said to *exemplify* each of these various forms. For example, Roscoe Frostbite's valid argument about smoking, **E,** also exemplifies the obviously invalid form **G''**, for it is possible to replace the entire first premise sentence of his argument description **E,** namely, 'Anything that causes cancer is a public health menace' with '*A*'; the second premise sentence, 'Smoking causes cancer', with '*B*'; and the conclusion sentence 'Smoking is a public health menace' with '*C*'. One might naturally make such a replacement if, for example, he did not identify 'anything' as a logical phrase. In that case he would take 'Anything that causes cancer is a public health menace' to be a simple sentence just like 'Boston is a city' or 'Smoking causes cancer'.

Roscoe's valid argument **E** shares the invalid form **G''** with the obviously invalid argument **G'** (which has true premises and a false conclusion). Does this show that **G'** is a *counterexample* to **E**? No, it does not. **G'** is *not* a counterexample to **E** because **E** *also* has a logically valid form, as was illustrated on p. 17. An argument is logically valid if and only if it has *at least one* valid form, and it is logically invalid if and only if it has *no* valid form. Thus **E** is valid because it has a valid form other than **G''**, and **G'** is invalid because it has no valid form. Because we are not yet in a position to distinguish precisely between logical and nonlogical phrases, we cannot distinguish one among the various forms of an argument as *the* logical form of the argument. However, it should be clear that when one speaks of an argument **D** as being a counterexample to another argument **A,** the *relevant logical form* they share is the one in which the most structure is taken into account. Although Roscoe's valid argument **E** *has* the invalid form **G''**, that is not the form of his argument in which the most structure is exposed. Rather, **E'** is that form. If there *were* a counterexample to **E,** then there would have to be some replacement of the nonlogical phrases in **E**'s description in accordance with **E'**, which results in true premise sentences and a false conclusion sentence, and, as we have said, there is no such replacement. When we look for a counterexample to an argument, we must always first find that form of the argument in question in which the most structure is exposed.

2.1 Exercises

In answering the following questions, you may find it helpful to refer to the summary of concepts and definitions introduced in this chapter (p. 45). Starred exercises are answered in Appendix III.

1. Although sentences are not the same as propositions, some of the same things can be said of both: for example, that they are true or false. Similarly, although arguments, their written expressions, and the inferences they represent are not to be confused with one another, one can say of each sort of thing that it has a certain logical form, that it is valid or

invalid (fallacious), and that it is sound or unsound. Under what conditions is it correct to say that:
  a. An inference is sound?
  b. An argument description is invalid?
  c. A sentence is true?
  d. An argument is fallacious?
  e. Two argument descriptions have the same logical form?
  f. Two arguments have the same logical form?
2. What, briefly, is the difference between logical and nonlogical phrases? What is a propositional connective?
3. Explain what is meant by the claim that validity is a matter of logical form. Give an example of a valid argument and an example of an invalid argument in the course of your explanation.
4. Do the following statements hold for *every* argument **A** and its conclusion C? Defend your answers and give examples wherever necessary.
  a. If **A** is sound, then C is true.
  b. If **A** is unsound, then C is false.
  c. If **A** is valid and C is false, then **A** is unsound.
  d. If **A** is invalid, then C is false.
  e. If **A** is valid, then C is true.
5. Suppose that arguments **A** and **B** have a form in common.
    a. If **A** is valid, what, if anything, can one conclude about **B**?
  ★b. If **A** is invalid, what, if anything, can one conclude about **B**?
    c. If **B** is valid, what, if anything, can one conclude about **A**?
  Suppose that **A** and **B** have in common the logical form that results from replacing *every* nonlogical phrase in their argument description(s) with an appropriate uppercase letter 'A', 'B', and so on. Does that change any of your answers?
6. Display the logical form of each argument below which results from replacing each distinct simple sentence in the argument description with a distinct uppercase letter, 'A', 'B', and so on.
    A   (1) If Los Angeles is a city, then California is a state.
          (2) If California is a state, then Chicago is a city.
          (3) Therefore, Chicago is a city.
    B   (1) Jesus made significant statements only if he was more than a man.
          (2) If he rose from the dead, then he was more than a man.
          (3) He did rise from the dead.
          (4) Therefore, Jesus made significant statements.
  ★**C**   (1) If more fertilizer is produced from crude oil, then the Green Revolution will succeed in the Third World.
          (2) Either we cut back on petroleum consumption in other forms or more fertilizer will not be produced from crude oil.

> (3) We will not cut back on petroleum consumption in other
>   forms.
>
> (4) Therefore, the Green Revolution will not succeed in the Third
>   World.

★7. Find a counterexample to each of the arguments in Exercise 6.

★8. Suppose you are correctly informed that a particular argument is invalid but that no one can find a counterexample. Would it be true, nevertheless, that a counterexample exists? Why or why not?

Difficult

9. Consider the following arguments:

   A (1) Nixon is present President of the United States and it is not the
           case that Nixon is present President of the United States.

      (2) Therefore, "Tricky Dick" is deceiving us about his present ac-
          tivities.

   B (1) The moon is roughly 250,000 miles from the Earth.

      (2) Therefore, either grass is green or it is not the case that grass is
          green.

   What can you say about the validity or invalidity of **A** and **B**? Their soundness or unsoundness? What do these examples show about the "connection" between premises and conclusion of valid arguments?

10. In our use of the uppercase letters 'A', 'B', and 'C', we have generally made the restriction that they are to represent *simple* sentences, but often one wants to talk about sentences in general, making no assumptions about their simplicity or complexity. In answering the following question, do *not* assume that 'A', 'B', and 'C' designate only simple sentences. Suppose that you are given three arguments of the following forms:

    A (1) *A*.   **B** (1) *B*.

       (2) Therefore, *B*.   (2) Therefore, *C*.

    C (1) *A*.

       (2) Therefore, *C*.

    Now suppose that **A** and **B** are valid and that **B** is unsound. What can you conclude about the validity of **C**? About the soundness of **C**? Defend you answers.

11. Show that the following two statements are true of any argument **A**:

    a. If **A** is invalid, then it has a counterexample.

    b. If **A** has a counterexample, then it is invalid.

12. Assume that the conclusion of a one-premise valid argument is false and that the result of consistently replacing all the simple sentences contained in the argument description always yields a false conclusion sentence. What, if anything, can you conclude about the premise of this argument? Defend your answer.

13. Consider argument **A** on p. 11. Now replace the premise sentence with
    (1') Chicago is a city.
    and the conclusion sentence with
    (2') Cows are carnivorous.
    Is the resultant argument,
    A' (1') Chicago is a city.
        (2') Therefore, cows are carnivorous.
    a counterexample to **A**? Why or why not? Defend your answers by means of the definitions of *validity* and *counterexample*.

3.
INFORMAL FALLACIES

It is widely held that there is an important class of fallacies called "informal fallacies." These are contrasted with formal fallacies either because they involve mistakes in reasoning that are not due to the logical form of the argument in question or because the logical form is not discernible. Usually, one is instructed to memorize examples of arguments that demonstrate the various "fallacies" to enable one to identify other instances of them when encountered. This is a questionable enterprise for two reasons. First, it creates the false impression that logic is a very devious business indeed and that only the cleverest and most subtle persons will ever develop sufficient skill to recognize the myriad "fallacies" to which they may be subjected. Logic certainly is not devious. Only two things can go wrong with an argument—it can be invalid or it can be unsound. If an argument is invalid, then it has a counterexample; whether or not it is *also* an instance of an "informal fallacy" is beside the point. The second problem with this taxonomic approach to logic is theoretical: Even when one learns to recognize alleged examples of the various "fallacies," it is difficult to see what common factor makes them all instances of the *same* fallacy. A formal fallacy, as was explained in Section 2, is the logical form of an invalid argument. Recall arguments **C** and **D,** for example, both of which had the invalid form

C'   (1) *A or B.*
     (2) *Therefore, B.*

Now it is easy to tell when two arguments, such as **C** and **D,** are instances of the *same* formal fallacy. If replacement of their simple sentences with uppercase letters results in the same pattern of logical phrases and letters as occurred in **C'**, then the arguments have, or are instances of, the same form. If that form happens to be a formal fallacy, as in **C'**, then they are both instances of the same fallacy. But in the case of "informal fallacies," it appears to be impossible to say when two arguments commit the same fallacy, as the following discussion illustrates.

During the House Judiciary Committe hearings on the impeachment of former president Nixon, one of the committee members, Delbert Latta of Ohio, offered (roughly) the following defense of Mr. Nixon:

> *Mr. Jenner (the Republican counsel for the committee) says that evidence E is strong evidence that Mr. Nixon is guilty of obstruction of justice. But Mr. Jenner's views can be ignored because he was a member of a commission that recommended the legalization of prostitution.*

Latta's unacceptable argument appears to be

(1) *Mr. Jenner claims that evidence E is strong evidence that Mr. Nixon is guilty of obstruction of justice.*
(2) *Mr. Jenner was a member of a commission that recommended the legalization of prostitution.*
(3) *Therefore, E is not strong evidence that Mr. Nixon is guilty.*

This is certainly an invalid argument. It has the form

(1) *A.*
(2) *B.*
(3) *Therefore, it is not the case that C.*

It is easy to find a counterexample. Choose any true sentences to replace 'A' and 'B' and 'C'. This makes the premises true and, since the negation of a true sentence is false, the conclusion false.

Those who are interested in informal fallacies would not be content to let the matter rest here. They would quite likely offer the following explanation of what went wrong in the original argument: It is a mistake in reasoning to attempt to discredit a person's views by discrediting his character. Thus, they would say, Latta's mistake was trying to show that what Jenner claimed was false (or "could be ignored") because, in Latta's view, Jenner once recommended something immoral. They might explain that it simply does not follow from the fact that someone once advocated something immoral that what he says now is false. Unfortunately, truth is not the special prerogative of those with approved morals. Such a mistake in reasoning is labeled *argumentum ad hominem* ("argument against the man" rather than against what he maintains. Notice that this sense of 'argument' is actually equivalent to 'dispute'; it is not this sense of the word with which we are concerned).

We agree that anyone who made the inference represented by Latta's argument would be making a mistake in reasoning because the argument is invalid, as is shown by its counterexample. The difficulty resides in attempting to give any further useful characterization of *the mistake* in reasoning or of *the fallacy of argumentum ad hominem* of which Latta's argument is supposed to be an *instance*. To see the difficulty more clearly, consider the following argument:

(1) *Jones maintains that socialism is wrong.*
(2) *Jones is a rich stockbroker.*
(3) *Therefore, it is not the case that socialism is wrong.*

Of course, the size of Jones's bank account has nothing to do with the truth of his opinions; someone who gave this argument would probably be trying to persuade us that socialism is not wrong by getting us to distrust or dislike Jones. This argument has the same logical form as Latta's:

(1) *A.*
(2) *B.*
(3) *Therefore, it is not the case that C.*

So it is indeed invalid. Since they share the same invalid form, they are instances of the same formal fallacy, but this does nothing to characterize the informal fallacy of *argumentum ad hominam* because these two arguments also share the same form with

(1) *The sky is blue.*
(2) *Grass is green.*
(3) *Therefore, it is not the case that tigers are carnivorous.*

This argument, although it is an instance of the same *formal* fallacy, has nothing to do with attempting to discredit a person's views by discrediting his character. Thus, if there is a fallacy of *argumentum ad hominem,* there must be a way of characterizing it according to which the first two arguments above are instances but the third is not. It is, however, difficult to see that those two arguments have *anything* in common other than their logical form and the fact that those who offered them had certain base motives, namely, to discredit someone's views by discrediting his character.

Although anyone persuaded by either argument would make a mistake in reasoning, we doubt that it is possible to give a general characterization of arguments that might represent attempts to discredit a person's views by discrediting his character. For a general characterization would have to appeal either to the form of such arguments or to their content. That appeal to form is inadequate is shown by the third argument above. Those who are interested in informal fallacies have not given an alternative account of the form of such arguments; indeed, by calling them *informal* fallacies, they seem to suggest that no general account of their form can be given. On the other hand, it does not seem that appeal to content will provide a general account either because some attempts to discredit a person's views by discrediting his character involve valid arguments. Suppose, for example, that the arguer above had said:

(1) *Jones maintains that socialism is wrong.*
(2) *Jones is a rich stockbroker.*
(3) *If Jones is a rich stockbroker and he maintains that socialism is wrong, then he is lying.*
(4) *If Jones is lying, then socialism is not wrong.*
(5) *Therefore, socialism is not wrong.*

This argument has the valid form

(1) *A*
(2) *B*
(3) *If A and B, then C.*
(4) *If C, then it is not the case that D.*
(5) *Therefore, it is not the case that D.*

(We leave it as an exercise for the reader to show that there cannot be a counterexample to this argument.) For this reason many people would not want to count this argument as an instance of the *fallacy* of *argumentum ad hominem.* Yet its content would certainly be appropriate to instances of that "fallacy" because it represents an attempt to discredit a person's views by discrediting his character [note premise (3)]. Thus one has either to hold that some valid arguments can be instances of informal fallacies or that one cannot characterize this fallacy in terms of content. If one takes the first tack, then it is difficult to see what could be the point of knowing whether an argument commits the informal fallacy; one would still have to determine whether or not the argument is valid. If one takes the second tack, then he is left without a general characterization of the fallacy.

Notice that it would not help to suggest that only *invalid* instances of arguments attempting to discredit a person's views in this way are instances of the fallacy of *argumentum ad hominem* because that would also require an independent demonstration of invalidity. The whole point of memorizing alleged examples of the fallacy in the first place is to help one identify unacceptable arguments. So if one must decide whether an argument is invalid in order to determine whether it is an instance of an informal fallacy, then it is pointless to try to identify informal fallacies at all. No *more* force attaches to the claim that a certain argument exhibits an informal fallacy than attaches to the claim that it is invalid—that a counterexample can be given.

So far, we have discussed only one of the alleged informal fallacies. Not all of the previous objections apply directly to other alleged informal fallacies, but similar objections can be raised against any attempt to give a general account of informal fallacies. Perhaps after all, one is better off *distinguishing* between errors in reasoning, and fallacies in the arguments that might represent such reasoning. That is, there may be errors in reasoning that have nothing to do with the arguments representing the reasoning, even though, of course, any logically invalid argument will correspond to *some* error in reasoning. The preceding distinction is nicely brought out in the case of the "fallacy" of *petitio principii* (begging the question, or circular reasoning). This fallacy is said to be committed by a person who smuggles in the conclusion he wants to prove (or a disguised version of it) as a premise of his argument. This certainly seems to involve an error of some sort, but the argument that represents such reasoning has to be valid. The logical form would look like this:

(1) A.
(2) ·
   ·
   · ·
   ·
(n) ·
$(n + 1)$ *Therefore, A.*

Clearly, there can be no counterexample to an argument with this form. No sentence can (in the same context) express both a true and a false proposition, so there is no replacement of 'A' that results in true premises and a false conclusion. Thus no such argument is fallacious, but anyone who argued in this way would be making some sort of mistake.

We are not suggesting that there is no value in investigating the various sorts of mistakes in reasoning that people are prone to make; on the contrary, this is an area where interesting and fruitful discoveries are waiting to be made. Rather we are suggesting that until a general characterization of informal fallacies can be given which enables one to tell with respect to any argument whether or not it exhibits one of the informal fallacies, knowing how to label certain paradigm cases of this or that mistake in reasoning is not really useful for determining whether a given argument is acceptable.

3.1 Exercises

In answering the following questions, you may find it helpful to refer to the summary of concepts and definitions introduced in this chapter (p. 45). Starred exercises are answered in Appendix III.

1. Is it worse to commit a formal fallacy than an informal fallacy? Vice versa? Explain.

2. Can an argument that exemplifies the informal fallacy of *argumentum ad hominem* (attacking the man) ever be sound? Explain.

★3. Consider the following argument form:

   (1) A.

   (2) Therefore, A.

   (where 'A' may designate a simple or complex sentence). Arguments having this form are sometimes called "circular arguments" because, intuitively, they represent reasoning "in a circle" where one concludes the same proposition that one has cited as the *evidence* for what one wishes to conclude. Since we do not, in general, believe that a proposition "proves" *itself,* it seems proper to say that a person who reasons in this way sometimes commits some sort of error in reasoning. Nevertheless, it is another question altogether whether an argument representing such reasoning is valid. Based on the account of validity given in Section 2, are such arguments valid or invalid? Sound or unsound? Explain.

★4. Suppose that argument **A** exemplified an informal fallacy and argument **B** exemplified a formal fallacy. What, if anything, can you conclude about their validity or invalidity?

Difficult

5. Suppose that someone tried to distinguish between formal fallacies and informal fallacies by appealing to the content of the arguments that exemplify the informal fallacies in contrast to their logical form. Is this a good theory about the difference between informal fallacies and formal fallacies?

4.
ARGUMENTS, INFERENCES, AND BELIEFS

We have said what arguments are—they are structured collections of propositions—we have distinguished them from their written expressions (i.e., argument descriptions), and we have explained their two most important properties, validity and soundness. Now we turn to a discussion of why arguments are important.

The major reason arguments are important is that, when expressed verbally or in writing, they can be *records* of inferences. Inferences, in turn, are important for three reasons:

1. They can *cause or generate* beliefs.
2. They can *support* beliefs.
3. They can *justify* beliefs.

What are inferences? How do inferences differ from arguments? How do inferences cause, support, and justify beliefs? These are among the questions to be answered in this section.

Making an inference is something a person does. Like running, making an inference is an activity, but unlike running, a physical activity, inferring is a mental activity. In Section 1 we gave as an example of a process of reasoning, Roscoe's coming to believe that smoking is a public health menace. In that example, Roscoe's mental transition from his original beliefs that smoking causes cancer and that anything that causes cancer is a public health menace to his new belief was a case of his making an inference. Arguments are unlike inferences because they are not activities of any kind; rather they are abstract things, composed of propositions. An argument *represents* an inference if its premises consist of the propositions that someone begins by considering (or believing), and its conclusion is the proposition that he ends by inferring consciously or unconsciously from those premises. An argument *records* an inference if it represents that inference and someone expresses it in writing with the intention thereby of representing the relevant inference.

Inference is often confused with implication, but it is important to recognize that in the sense in which logicians use these two words, they designate completely different notions. Implication is not an activity of any sort; it is a *relation* between propositions.[2] In particular, it is that

---

[2] There are other senses of the word 'implies'. It can be said that a *person* implies rather than asserts that something is the case, but we are concerned only with the sense of this term in which it relates propositions.

relation obtaining between the premises and the conclusion of a *valid* argument. For example, in the argument

(1) *Boston is a city and Boston is in the United States.*
(2) *Therefore, Boston is in the United States.*

the proposition expressed by (1) *implies* that expressed by (2). In this case there is only one premise, but in the case of valid arguments with multiple premises, the *set* of premises implies the conclusion. For example, in

(1) *Anything that causes cancer is a public health menace.*
(2) *Smoking causes cancer.*
(3) *Therefore, smoking is a public health menace.*

the set consisting of the propositions expressed by (1) and (2) implies the single proposition expressed by (3).

Implication holds (or fails to hold) independently of any human activity. No one need ever have inferred the proposition expressed by (3) from those expressed by (1) and (2) or have expressed them or even have thought of them. Even if there were no human race, the premises of both of the foregoing arguments would imply their conclusions.

Nor do propositions ever do any inferring. This is an activity performed only by organisms (and, perhaps, computers), but there is an intimate connection between the activity of inference and the relation of implication. Whether or not the relation of implication holds is a measure of the *correctness* of inference. Where S is a person, B a proposition, and A a proposition or set of propositions, *it would be correct* for S to infer B from A if and only if A implies B.[3] If we imagine a set A of propositions to consist of the premises of an argument which records an inference and B to be the conclusion of that argument, then an important relationship between the activity of inference and the recording argument emerges: The inference is correct if and only if the recording argument is valid. Of course, one can make incorrect inferences (i.e., those that would be recorded by invalid arguments), but the point is that a person usually infers one proposition from others only because he *thinks* consciously or unconsciously that those propositions imply the one he infers from them.

Inference is a means of generating beliefs; if one already has certain beliefs, then he can come to believe new propositions by inferring them from his original beliefs. Let us now see how inference can support and

[3] The exception of inductive inference is discussed in Appendix I.

justify beliefs. Inference, of course, is not the only way one can justify beliefs. A very common means of justifying belief with which we are all familiar is observation. Let us begin by comparing two instances of justifying beliefs, one by observation and one by inference. Both concern that well-known professor, Roscoe Frostbite.

Professor Frostbite, aware of the disproportionately large percentage of clocks from the Black Forest making cooing noises came to believe that there must be a disproportionately large number of cuckoo birds in the Black Forest. When his belief was challenged by an ornithologist who claimed that there is no species of cuckoo birds in the Black Forest, he immediately booked a flight to Swabia and went out, binoculars in hand, to the Black Forest. And indeed his belief was justified by his observing millions of cuckoos in every direction.

On another, less happy, occasion Professor Frostbite overheard a phone conversation between his wife, Crustacea, and her mother. During that conversation Crustacea learned for the first time of a meeting in a cave in the Himalayas between Roscoe and her dearest and closest friend, the famous female explorer Apassionata L'amour. "Good Lord," Roscoe thought to himself, "if I tell Crustacea that the meeting was strictly professional and that all we did was discuss why Baked Alaska is the staple diet of the Abominable Snowman, she will believe the worst. On the other hand, if I don't tell her that, Crustacea will believe the worst." Realizing that Crustacea would believe the worst, Roscoe shrugged his shoulders and resumed playing his violin.

Roscoe's belief about Crustacea's believing the worst is a new belief generated by his inferring it from his two earlier beliefs. The argument recording his inference is this:

(1) *If I (Roscoe) tell Crustacea that the meeting with Apassionata was strictly professional, etc., then Crustacea will believe the worst.*
(2) *If I (Roscoe) do not tell Crustacea that, etc., then Crustacea will believe the worst.*
(3) *Therefore, Crustacea will believe the worst.*

Further, because the inference is correct, it *supports* his belief in the proposition (3) expresses. A correct inference is said to support a belief in the sense that whatever reason one could have for believing the premises of the argument that could record that inference is also a reason for believing the conclusion. That is because a correct inference is one that would be recorded by a valid argument, so whatever *risk* one runs of being mistaken in the premises is never increased by transferring one's belief to the conclusion. Further, if Roscoe is *justified* in believing the premises of this argument, then he is also *justified* in believing the conclusion.

One's justification in believing the premises of an argument may come from a number of sources. For example, one may be justified by observation, as in the case of Roscoe and the cuckoos, or one may have inferred the relevant premises from other beliefs in which one was justified. On the other hand, one might have remembered that the premise is true or have been told it by a reliable source. We are not concerned here with the conditions under which one is justified in believing the premises of an argument; all we are saying is that *if* one is justified in believing the premises of a valid argument, *then* he is justified in believing the conclusion. In this particular case, we may suppose that Roscoe is justified in believing the premises of the preceding argument on the basis of his intimate knowledge of his wife's psyche. Therefore, since his inference was correct, he is justified in believing that Crustacea will believe the worst.

To sum up, the intimate connection between inferences and arguments is precisely this: An inference is *correct* if and only if the premises of the argument recording it imply the conclusion. If one generates a belief by inferring it from previous beliefs, then one's inference *supports* that new belief just in case the inference is correct. Finally, if one's inference supports a belief, one is *justified* in that belief just in case one is justified in believing all the propositions from which it was inferred (i.e., the premises of the argument that records the inference). Inference, like observation, is a legitimate way to generate beliefs, and is used extensively by mathematicians, philosophers, lawyers, and scientists. In science, both observation and inference are used to generate beliefs (or theories); both are indispensable to the scientific enterprise. In philosophy, observation is somewhat less extensively used to justify beliefs (or philosophical theories).

4.1 Exercises

In answering the following questions, you may find it helpful to refer to the summary of concepts and definitions introduced in this chapter (p. 45). Starred exercises are answered in Appendix III.

★1. Suppose that the wind has carved out on the face of Mt. Rushmore the following argument description:
(1) The weed of crime bears bitter fruit.
(2) If the weed of crime bears bitter fruit, then crime does not pay.
(3) Therefore, crime does not pay.
Does the argument expressed by this argument description *represent* either an actual or a possible inference? Does it *record* an inference? Why or why not?

★2. Consider the following sentence: "In saying that no one *presently* employed by the university is engaged in classified research, President Kingster Brewman implied that some *former* employees of the university may have been so engaged." Is this the use of the word 'imply' employed in this text? Explain.

3. Suppose that a person offers an argument in which the premises do not imply the conclusion. Could his inference from the premises to the conclusion be correct? Explain.

4. Suppose that a certain one-premise argument is invalid. Does this mean that no one could ever be justified in inferring the *premise* from the *conclusion?* Explain.

5. Suppose that Roscoe comes to have a belief in the conclusion, *C*, of argument **A** as a result of his inferring it from **A**'s premise, which he already believes. Are the following statements true or false? Explain.
   (1) Roscoe is *justified* in believing *C* if and only if *C* is true.
   (2) *C* is true if and only if Roscoe's inference was *correct.*
   (3) Argument **A** *establishes* the truth of *C* if and only if Roscoe's inference was *correct* and he was *justified* in believing the premises of **A**.

6. Roscoe Frostbite's fear of snakes caused him to believe that a rattlesnake's bite is invariably lethal. How was Frostbite's belief generated? Is it supported or justified in any way?

7. Suppose that Jones believes the premises of a certain argument. Is there anything in the concept of *inference* which makes it impossible for him to infer a proposition other than the conclusion of that argument? If so, what? If not, why not?

8. Suppose that Roscoe comes to believe the conclusion of a particular argument by inferring it from the premises and, further, that his inference does not justify his new belief. Does it follow from this that Roscoe could not become justified in believing the conclusion of that argument? Explain.

Difficult

9. Suppose that Roscoe acquires a belief in the conclusion of an argument **A** by inferring it from **A**'s premises, which he already believes and, further, that his inference *supports* his new belief (in the conclusion). Under what conditions would Roscoe be *justified* in *rejecting* one of the premises of **A**? Explain.

5.
INFERENCE AS A LEGITIMATE GROUND OF BELIEF

Inference is a legitimate way to generate beliefs because it can support and justify them. But what exactly does 'legitimate' mean? Unfortunately, it is difficult to give a definition of 'legitimate', but we can at least compare inference to other proper methods of generating beliefs and contrast it with improper methods. For example, observation is known to be a proper means of generating beliefs and emotion is known to be an improper means.

First, emotion *does* generate beliefs—if one detests a person enough, it is easy to believe him guilty of nearly any outrage. For example, after learning of the sojourn with Ms. L'amour, Crustacea regarded Roscoe with something more than contempt. And because of this, let us suppose, she came to believe that Roscoe had *always* been unfaithful to her. Here Crustacea's emotions got the better of her and dictated a certain belief. If Roscoe is to be believed, however, he was *never* unfaithful to her. The important point here is that whether or not Roscoe *should* be believed depends, in this case, upon observations of his behavior and not Crustacea's consuming detestation for him. It is just coincidence that her earlier belief in Roscoe's fidelity, based as it was on trust in the worthy musician, was true. However true, it was not *justified* by her emotions. Her later emotions did not change the correctness of her earlier belief in Roscoe's fidelity; it merely altered her belief. Suppose it were revealed that Roscoe had, after all, always been unfaithful. Still it would be nonsense to say that Crustacea's later hatred for him led her to *rectify* her earlier belief. All that could sensibly be said in that case is that her emotions caused her to *change* her beliefs from what was false to what, quite by coincidence, happened to be true.

The case of observation is very different. You look across the campus and see Basil Hassleforth, whom you have not seen in a long time. Running across the campus, oblivious of your conspicuousness, you grab him by the shoulder and exclaim, "Basil! Old pal . . . ," only to see a total stranger. Your first belief that the person across the campus was Basil was based on visual observation, and so is your new, somewhat painful, belief that that person is not Basil. Of the two beliefs, both generated by observation, the first is false and the second true. But the crucial point is that, in contrast to emotion, observation has not only changed your belief, it has *rectified* your old belief. Thus in reporting the incident to a friend, you might say, "When he turned around and I saw it wasn't Basil, I was mortified."

Although both observation and emotion can cause or generate beliefs, only observation can rectify a belief generated by an earlier use of the same; the fact that it does not make any sense to speak of "mis-emotions," whereas it makes perfectly good sense to say that one has mis-observed or has mistakenly observed something is strong evidence for this point. It is this capability of being used correctly or incorrectly that characterizes a means of generating beliefs as legitimate or proper.

Inference is like observation and unlike emotion. Observation and inference are legitimate means of establishing beliefs because they justify beliefs. It is because inference justifies beliefs that beliefs based on incorrect inferences can be rectified. For an example of an incorrectly drawn conclusion corrected later by a properly drawn conclusion, return again to the drama involving Roscoe, Crustacea, and Apassionata. The situation, having become very acrimonious, caused Crustacea to meet with an unnatural demise. The investigating detective, after viewing the scene of her death and collecting all the facts, reasoned as follows: "Roscoe didn't murder his wife unless he knows something about poison; but then, among his many other accomplishments, he is also a first-rate pharmacologist, isn't he? So it must be Roscoe. Hold on, that conclusion cannot be right. For if Roscoe murdered Crustacea, he had to be home between midnight Tuesday and 2:00 A.M. Wednesday, but we know that he was not home then because he was seen counting cuckoos in Laguna Beach from 8:00 P.M. Tuesday till 4:00 A.M. Wednesday."

The first, incorrect, inference by the detective is recorded by the following argument:

A (1) *Roscoe didn't murder Crustacea unless he knows something about poison.*
   (2) *Roscoe knows something about poison.*
   (3) *So, Roscoe murdered Crustacea.*

The second, correct, inference by the detective is recorded by the following argument:

B (1) *If Roscoe murdered his wife, then he had to be home between midnight Tuesday and 2:00 A.M. Wednesday.*
   (2) *Roscoe was not at home between midnight Tuesday and 2:00 A.M. Wednesday.*
   (3) *Therefore, Roscoe did not murder his wife.*

Assuming **B** to be sound, the latter inference rectifies the detective's original belief that Roscoe murdered Crustacea.

The sound inference recorded by **B** rectifies the detective's faulty belief in the conclusion of **A**, but this should not give the impression that correct inferences taken by themselves always lead to *true* beliefs. Let us suppose that a second detective, who is independently investigating the case, also knows that Roscoe was counting cuckoos in Laguna Beach. He reasons as follows:

C (1) *Roscoe was counting cuckoos in Laguna Beach.*
   (2) *If Roscoe was counting cuckoos in Laguna Beach, then he is psychotic.*
   (3) *If Roscoe is psychotic, then he murdered Crustacea.*
   (4) *Therefore, Roscoe murdered Crustacea.*

Both **B** and **C** are valid arguments, so the inferences they record are correct. Yet their conclusions cannot both be true. This shows that some correct inferences lead to false beliefs. And this is exactly what we would expect, for in Section 2 we said that a valid argument corresponds to a correct inference, and a valid argument, assuming that it has at least one false premise, can have a false conclusion.

Nor should it be supposed that if a belief is *justified* either by observation or by inference, then it is *true*. Consider the case of observation. Suppose that I am stopped by a police car and that a man dressed in a police uniform alights from the car, approaches me, and begins to remonstrate with me for having exceeded the speed limit. In such a case I surely would be justified in believing that the man is a policeman. Yet it is possible that it was all a practical joke, that the man is really an impostor. In this case I would be justified in believing that he is a policeman, but my belief would be false.

Second, recall the case of the two detectives' valid inferences, those recorded by **B** and **C** above. It may well be that both detectives were justified either by observation or knowledge of psychology in believing all the premises of their respective arguments, yet since one of their conclusions is false, it must be that some false beliefs are justified by inference.

A sound argument *establishes* the truth of its conclusion, but again, this must not be confused with the question of whether *a person* who inferred the conclusion from the premises is thereby *justified* in believing the conclusion. It may well be that the following argument is sound:

(1) *If the sum of all the phone numbers in Paris exceeds the sum of social security numbers of brown-eyed residents of New York, then there is an undiscovered moon of Jupiter.*

(2) *The sum of Paris phone numbers does exceed the sum of social security numbers of brown-eyed residents of New York.*

(3) *Therefore, there is an undiscovered moon of Jupiter.*

This argument is certainly valid, so whether or not it is sound depends on whether (1) and (2) are true. If they are true, then this argument establishes the truth of (3). Yet it is difficult to imagine anyone's being justified in believing either of the premises. Thus if one came to believe the conclusion by inferring it from the premises in which he already believed (for some reason best known to himself), his inference would support his new belief, but it would not justify it because he would not have been justified in believing the premises.

Notice that legitimate grounds of beliefs are not only rectifying but are mutually rectifying;[4] for example, inferences can rectify beliefs based on observations, and vice versa. Let us alter the example about Basil Hassleforth. You see a person in Los Angeles that you initially think is Basil, but then you realize that this is not true because you know that Basil is in London. Here the inference based on the principle that an object cannot be in two places at the same time corrects your mistaken observation.

Finally, it should not be thought that because a belief is generated by improper means it cannot be justified by some other means. A belief could be generated by emotion, for example, but later justified by inference or observation. Suppose that the detective investigating Crustacea's death likes Roscoe and *wants* to believe that he is innocent. His desire to believe Roscoe innocent may be sufficiently strong to cause such a belief. Clearly, his belief is not thereby justified, but he could then justify his belief by first coming to have justified beliefs in the premises of argument **B** above and then inferring the desired conclusion. Contrariwise, if he dislikes Roscoe and thereby comes to believe that Roscoe is guilty, he can justify this belief by getting the goods on him.

So inference and observation are proper and, indeed, indispensable ways of creating beliefs. They are proper ways of generating beliefs because they, unlike emotion, can justify beliefs. Verbal and written arguments, therefore, are important records of how some beliefs—those involving inference—are justified. If the inferences are complex and

---

[4] Being self-rectifying and mutually rectifying are, in effect, features of legitimate grounds for belief stressed by Henry Leonard. See his *Principles of Reasoning* (New York: Dover Publications, Inc., 1967), Units 7 and 8.

lengthy, the arguments recording these inferences take on even greater importance. So it is that law, mathematics, and philosophy journals abound in arguments. Indeed, verbal and written arguments are just as important as recorded observations in the various empirical sciences.

5.1 Exercises

In answering the following questions, you may find it helpful to refer to the summary of concepts and definitions introduced in this chapter on (p. 45). Starred exercises are answered in Appendix III.

1. What marks a method of generating beliefs as legitimate? What distinguishes such methods from improper ways of generating beliefs?
2. What is the difference between one's *changing* an earlier belief and one's *rectifying* an earlier belief? Give an original example of a false belief's being rectified by two different legitimate methods of generating beliefs.
3. We have said that correct inferences do not always lead to true beliefs. What additional conditions must be met to ensure that a correct inference does genuinely "rectify" a false belief (i.e., lead to a justified true belief)?
4. Suppose that Jones infers B from A. Which of the following statements are true and which false? Defend your answers.
    a. If Jones's inference is correct, then B is true.
    b. If Jones's inference is correct and A is true, then B is true.
    c. If Jones's belief in B is justified by his inference, then B is true.
    ★d. If Jones's inference justifies a belief in B and B is false, then Jones would be justified in disbelieving A.
    e. If Jone's inference is correct, then he is justified in believing B if he is justified in believing A.
    f. If the argument recording Jones's inference establishes B and Jones believes A, then he is justified in believing B.
5. Consider argument **B** on p. 36. Suppose that the detective's superior, Inspector Hindsight, *observes* that Crustacea was not dead after all, but that she only swooned. Would Inspector Hindsight's belief in what (3) expresses be justified? Would this show that the detective's belief in what (3) expresses was *not* justified? Explain.

Difficult
6. Suppose that Jones is justified in believing B on the basis of his inference of B from A and that B is false. Does it *follow* from this that Jones is justified in rejecting A? Explain.

6.
SOME OTHER USES OF ARGUMENTS

One of the major uses of arguments is to persuade, and rightly so. If a person has a false belief, often he can be persuaded to rectify his belief by being given a good argument. For example, in Section 5 we considered a case where the detective investigating Crustacea's death first believed that Roscoe was guilty and then rectified his mistaken belief by making a second inference. In this case the detective rectified his own faulty belief, but anyone else might have offered the second argument in an attempt to persuade him of Roscoe's innocence. Indeed, if one believes the premises of a valid argument, he *ought* to be persuaded in the conclusion (unless he is prepared to give up at least one of his premises). Unfortunately, however, because arguments do have great persuasive force, they can be misused. That is, it is possible to persuade someone in the conclusion of an invalid argument. It is dangerous to speculate on just why invalid arguments are persuasive, but one might hazard the guess that many people just assume that if they are presented with the outward form of an argument it is valid and, being undisciplined, do not bother to examine it in sufficient detail to determine that it is, in fact, not valid. Then, if they happen to believe the premises, they become persuaded in the conclusion. For example, a common argument against abortion attempts to show that fetuses are human beings (and thus should be accorded the "right to life") because they have brain waves just like human beings. The argument seems to be this:

(1) *All humans have brain waves.*
(2) *All fetuses have brain waves.*
(3) *Therefore, all fetuses are humans.*

It seems that this argument is persuasive. Yet it is invalid, as is shown by the following counterexample. Replace the descriptive terms 'human' with 'cat', 'fetus' with 'dog', and 'brain wave' with 'tail'. The result is

(1) *All cats have tails.*
(2) *All dogs have tails.*
(3) *Therefore, all dogs are cats.*

which has true premises and a false conclusion.

This is an example of an invalid argument used to persuade one in the truth of the conclusion. Quite a different use of an invalid argument is to persuade one in the truth of a *premise* rather than the conclusion. Advertisers, for example, often try to induce people mistakenly to infer that they will share the benefits bestowed upon the members of some other group of people who buy a certain product if they also buy that product. For example, General Mills cereal company advertises that a high percentage of successful athletes eat their product—the Breakfast of Champions. The suggestion is clear—one is expected to infer that personal success will occur as a result of eating Wheaties. The argument (slightly simplified) is this:

(1) *All successful athletes eat Wheaties.*
(2) *I (will) eat Wheaties.*
(3) *Therefore, I will be successful.*

Indeed, this is a bad argument—as the following counterexample shows: Replace 'successful' with 'fat', 'athlete' with 'cat', 'eat' with 'drink', and 'Wheaties' with 'water'. This result is

(1) *All fat cats drink water.*
(2) *I (will) drink water.*
(3) *Therefore, I will be fat.*

In the case of the foregoing "Wheaties argument" one is not meant to become persuaded in the truth of the conclusion because, presumably, he does not already believe premise (2). The advertisement is directed at those who do not already eat Wheaties. The point, rather, is to get one to *make* that premise true by buying Wheaties. In this case, then, one is persuaded in the *premise* because he is encouraged (mistakenly) to infer the *conclusion*.

Invalid though the argument is, such arguments are, as a matter of fact, very persuasive. Perhaps this is so because one is apt to confuse them with arguments such as the following valid argument:

(1) *All successful athletes eat Wheaties.*
(2) *I am a successful athlete.*
(3) *Therefore, I eat Wheaties.*

This argument is valid. Therefore, if one were justified in believing its premises, then he would be justified in believing its conclusion. Perhaps it is because this second argument could be used to justify a belief in its conclusion that one can be led to accept premise (2) of the original argument. Note, however, that the latter argument, unlike the original, does not purport to provide a recipe for becoming successful.

Quite a different use of arguments is to test hypotheses or assumptions. Here the point is not to convince one of the truth of the conclusion, but rather to gather evidence for or against one of the premises. For example, an important experiment which tended to establish the hypothesis that light is composed of particles having mass involved the realization that if light has mass, then it will be affected by gravity. Scientists then thought that if light is affected by gravity, one could wait for Alpha Centauri, a distant star, to move behind the sun. Then, when calculations showed that the star should not be visible, one would know that its light has been bent if it is still seen from earth. The accompanying figure shows the real position of Alpha Centauri established by calculation versus its apparent position as observed by telescope from earth. The hypothesis that light has mass, together with our knowledge that if it has mass it will be affected by the sun's gravity and the expected experimental results, permits one to infer that Alpha Centauri will appear to be at point *a*, but, as we shall see, the purpose of the inference is not to justify a belief in the conclusion:

(1) *Light has mass.*
(2) *If light has mass, then it will be affected by gravity.*
(3) *If light is affected by gravity, then if one observes Alpha Centauri at point r, it will appear to be at point a.*
(4) *We do observe alpha centauri at point r.*
(5) *Therefore, Alpha Centauri appears to be at point a.*

Although this argument is valid, the scientist does not use his inference to generate or justify a belief in (5) because, first, he does not already believe (1), and second, if he comes to believe (5), it will be on the basis of observation. He does not already believe (1) because that is just the claim he wants to test. He does, of course, already believe (2) and (3) on the basis of previous knowledge of the behavior of gravity and as-

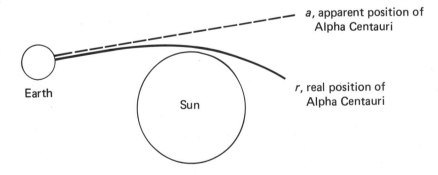

a, apparent position of Alpha Centauri

Earth

Sun

r, real position of Alpha Centauri

tronomy, and he *comes* to believe (4) by following through on his experiment.

There are only two possible outcomes of the experiment described in premise (4): Either Alpha Centauri appears to be at point *a* or it does not. Suppose, first, that Alpha Centauri does not appear at point *a*. Then the scientist can determine that at least one of his premises is false because he knows that a valid argument with a false conclusion must have at least one false premise. He knows that premises (2) to (4) are not false, for reasons already given. So he knows that his hypothesis [namely, (1)] is false; it is the only thing left that can be false. Now suppose that the outcome of the experiment is as expected and the conclusion of the foregoing argument is true. In this case it would be wrong to think that (1) has been proved to be true because a valid argument with a true conclusion can have a false premise (i.e., can be unsound), but at least the scientist has found out that one way his hypothesis might have been disproved failed to materialize. So he knows that his hypothesis has some likelihood of being true. Note that in neither case would this argument have had anything to do with generating or justifying a belief in the conclusion.

The last use of arguments to be mentioned is that of providing an explanation of some state of affairs. In such cases the argument may or may not also record an inference. But if it does record an inference, its purpose is neither to establish a belief nor to test a hypothesis. Suppose that you see your cat sleeping on the back of his head and you wonder why he does that. Then you remember that cats in a deep sleep phase always sleep on the backs of their heads and you also remember that your cat has been asleep for about thirty minutes. The argument that revealed this explanation is

(1) *Cats in the deep sleep phase always sleep on the backs of their heads.*
(2) *My cat is in the deep sleep phase.*
(3) *Therefore, my cat sleeps on the back of his head.*

Your discovery of an explanation of why the cat sleeps the way it does consists only in your having realized that (3) follows from (1) and (2). There is no question of any beliefs being generated here because your beliefs in (2) and (3) were generated by observation and your belief in (1) came from your once having read a psychology text.

6.1 Exercises

In answering the following questions, you may find it helpful to refer to the summary of concepts and definitions introduced in this chapter on p. 45. Starred exercises are answered in Appendix III.

1. Suppose that an argument is used to explain a phenomenon. Could it also record an inference? Explain, giving an example.

2. Suppose that Cardinal Biggles is asked to justify his position that advocates of abortion may not rightfully receive the sacraments of the Church and he replies: "I am the Cardinal and the power is vested in me by the Holy Catholic Church to pronounce on matters of morality and I say advocacy of abortion is just as immoral as abortion itself." To what use is this argument being put? Explain.

3. On p. 4 we said that we were not interested in arguments in the sense of that word reflected in the sentence "We'd better not invite McMurraghue to the party; he'll try to start an argument with Austin Smith-Jones and that will ruin the entire evening." Does it follow from this that arguments (in the sense of that word in which we are interested) cannot be used to make someone angry? Explain.

★4. Could an argument be used to persuade someone even though he did not actually make the inference the argument represents? Explain. Could an argument be used to test a hypothesis or explain something without also recording an inference? Explain.

5. On p. 43 it was said that a valid argument with a false conclusion must have at least one false premise. Explain why this is so.

Difficult

6. Could an argument used to explain a certain phenomenon ever justify a belief in one of the premises? How? Explain fully, giving an example.

7.
SUMMARY OF IMPORTANT DEFINITIONS AND CONCEPTS IN CHAPTER 1

Below are explanations and definitions of the central concepts introduced in this chapter. Each is followed by the page number on which it was introduced.

1. A *proposition* is an abstract object expressible by a declarative sentence. (p. 5)
2. An *argument* is a structured collection of propositions, one of which is the conclusion and the others the premises. (p. 6)
3. In the most common use of arguments,
    (1) the *conclusion* is the proposition to be established.
    (2) the *premises* are the propositions offered as evidence for the conclusion. (p. 4)

Where **A** is any argument with premises $P_1, \ldots, P_n$ and conclusion C, then:

4. A set of sentences, S, constitutes **A**'s *argument description* if and only if both
    (1) S constitutes a written expression of **A**, and
    (2) S contains all and only those sentences expressing $P_1, \ldots, P_n$ and C. (p. 6)
5. **A** is *valid* if and only if there is no replacement of the nonlogical phrases (names, predicates, or simple sentences) in its argument description(s) with (perhaps different) nonlogical phrases, the same replacement for the same phrase throughout a given argument description such that the resulting argument description expresses an argument with true premises and a false conclusion. (p. 16)
6. $\{P_1, \ldots, P_n\}$ *implies* C if and only if **A** is valid. (p. 31)
7. **A** is *sound* if and only if both
    (1) **A** is valid, and
    (2) $P_1, \ldots, P_n$ are all true. (p. 18)
8. **A** is *deductive* if and only if either
    (1) **A** is valid, or
    (2) **A** is invalid, but represents an inference from $\{P_1, \ldots, P_n\}$ to C that is intended to be valid. (p. 4)

45

9. **A** is *inductive* if and only if both
   (1) **A** is not deductive, and
   (2) **A** represents an inference from $\{P_1, \ldots, P_n\}$ to C that is intended to support C to some extent. (p. 4)
10. **A** is *fallacious* if and only if both
    (1) **A** is deductive, and
    (2) **A** is invalid. (p. 18)
11. **A**'s *logical form* is the pattern of logical and nonlogical phrases in **A**'s argument description. (p. 13)
12. Where **D** is an argument, **D** is a *counterexample* to **A** if and only if **D** has the same logical form as **A** and **D**'s premises are true and **D**'s conclusion is false. (p. 18)
13. A *formal fallacy* is the logical form of a fallacious argument. (p. 18)

Let S be any person, C a proposition, and $\{P_1, \ldots, P_n\}$ any set of propositions. Then:

14. *It would be correct* for S to infer C from $\{P_1, \ldots, P_n\}$ if and only if $\{P_1, \ldots, P_n\}$ implies C. (p. 31)
15. If S generates a belief in C by inferring C from previous beliefs in $\{P_1, \ldots, P_n\}$, then S's inference *supports* his belief in C if and only if his inference was correct. (p. 32)
16. If S's inference from $\{P_1, \ldots, P_n\}$ to C both generates and supports his belief in C, then S is *justified* in believing C on the basis of that inference if and only if S was justified in believing all of $P_1, \ldots, P_n$. (p. 32)

CHAPTER

2

The Identification and Clarification of Arguments

1.

PRELIMINARY REMARKS: GROSS STANDARD FORM

The various argument descriptions discussed in Chapter 1 all had in common a certain superficial structure. In each case there was

1. A vertical list of sentences, the last of which expressed the conclusion and the others of which expressed the premises.
2. Each sentence was numbered.
3. The conclusion sentence was preceded by a word, called the "illative particle," such as 'therefore', 'thus', 'so', or 'hence'.

The illative particle marks the presence of an actual or possible inference from the premises to the conclusion. When an argument is expressed by an argument description meeting these conditions, we shall say the argument is in *gross standard form.*[1]

When an argument is in gross standard form, the premises and conclusion are clearly demarcated. Thus the task of *identifying* an argument is accomplished when it is put into gross standard form. Unfortunately, most arguments are not born in gross standard

[1] The term 'gross standard form' is Henry Leonard's [*Principles of Reasoning* (New York: Dover Publications, Inc., 1967)].

form. That is, apart from textbook examples, arguments are seldom found already expressed in gross standard form. In normal contexts of use, arguments are expressed in a highly informal, discursive manner that usually obscures their logical form, making it difficult or impossible to determine validity or invalidity. It may even be difficult to tell precisely what the premises and conclusion are. When an argument is presented in an informal discursive manner, some examples of which are to follow, we shall say that it is in its *natural habitat*. [2]

The useful application of the concepts of validity and soundness elucidated in Chapter 1 presupposes that an argument is first *identified*, that is, its premises and conclusion are demarcated; and second, *clarified*, that is, its logical form made explicit. Accordingly, this chapter has two goals, the identification and clarification of arguments in their natural habitats.

Paraphrasing an argument from its natural habitat into gross standard form involves determining which propositions belong to the argument, and determining which of those are premises and which the conclusion. (It is not necessary to accomplish these tasks in order; usually one does them both at once. More often than not, the best way to begin is to look for a conclusion, and then see how it is supported.) To see what propositions belong to an argument, one studies its written expression in the natural habitat and then undertakes to answer the following three questions:

1. Of the propositions actually expressed in the passage, which are part of the argument, either as premises or conclusion?
2. Of the propositions actually expressed in the passage, which are irrelevant to the argument?
3. Are there any propositions not actually expressed by any sentence in the passage that are nevertheless part of the argument?

Once one has answered these questions, and thus has determined which propositions are premises and which conclusion, the argument may be put in gross standard form. When an argument is reexpressed in this way, it has been *extracted* from its natural habitat. This completes the task of identification.

The clarification of arguments requires the help of a symbolic language, called *the official idiom*, especially designed to display the formal relations among premises and conclusion upon which validity and invalidity depend. Because the official idiom is so designed, it is useful not

---

[2] The term 'natural habitat', as applied to arguments, is Howard Pospesel's [*Arguments* (Englewood Cliffs, N.J.: Prentice-Hall, Inc., 1971)].

only for the practical task of clarifying arguments, but also for enabling us to make precise our informal account of validity in Chapter 1. This, in turn, paves the way for the development of techniques for evaluating arguments, the topic of Chapter 3. To clarify an argument, then, is to paraphrase it from gross standard form into the symbolic language of the official idiom. When a proposition or an argument is expressed in the symbolism of the official idiom, we shall say that it is in *official standard form*.

Logic's utility in identifying and clarifying arguments is revealed above by the two-stage process of paraphrase of arguments from natural habitats into the official idiom. This process is called *paraphrase* rather than *translation* because no attempt is made to preserve all the *meaning* of the original argument expressions. We are ultimately interested only in the validity or invalidity of arguments, and this depends on their logical form, not on the meaning of their English expressions. The usefulness of paraphrase in identifying, clarifying, and, ultimately, evaluating arguments resides as much in discarding what is not relevant to validity as in retaining what is essential. In the first step—paraphrase into gross standard form—most of the rhetorical force of the original is lost; and in the paraphrase from gross standard form into official standard form, only the formal properties of the original are retained. In this chapter we shall stress the important clarificatory function of logic and, in particular, we shall be painstaking in our development of the official idiom; for the ability to use logic to clarify arguments requires a precise understanding of how arguments expressed in their natural habitats relate to their counterparts in official standard form. Further, one can fully appreciate the theoretical role of a language like the official idiom only if one understands how it relates to a natural language such as English.

1.1 Exercises

In answering the following questions, you may find it helpful to refer to the summary of concepts and definitions introduced in this chapter on p. 169. Starred exercises are answered in Appendix III.

1. Which of the following argument descriptions are arguments in gross standard form and which are not? Defend your answers.
   a. Brutus killed Caesar; so, someone killed Caesar.
   b. (1) Brutus is evil.
      (2) Brutus killed Caesar.
      (3) So, if Brutus killed Caesar, then Brutus is evil.

    c. (1) If anyone killed Caesar, then he was evil.
      (2) Brutus killed Caesar.
      (3) Thus Brutus was evil.
      (4) Brutus was Caesar's best friend.
      (5) Therefore, Brutus was Caesar's best friend and he was evil.
  ★d. (1) Brutus killed Caesar.
     Thus someone killed Caesar.
    e. (1) Brutus killed Caesar.
      (2) Therefore, the moon is made of cheese.
    f. (1) Brutus killed Caesar.
      (2) Therefore, Brutus did not kill Caesar.
    g. Brutus killed Caesar.
     Therefore, someone killed Caesar.

2. Arguments are rarely found expressed in gross standard form. What advantages are there in having arguments expressed in gross standard form rather than in their "natural habitats"?

3. Which of the following passages contain arguments and which do not? List the conclusions of those that contain arguments.

    a. "Civilization had made man if not more bloodthirsty, certainly more vilely, more loathsomely bloodthirsty. In former days he saw justice in bloodshed and with his conscience at peace exterminated those he thought proper to kill. . . . We now think bloodshed abominable and yet engage in this abomination, and with more energy than ever. Which is worse?"

               Fedor Dostoevski, *Notes from the Underground*

    b. "As Gregor Samsa awoke one morning from uneasy dreams he found himself transformed in his bed into a gigantic insect. He was lying on a hard, as it were, armorplated, back and when he lifted his head a little he could see his dome-like brown belly divided into stiff-arched segments. . . . His legs, which were pitifully thin compared to the rest of his bulk, waved helplessly before his eyes."

               Franz Kafka, *The Metamorphosis*

    c. "There is one final crowning irony to the abortion debate. While attempts to ban abortion are characteristically led by people who call themselves conservatives, their position is actually a flat contradiction of conservative doctrine. For nothing could interfere more directly with a woman's personal life than state action telling her whether she will or will not give birth. Yet the basis of all conservative doctrine is resistance to state interference with one's personal life."

               Letter to the Editor,
               The Los Angeles Times

2.
THE FORMALIZATION PROCEDURE: STAGE 1

The first step in formalization is paraphrase into gross standard form. We shall illustrate some of the main principles involved by means of seven examples.

EXAMPLE 1

Suppose that the following passage were found in an article in *Foreign Affairs:*

Another common argument in favor of requiring Third World recipients of foreign aid to institute rigorous birth control measures is as follows:

> (1) *If aid is granted without requiring a concomitant birth control program, then the population of the recipient country will increase without any improvement in the standard of living.*
> (2) *If the population of the recipient country increases without any improvement in the standard of living, then there will be an increase in the general misery.*
> (3) *If there is an increase in the general misery, then aid is worse than useless.*
> (4) *Therefore, if aid is granted without requiring a concomitant birth control program, then aid is worse than useless.*

Senator Sarky, who gave this argument in a recent Senate debate, also favors the following safeguards in the foreign aid program. . . .

In this case there is no difficulty in detecting the argument because it is already in gross standard form. The natural habitat is nothing more than the surrounding information in the *Foreign Affairs* article, including a statement that an argument is about to be given. Paraphrase into gross standard form is very easy in this case; one simply recopies sentences (1) to (4) just as they appear above, eliminating the rest of the passage.

In the previous example it was easy to extract the argument because the natural habitat did not contribute anything to the argument. Often, however, the natural habitat includes intricate networks involving the arguer's motives, his rhetorical style, what is known or believed or presumed to be known or believed by the arguer or listener, the complexity of the topic, and so forth, upon which one must rely to identify the argument being given. These networks are called *contexts*. We will consider a case where contextual factors come into play.

EXAMPLE 2

Recall Roscoe Frostbite's argument about smoking at the beginning of Chapter 1. Had he expressed it in a normal conversational way, he might have expressed the argument as follows:

I just read the Surgeon General's report. Everything I like is bad for you! Now it seems that even smoking is a public health menace. Since it causes cancer and, as is obvious, anything that causes cancer is a public health menace, it's a menace too.

This passage expresses, or contains, an argument because Roscoe advances a proposition and tries to support it with other propositions. We already know, by hypothesis, what his argument is in gross standard form. As represented in Chapter 1, it is

(1) *Anything that causes cancer is a public health menace.*
(2) *Smoking causes cancer.*
(3) *Therefore, smoking is a public health menace.*

We can study the influence of contextual factors by comparing the two ways of expressing this argument. First, the argument in its natural habitat, a conversation with someone, is an example of an "inflated" argument expression. Some sentences express propositions that are neither premises nor conclusion. The proposition expressed by the first sentence in the passage, for example, is neither his conclusion nor part of his evidence. His purpose in asserting it was not to *support* his conclusion, but to introduce the topic, or provide an occasion for giving his argument. Similarly, the second sentence merely serves to express Roscoe's dismay at what he learned by reading the Surgeon General's report; the proposition expressed is not part of his argument. The first proposition belonging to Roscoe's argument is that expressed by the third sentence. As can be seen in the gross standard form of the argument, this proposition is his conclusion. In conversation it is fairly common first to state one's conclusion and then to give the evidence.

Note, however, that some words in the conclusion sentence are omitted in its paraphrase. The phrase 'now it seems that . . .' is not part of Roscoe's assertion—he is not asserting that *right now, at this very moment, it seems that* smoking is a public health menace. Rather, he is asserting precisely the proposition that smoking is a public health menace. Only a sentence expressing the proposition he is actually asserting appears in the gross standard form of the argument. The phrase 'now it seems that . . .' is what is called a conversational modifier. Conversational modifiers have many and varied uses, too numerous to discuss here. Suffice it to say that such phrases are part of one's rhetorical style. Their function generally is to draw attention to propositions actually being asserted, but they do not themselves correspond to parts of those propositions. Whether or not a given phrase is a conversational modifier or part of an assertion depends on its use on a particular occasion; one simply has to be sensitive to nuances of use to tell the difference. In this case it is quite clear that Roscoe uses the phrase 'now it seems that . . .' only to indicate that he has come to be convinced of the truth of his conclusion on the basis of evidence he is about to give. On the other hand, it is possible that in a different context someone might use the phrase differently. Consider, for example, someone giving a running commentary on a magic show. He might well want to report on *the way things now seem,* for example, "It now seems that the lady is sawn completely in half, a very clever trick indeed." In this case the phrase would not be a conversational modifier.

Similarly, 'even' in the same sentence does not contribute to what Roscoe is actually asserting; he uses it merely to indicate a certain degree of frustration about the number of generally accepted habits that turn out to be dangerous. One of the most important functions of paraphrase into gross standard form is the stripping away of such rhetorical devices to get down to what is essential in an argument. So one has to develop a sensitivity about such uses.

The last sentence of the passage contains Roscoe's two premises. The paraphrase into gross standard form alters this sentence in four respects. *First,* the illative particle, 'since', is removed from the premise sentence and placed before the conclusion sentence. Because all illative particles are equivalent in function, we replaced 'since' with the more idiomatic 'therefore' to indicate that it does not matter which illative particle is used. Although the illative particle was originally in the premise sentence, its function in the natural habitat is just the same as in the gross standard form of the argument: to indicate an inferential relation between Roscoe's premises and his conclusion. So this relation is marked in gross standard form by placing it in its proper position. *Second,* the phrase '. . . as is obvious . . .' is "paraphrased away" because it functions as a conversational modifier. It is not part of Roscoe's argument that *it is obvious that* anything that causes cancer is a public health menace. He is *asserting* that anything that causes cancer is a public health menace while *signaling* to his interlocutor that it would not be sensible, in his opinion, to challenge this premise. *Third,* the original premise sentence is broken up into two premise sentences in gross standard form. It seems better to represent Roscoe's argument as containing two premises because the modifier '. . . as is obvious . . .' appears to break the sentence into two distinct thoughts. This is largely a matter of convenience, however. The validity or invalidity of an argument is not affected by conjoining the premise sentences or listing them separately. This is because *all* arguments of the forms

(1) *A and B.*
(2) *Therefore, A.*

and

(1) *A.*
(2) *B.*
(3) *Therefore, A and B.*

are valid. *Finally,* the reference of the various occurrences of the pronoun 'it' is fixed by replacing that word with 'smoking'. For example, the sentence 'Since it causes cancer . . .' becomes 'Smoking causes cancer . . .' in the paraphrase. The reason for this is to make clear what proposition is expressed by 'it causes cancer'. Roscoe's argument in gross standard form has now been extracted from its context. This means that the information relevant to that argument and supplied by contextual factors in the natural habitat is now presented explicitly in the gross standard form.

To sum up, the discursive passage above does contain an argument. In it Roscoe concludes the proposition that smoking is a public health menace and offers as evidence the propositions that smoking causes cancer and that anything that causes cancer is a public health menace. Roscoe exploits various *contextual features* of the natural habitat to help his listener identify his premises and conclusion. Contextual features are not themselves part of an argument; they are neither premises nor conclusions. Rather, they are *elements of the situation in which an argument is presented (sometimes including the particular way it is expressed) that may help (or hinder) a listener or reader to tell exactly what the premises and conclusion are (i.e., what the argument is).* In this case the contextual features include the following: (1) Roscoe's presupposition that his hearer knows something about the Surgeon General's report on smoking, at least that 'the Surgeon General's report' refers to his report on *smoking;* (2) his use of the conversational modifiers 'it now seems that . . .', '. . . even . . .', and '. . . as is obvious . . .'; (3) the placement of the illative particle to mark an inferential relation between premises and conclusion; and (4) Roscoe's hints about his attitudes toward the truth of the propositions that he is asserting. This last item, although it is a contextual feature, does not tell us anything about the argument itself, and thus is irrelevant. Because most of the contextual factors at work do help identify the premises and conclusion, we are able to use them to *extract* Roscoe's argument from its natural habitat and reexpress it in gross standard form. In this step of the paraphrase, everything that is not essential to the argument is "paraphrased away."

Example 2 involved an inflated argument expression in its natural habitat. A more complicated case involves an incomplete expression. In the case of inflated expressions of arguments, one has only to discard what is irrelevant, but using contextual features to determine what is left out of an incomplete expression of an argument is more difficult.

EXAMPLE 3

Huey Long, the notorious late governor of Louisiana, is said to have complained to a group of rural southern Louisianians, during the course of an election campaign, that his bachelor opponent (let us call him Roscoe Frostbite) was "guilty of living for years in open celibacy with his sister." Apparently, Long was trying to persuade his audience that Frostbite had an impoverished moral sense. Probably, it was Long's purpose to convey this information by deceiving people into believing that the following invalid argument (in gross standard form) is sound:

(1) *Frostbite lived in open celibacy with his sister.*
(2) *Therefore, Frostbite is immoral.*

Note that although Long did not explicitly express this conclusion, it is strongly suggested by the context, namely, knowledge of Long's goal of defeating Frostbite, the presumed ignorance or emotionality of the listeners, Long's rhetorical style (outrage), and so on. So here is a case where an unscrupulous person manipulates contextual factors to *deceive* his audience into accepting a bad argument. We are not principally concerned here with the invalidity of this argument; we want mainly to consider the problem of identifying it. In this case the most important contextual features are Long's pompous outrage, which tells us what his unexpressed conclusion is, and his obvious confidence that his listeners did not know what 'celibacy' means, which, together with his outrage, suggests to the audience that whatever it may be it has to do with immorality.

These contextual factors seem to point to the preceding representation of his argument in gross standard form, but because Long's manipulation of them is subtle, one might think his argument is best represented in gross standard form by the following:

(1) *Frostbite lived in open celibacy with his sister.*
(2) *Anyone who lived in open celibacy with his sister is immoral.*
(3) *Therefore, Frostbite is immoral.*

Unfortunately, the deceased Mr. Long cannot be asked which argument he intended. All one has to go on are the hints he gave: his tone of outrage, his evident confidence that his audience did not know the meaning of 'celibacy', and so on. These hints may not be sufficient to determine what his argument actually was. Under such circumstances the best one can do is to present a range of permissible alternatives, noting that a more precise determination requires further investigation. For example, examination of Long's notes for his never-published autobiography might reveal enough information about the incident to decide between the two versions; he might say, for example, that he defeated poor Frostbite by tricking campaign audiences into believing that he was immoral. Note, however, that even in the absence of further information, and this is the crucially important point about such cases, if an argument is presented so obscurely that one cannot even tell what it is, one would be foolish to be persuaded of the truth of its conclusion.

Having issued this warning, it is nevertheless important to see what *would be relevant* to deciding between the two versions, that is, to deciding for or against the inclusion of premise (2). Properly to decide for or against the inclusion of that premise, one would need to know whether Long supposed that his audience actually *believed* the proposition expressed by (2) or whether he just thought that they would accept merely that the sentence expressed some true proposition or other without really understanding it. Such considerations suggest the following criteria governing the inclusion of unasserted premises (or a conclusion) in an argument:

1. *The criterion of obviousness:* Even if an arguer fails to assert a proposition, it is a *premise* of his argument if both

(a) his argument needs that proposition to be valid.
and
(b) it is obvious (at least to the arguer).

or

2. *The criterion of belief:* Even if an arguer fails to assert a proposition, it is part of his argument if both
(a) his argument needs that proposition to be valid.
and
(b) it is clear from what the arguer actually says that he believes it or expects the reader or listener to believe it or (in the case of unasserted conclusions) that he inferred it or expects the listener to infer it from the premises.

Long did not actually assert that anyone who lives in open celibacy with his sister is immoral. The question is: Is this proposition nevertheless a premise of his argument? Consider the criterion of obviousness. Long's argument does require this proposition as a premise to be valid; so condition (a) is met. But the proposition is not obviously true; in fact, it is obviously false. So condition (b) is not met. In the case of the criterion of belief, condition (a) is also met, but there is no reason to think either that Long himself believes that living in open celibacy with one's sister is immoral or that he expects his audience to believe it. On the contrary, it seems clear that the wily politician is well aware that anyone who *understands* this sentence will *disbelieve* the proposition it expresses but is confident of his ability to *confuse* his audience. So condition (b) of the criterion of belief is not met either. Since neither criterion justifies adding this premise, we probably should accept the original gross standard formulation of Long's argument.

These criteria should be regarded only as guidelines; they do not cover every conceivable case. Consider a correct use of these criteria wherein Jones gives the following argument:

Am I rational? Of course, I'm rational. All men are rational, so I am, too.

At first glance, the argument in gross standard form appears to be this:

(1) *All men are rational.*
(2) *Therefore, Jones is rational.*

Now this argument is invalid, but if the premise that Jones is a man were added, it would be valid. Furthermore, condition (b) of both criteria is met, so each criterion separately seems sufficient to license the addition of this premise. Thus the correct formulation of Jones's argument in gross standard form would appear to be

(1) *All men are rational.*
(2) *Jones is a man.*
(3) *Therefore, Jones is rational.*

Indeed, this illustrates the proper use of the criteria of obviousness and belief, but if we alter the situation a little, these criteria can be defeated. Suppose it is known on independent evidence that Jones *wrongly* believes that his first argument is valid and the second is invalid. Then, even though he believes the inserted premise and, indeed, it is obvious, the fact that he would emphatically *reject* the second argument as his own and insist on the first outweighs the criteria.

This shows again that paraphrase is not mechanical; one has really to see exactly what is going on in a particular context. This and the Huey Long case also raise the important issue of *charity* in paraphrase. The purpose of paraphrase is to clarify a person's argument so that it can eventually be evaluated. Since people do sometimes give invalid arguments, the proper use of the technique must retain the (perhaps buried) invalid form of the original. It may show admirable charity always to attempt to make a person's argument valid, but this simply would not be correct. The criteria of obviousness and belief are not licenses to add whatever premises an argument requires to be valid (one can, after all, always find such a premise for any argument simply by joining the original premises by the appropriate number of conjunctions '. . . and ____' and then prefixing the complex sentence so produced by 'if . . .' and the conclusion of the original by 'then ____'). But they are meant to permit us to add only those propositions that are really presupposed *as premises* by the arguer.

Example 3 concerned an argument with an unexpressed conclusion. Contextual features told us what the conclusion was and also ruled out the addition of a certain premise that would have rendered it valid. Note that even if this premise were admitted, thereby making Long's argument valid, the argument would remain unsound because of the obvious falsity of the premise. So he still could not have established the truth of his conclusion. Now we shall turn to an argument that falls between the first two cases. That is, a putative conclusion is indeed expressed but is not really the conclusion of the argument. In other words, the real conclusion is different from that actually expressed and has to be determined from contextual features.

EXAMPLE 4

On a television program during the 1972 national election campaign, George Meany, the president of the AFL–CIO, said that he had concluded that the AFL–CIO should adopt a neutral stance between presidential candidates McGovern and Nixon. When questioned by reporters about the grounds for this conclusion, he replied that McGovern was only slightly pro-labor, that he was an apologist for the communist world, that he advocated certain social policies that Meany found repugnant, and so on, but that, on the other hand, Meany had good personal relations with President Nixon, that Nixon's policy toward the communist world was like an admirable chess strategy, the platform of the Republican party was not very much against labor, and so on. Now a little reflection will show that the conclusion Meany claimed to have drawn is not the one he really drew and intended his audience to draw. His real conclusion was not that the AFL–CIO should adopt a neutral stance on the choice of U.S. President, but that it should adopt a positive attitude toward Nixon as the presidential choice. This conclusion was, of course, left unexpressed, and indeed it is contrary to the stated conclusion, but the context of Meany's remarks (e.g., our knowledge of Meany's personal dislike of McGovern, his anticommunist views, his position as spokesman for labor, etc.) suggests an application of the criterion of belief: To be valid, Meany's argument requires the conclusion that the AFL–CIO should support Nixon and the context provides very strong evidence that he does believe this conclusion rather than that the AFL–CIO should remain neutral. Therefore, although his *stated* argument is invalid, we have good reason to think his *real* argument is valid. There is only the slightest doubt that his real argument in gross standard form was

(1) *The AFL–CIO should support whichever candidate is superior in the respects of being pro-labor, having a good foreign policy, and so on.*
(2) *Nixon is superior in these respects.*
(3) *Therefore, the AFL–CIO should support Nixon.*

Now consider a case where an unexpressed premise may be inserted.

EXAMPLE 5

The logicians Bertrand and Alexis are having a disagreement. Bertrand says,

You, Alexis, claim that arguments of the form
  A   *(1) Jimmy doesn't scowl.*
      (2) Therefore, there exists something that doesn't scowl.

are valid. But you are wrong, as the following counterexample shows:
  B   *(1) The Round Square of Phineas doesn't exist.*
      (2) Therefore, there exists something that doesn't exist.

*The premise of **B** is true, but its conclusion not only is false, but also is contradictory.*

Normally, we should be justified, on the basis of the criterion of belief, in granting Bertrand the unexpressed premise that **A** and **B** do, in fact, have the same form. Bertrand's argument does require it, and that he believes it is made clear by his remark that **B** is a counterexample to **A** because, being a logician, Bertrand knows that a counterexample to an argument is another argument of the same form as the original, with true premises and a false conclusion. By a second application of the criterion of belief, we may also grant Bertrand the premise that if **B** is invalid, then **A** is, also. So, the gross standard form of Bertrand's argument should be:

(1) *The following two arguments have the same form:*
  A   *(1) Jimmy doesn't scowl.*
      (2) Therefore, there exists something that doesn't scowl.
  B   *(1) The Round Square of Phineas doesn't exist.*
      (2) Therefore, there exists something that doesn't exist.
(2) **B** *is invalid.*
(3) *If **B** is invalid, then **A** is invalid.*
(4) *Therefore, **A** is invalid.*

In point of fact, as we shall see later,[3] Bertrand's argument may be unsound due to the possible falsity or premise (1). Historically, Bertrand Russell's *challenge* of this premise helped to motivate his famous theory of definite descriptions. Russell's theory in part is an analysis of the form of sentences such as 'The round square of Phineas doesn't exist' and his theory is believed by many to have sired twentieth-century analytic philosophy.

---

[3] See Chapter 2, Section 11.

In some cases the premises and conclusion of an argument are fairly explicit, but the logical form of the argument is distorted by contextual features. The next example involves a case where we are made to think that the logical form of an argument is entirely different from what it really is.

EXAMPLE 6

When asked whether he had ever met Winston Churchill, Groucho Marx is alleged to have remarked, vaguely, "Churchill and I once dined at the Connaught." When it was objected that Marx and Churchill were never at the Connaught at the same time he replied, "I didn't say I dined *with* Churchill. He ate there once and so did I." In this case, Marx's use of the word 'and' suggested some sort of connection between him and Churchill which Marx later claimed he had not actually *asserted* to hold. The argument Marx appeared to offer is

(1) *Marx and Churchill once dined together at the Connaught.*
(2) *If any two people dined together, then they met each other.*
(3) *Therefore, Marx met Churchill.*

But his real argument, as evidenced by his response to the objection, was

(1') *Marx once dined at the Connaught and Churchill once dined at the Connaught.*
(2') *If any two people dined together, then they met each other.*
(3') *Therefore, Marx met Churchill.*

The first argument is perfectly valid, but there is an obvious counterexample to the second. The joke depends on one's taking Marx's argument to be the first when in fact he was offering the second. The relevant contextual features that Marx manipulated to produce the joke include his audience's expectation that his remark would actually answer the question posed (a fatal error in any conversation with Groucho Marx), together with his use of the word 'and', which has the peculiarity that it functions differently when it is being used to form compound sentences, as in (1'), than when it merely forms a compound subject, as in (1). This difference, which reveals his real argument, is brought out by his emphasis on the contrast between *with* and *and* in response to the objection.

EXAMPLE 7

For the final example, imagine the following context. A few years ago there was a period of dramatic and rapid increase in the rate of inflation for food products. Among the items that inflated most were fish and meat. In response to widespread consumer dissatisfaction, the Secretary of Agriculture, Earl Butz, suggested that if consumers objected to the cost of meat, they should give it up and eat fish instead. Unfortunately, fish had inflated so rapidly that it was not cheaper than meat. The natural habitat of the following argument, then, is a conversation between two angry consumers examining prices at the fish market. One says,

> *Earl Butz says that in order to save money we should eat more fish. But what would be the point of that unless fish were cheaper than meat? In fact, meat is cheaper than fish!*

The speaker's rhetorical question in the second sentence of the passage makes clear his intention to refute a claim made by Earl Butz. Butz's claim, referred to by the speaker's use of 'that', is: To save money, we should eat more fish. Although the speaker's rhetoric makes his intention clear and he supplies evidence for his position in that and the succeeding sentence, his conclusion is left unexpressed. Because we know his intention, we can determine that his conclusion is the denial of Butz's claim:

> *It is not the case that to save money we should eat more fish.*

Note that it is not part of the conclusion that Earl Butz *said* that to save money we should eat more fish. This is just a contextual feature helping the listener to identify the conclusion, the denial of *what* Butz said, and perhaps reminding him of the broader context of the government's failure to control inflation.

Let us discuss this point in greater detail. Normally, a report about who advances a certain position is irrelevant to an argument, and such mention, therefore, is not carried over into the paraphrase. The reason for this, although simple, is important. Any paraphrase into gross standard form must preserve validity or invalidity. As was mentioned above, the point of paraphrase is to put a person's argument in a clear way, so a paraphrase, unlike the original with respect to validity, is unacceptable. Now, to add to a premise or conclusion the additional information that someone espouses it could alter the validity of his argument. For example, consider the following argument:

(1) *If there is a fuel shortage, then a recession will occur.*
(2) *There is a fuel shortage.*
(3) *Therefore, a recession will occur.*

which has the form

(1) *If A, then B.*
(2) *A.*
(3) *Therefore, B.*

This argument has no counterexample, as the reader can determine. But suppose one adds the information that Earl Butz *said* there is a fuel shortage. The resultant argument,

(1') *If there is a fuel shortage, then a recession will occur.*
(2') *Earl Butz says there is a fuel shortage.*
(3') *Therefore, a recession will occur.*

is invalid. Premise (2') contains no logical words, so the form of this argument is

(1') *If A, then B.*
(2') *C.*
(3') *Therefore, B.*

to which a counterexample may readily be found. The intuition behind this, of course, is that Earl Butz could be mistaken; it never follows from the fact that a person, however trustworthy, says something that it is true.

In our example, information about Earl Butz is merely a contextual feature, but that does not mean that such information *could* not be part of an argument. Imagine the following argument:

(1) *If the Pope says that abortion is wrong, then it is wrong.*
(2) *The Pope says that abortion is wrong.*
(3) *Therefore, abortion is wrong.*

Here the arguer offers the fact that the Pope said something as part of his evidence for his conclusion, so it would destroy his argument to leave that information out. Indeed, the utterly trivial argument

(1') *If abortion is wrong, then abortion is wrong.*
(2') *Abortion is wrong.*
(3') *Therefore, abortion is wrong.*

would result. Note, however, that even in the first argument (3) is not alleged to follow from (2) alone, but from (2) together with another premise, which, if true, guarantees the Pope's veracity. That a report about someone's having asserted something may sometimes be relevant and sometimes irrelevant emphasizes again that there is no mechanical way to paraphrase an argument; one must develop a sense of what is intended by the arguer.

Let us return to the argument concerning Earl Butz's advice. We have now to extract the premises. First, the speaker's use of 'unless' in his rhetorical question makes it clear that he means not only to reject Butz's claim, but also he is alluding to a claim he thinks supports his own contrary conclusion. What alleged fact does the speaker put forth here? His reference back to Butz's claim, together with the connective 'unless', indicate that he thinks there is a connection between Butz's claim and the proposition that fish is cheaper than meat. Indeed, it is pretty clear that the speaker thinks fish is cheaper than meat if Butz's claim is true. Thus one premise is

If in order to save money we should eat more fish, then fish is cheaper than meat.

The second premise is easy:

Meat is cheaper than fish.

The conversational modifier 'in fact' in the sentence expressing this premise does no more than emphasize that the speaker thinks that his next statement is true, and further, is relevant to the truth of the conclusion he draws. It can be omitted because our putting the argument into gross standard form already makes it obvious that the speaker is understood to think both that his premises imply his conclusion and that his premises are true. Usually, the enterprise of clarifying an argument presupposes that the speaker is trying to justify a certain belief he has, or thinks his audience should have. If so, then he is trying to say something true that implies his belief—he is trying to give a sound argument. Thus the argument in gross standard form is

(1) *If in order to save money we should eat more fish, then fish is cheaper than meat.*
(2) *Meat is cheaper than fish.*
(3) *Therefore, it is not the case that in order to save money, we should eat more fish.*

2.1 Exercises

Retain your answers to the exercises for this section. They will form the basis for future exercises. Starred questions are answered in Appendix III.

1. What is the difference between a contextual feature of an argument and a premise? What is an "irrelevant" contextual feature? Explain, giving examples.

★2. Consider the following passage:

"Man is unique among all the creatures of the earth. To make something as sacred as . . . a living fetus, which is still breathing and experiencing pain, the object of experimentation runs counter to the Judeo-Christian ethic, which has served this civilization well."

Letter from David A. Roberti, State Senator,
to The Los Angeles Times

Apparently, Roberti is arguing for the conclusion that experimentation on living fetuses is wrong. Is it part of his argument that fetuses *are* actually experimented upon, or is this a contextual feature (relevant or irrelevant?) Explain.

3. Suppose that Smith, in an obviously hostile manner, declares: "Jones is very untrustworthy. So it would be unwise to believe that he did not bribe the Police Chief merely on the basis of his protestations of innocence."

Is Smith's hostility a relevant contextual feature of his argument? Explain.

4. In the Prescript of this book, Carnap argues that illogical thought is an important factor in determining human behavior. Put his argument into gross standard form.

5. Put the following arguments into gross standard form:
   a. Rostow is guilty of an arrogance of power. But then so is Johnson if Rostow is. So, along with Johnson, Rostow is guilty of an arrogance of power.
   ★b. No one in his right mind would admire Hitler. But Wallace admires him—can you believe that? That is why I'm convinced that Wallace is mentally unstable.
   c. "This was the wall, and there was no way around, over or through it. If he did not resign, Richard Nixon would become the first president in history to be impeached, convicted and removed from office. If he left of his own choice, he would be the first to resign. For a man who prized his "historic firsts" this was the ultimate choking irony."

Saul Pett, The Los Angeles Times,
April 6, 1975

d. It is utterly pointless to ration gasoline. If gas is rationed, then more electricity will be used because people will stay home watching television. But if people use more electricity, the same amount of oil will then be used to generate additional electricity. Now obviously there is no point in rationing gasoline if the same amount of oil is used to generate additional electricity.

★e. If you take the final, then you pass Professor Black's course. If you pass his course, then you must take his final. So taking the final is both necessary and sufficient for passing his course.

f. It is not true that both the price of gold is fixed and people speculate on the price. People do speculate on the price of gold, so it is not fixed.

g. If the pizza is done, we will either split it with our friends or eat it all and get sick. Since we will not share it, we will get sick.

★h. "If number were an idea, then arithmetic would be psychology. But arithmetic is no more psychology than, say, astronomy is. Astronomy is concerned, not with ideas of the planets, but with the planets themselves, and by the same token the objects of arithmetic are not ideas either."

Gottlob Frege, *The Foundations of Arithmetic*

i. "The Kissinger–Nixon justification for going on in Vietnam is that we must preserve our credibility as a world power. But a great country can justify such relentless destruction of another only if its own safety, its vital strategic interest, is at stake, and virtually no one believes that about Vietnam anymore."

Anthony Lewis, a political columnist

j. "The key is blocking Nick Buoniconti. If you can block him, you can run on the Dolphins. If you can run on them, you can beat them."

Johnny Unitas, an athlete

k. "Kerensky once said, 'If there had been no Rasputin, there would have been no Lenin.' If this is true, it is also true that if there had been no hemophilia, there would have been no Rasputin."

R. K. Massie, *Nicholas and Alexandra*
(Rasputin gained influence with Nicholas,
the last Russian Czar, by claiming to be
able to cure the Czar's hemophiliac son)

l. If Vietnam is united under a communist government, then all of Southeast Asia will have communist governments. Why? Laos will become communist if South Vietnam does. If these become communist, then so will Cambodia. If Laos and Cambodia have communist governments, then Thailand will as well. And if these four countries have communist governments, all of Southeast Asia will.

m. "Police attempts to stamp out heroin by attacking drug suppliers may be counterproductive and lead to an increase in crime by addicts, two scientists believe. The two said that by aiming at the supply of the drug, police will force the price of heroin up. Addicts will have no choice but to pay the increase and will turn more and more to crime to do so."

From a news story

n. "Let C be the set of all objects that are not identical to themselves. We assume that every object is itself, so C is empty."

Seymour Lipshutz, *Set Theory and Related Topics*

o. "Even what a person has produced by his individual toil, unaided by anyone, he cannot keep, unless by permission of society. Not only can society take it from him, but individuals could and would take it from him, if society only remained passive: if it didn't interfere *en masse*, or employ and pay people for the purpose of preventing him from being disturbed in the possession [thereof]."

John Stuart Mill, *On Liberty*

p. "I do know that this pencil exists; but I could not know this if Hume's principles were true; therefore Hume's principles, one or both of them, are false."

G. E. Moore, *Some Main Problems of Philosophy*

q. The former CBS morning TV commentator, Sally Quinn, recounted the following tale. A female acquaintance of Ms. Quinn applied for an executive position in a prestigious New York City firm. She was on paper better qualified than many of her male competitors, had a very successful personal interview, and subsequently, along with other selected male candidates, was invited to meet with other members of the firm at a private club. The interviewer did not realize that it was a *Men Only* establishment, and, with considerable embarrassment, informed Ms. Quinn's acquaintance of the facts. Ms. Quinn's acquaintance did not attend the meeting. Two weeks later she received a letter informing her that the prestigious New York City firm had selected another candidate (male) for the position.

★r. "Sterilizing a woman on welfare who has two illegitimate children is not an imposition on her personal freedom," said the physician. "She has free choice between the following alternatives. She can choose to go off welfare and have as many babies as she wants. Or she can choose to get a welfare check every month and have no more babies."

s. "The same gentlemen who are accepting the most venal versions of what happened are prepared to hold President Nixon directly responsible for them. Professor Kenneth Galbraith, who has been neglecting his economics—an infrequent act of philanthropy—in order to campaign for McGovern, says it flatly: either Mr. Nixon was personally responsible for giving the orders to burglarize Watergate, in which case he should be defeated for moral venality, or if he did not know about it, he should be defeated for incompetence."

W. F. Buckley, Jr.,
"Some Added Observations About the Watergate Caper,"
The Los Angeles Times, October 11, 1972

t. "[Persuasion is] absolutely essential to successful living. Just look around you! In any profession, any enterprise, the man or woman at the top is almost always a master persuader."

Norman Vincent Peale,
Family Weekly, October 15, 1972

u. The priest was asked, "Shouldn't a belief in demonic possession be accepted only if there is some good evidence?" "No," said the priest, "In fact, justification for such a belief is either unnecessary or unachievable. For if one believes in demonic possession, justification is not needed; and if one does not believe in demonic possession, no evidence to the contrary, no matter how legitimate, will persuade the unbeliever."

v. ". . . You are wise;
Or else you love not; for to be wise and love
Exceeds man's might; that dwells with gods above."

William Shakespeare, *Troilus and Cressida*

w. "The economic argument is a parroting of the oil company line: "We need OPEC," because "OPEC is a blessing in disguise." The cartel, the argument goes, taught us how vulnerable we are, and by holding prices high, is forcing us to invest more intensively in domestic exploration and various energy alternates. This is like saying that we should be grateful to arsonists for making us vigilant against fires, and subsidize them as a way of encouraging people to install sprinkler systems."

Editorial, *The Los Angeles Times,*
December 12, 1978

x. "There is no problem with California's 59-year old indeterminate sentence law; the problem lies with the gubernatorial appointees to the Adult Authority. If the governor appoints men with a philosophy of early release for all, society will be endangered. If the governor appoints thoughtful men willing to protect society, the law can work very well."

Letter from Los Angeles Police Chief Ed Davis
to *The Los Angeles Times,* September 6, 1976

Difficult

6. There is a species of arguments resembling arguments in gross standard form but which differ in one important respect. In these arguments, usually called *derivations,* a number of subsidiary inferences are recorded before one reaches the final inference to the conclusion. The subsidiary inferences are to subconclusions, which appear as *lines* in the derivation, somewhat like *premises.* Normally, one identifies each genuine premise and then *justifies* each inference by writing the number of the line(s) from which each subconclusion is inferred. Here is an example of a derivation:

   (1) All creatures with livers are warm-blooded. (premise)
   (2) All creatures that are warm-blooded are mammals. (premise)
   (3) Smokey the Bear is a creature. (premise)
   (4) Smokey has a liver. (premise)
   (5) So, Smokey is a creature with a liver. [from (3) and (4)]
   (6) So, Smokey is warm-blooded. [from (1) and (5)]
   (7) So, Smokey is a creature that is warm-blooded. [from (3) and (6)]
   (8) So, Smokey is a mammal. [from (2) and (7)]

   Now explain why the derivation above is not an argument in gross standard form. This derivation, although not an argument in gross standard form, can be paraphrased into a *series* of arguments each of which is in gross standard form. Do so.

7. One can *always* find a premise which, when added to an invalid argument, converts it in into a valid argument. Thus, whenever a person gives an invalid argument, the first condition of the two criteria (of belief and of obviousness) for the inclusion of unasserted premises is met. Give an original example of an invalid argument that a person might give in support of some conclusion or other. Then

   a. Give an example of a proposition that satisfies the first condition of each criterion but fails the second condition in each case. Explain why it fails.

   b. Give an example of a proposition that could be imagined, in the proper context, to meet both conditions of either of the two criteria. Explain what contextual features are at work that justify your inclusion of this premise.

   c. Now consider an arbitrary invalid argument having the form
   (1) *A.*
   (2) Therefore, *B.*
   Give the form of a premise that, if added to this argument, would result in a valid argument.

3.
THE FORMALIZATION PROCEDURE: STAGE 2

Putting an argument into gross standard form sometimes both identifies and clarifies it. That is, one can tell from such a formulation what the premises and conclusion are and, as happened in a few of the examples discussed above, the logical form is sufficiently clear to permit determination of validity or invalidity; but this is usually not the case. Normally, the logical form is obscured by the literary style of the sentences expressing the argument in gross standard form.

To clarify arguments, we need some specialized machinery. To begin, we shall develop a symbolic, or *formal*, language called *the official idiom*, which is especially constructed to display precisely the formal relations among premises and conclusion upon which validity and invalidity depend. The distinction between formal and natural languages, very roughly, is this: A natural language, such as English or German, is one found "in nature," whereas a formal language is invented to serve a certain specialized purpose. A familiar example of a formal language is the symbolic language of arithmetic, which is valuable not because more can be said in it than in English, but because numerical relations can more clearly be displayed and, consequently, computation facilitated. In the case of the official idiom, the grammatical forms of its symbolic sentences are especially designed to display the *logical form* of sentences and arguments.

To clarify an argument, then, is to paraphrase it from gross standard form into the official idiom. When a sentence or argument is expressed in the symbolic language of the official idiom, it is in *official standard form*. The remainder of this chapter is devoted to the construction of the official idiom and paraphrase into official standard form.

Clarification and evaluation are intimately related. After an argument is clarified, determination of its validity or invalidity is not difficult. Conversely, to the extent to which an argument is imperfectly clarified, application of the preliminary definition of validity is hampered or even made impossible. The definition is difficult to apply in practice just because we have as yet no clear way to represent the logical form of arguments. A useful way to bring out the function of the official idiom, then, is to discuss some of the problems in applying the preliminary definition. As will be seen, the official idiom surmounts all these difficulties. The definition was

72

An argument **A** *is* valid *if and only if there is no consistent replacement of the nonlogical phrases (names, predicates, or simple sentences) in its argument description(s), the same replacements for the same nonlogical phrases throughout a given argument description, resulting in an argument description expressing true premises and a false conclusion.*

Recall that this definition stemmed from the intuition that arguments of the form

(1) *A and B.*
(2) *Therefore, B.*

for example, are valid and arguments of the form

(1) *A or B.*
(2) *Therefore, B.*

are invalid *because* of the way the propositional connectives ' . . . and ____' and '. . . or ____' function and not because of the content of sentences taking the place of '*A*' and '*B*'. This definition is simply a generalization of this intuition to *all* arguments and *all* logical words.

Three difficulties interfere with the practical application of this definition as it stands. First, it presupposes a precise distinction between the logical and nonlogical words occurring in argument descriptions. We have, to be sure, given clear-cut examples of both sorts of phrase, but we have not yet given a way of telling, with respect to *any* phrase whatever, to which class it belongs. In fact, as far as we know, there is no way to distinguish completely and precisely between the logical and nonlogical phrases of a natural language such as English. Second, this definition presupposes a thorough understanding, now lacking, of the function of the logical words. To put it another way, the definition seems to require us to examine *ad seriatum* every possible replacement of the nonlogical words in an argument description before we can determine whether or not an argument is valid. This is a most uncongenial task. The third difficulty is this: We are supposing that, given two different formulations of an argument in, say, gross standard form, we can tell whether or not they are formulations of the *same* argument. In general, two different argument descriptions are formulations of the same argument just in case

1. The same propositions are expressed.
2. They are related in the same way.

However, to determine whether or not the second condition holds, we require some means of telling how the propositions comprising an argument are related to one another. This is, of course, the same old question of how to detect its logical form.

The official idiom overcomes all these difficulties; indeed, one of the chief virtues of a formal language such as the official idiom is that it remedies such deficiencies of natural languages. First, in the official idiom, there is a sharp distinction between logical and nonlogical phrases. Second, a precise account of how the logical words of the official idiom function in arguments can be given. Because the official idiom regiments arguments in certain ways, paraphrase into official standard form enables one to reduce the impossible task of examining every appropriate replacement of nonlogical phrases in an argument description to a manageable, even mechanical, task. In other words, when an argument is in official standard form, it is possible to tell whether or not a counterexample exists without having to look at every argument of the same form to see whether or not one of them has true premises and a false conclusion. Finally, because the official idiom makes the logical form of arguments explicit, paraphrase into it answers the question: When are two argument descriptions formulations of the same argument?

There are two main stages in the construction of the official idiom. First, there is a specification of its *syntax*. This involves a listing of the symbols belonging to its *vocabulary* and specifying the *grammar*, or how the symbols can be put together. The vocabulary includes both logical and nonlogical symbolic phrases. In the beginning we shall be concerned only with arguments whose validity depends only on connections between propositions. So, for the present, we shall ignore the symbolic expressions for names, predicates, and quantifiers (i.e., words like 'all' and 'some'). The logical phrases with which we shall begin loosely correspond to the propositional connectives of English. They are called *logical constants*. The nonlogical vocabulary consists of an indefinitely large set of *sentence letters*, $'p'$, $'q'$, $'r'$ (with or without subscripts). Ordinarily, their function is to *abbreviate* simple English sentences such as 'Socrates sits' or 'Roscoe murdered Crustacea'. One would paraphrase such a sentence into the official idiom, simply, as $'p'$.

To give the official idiom a grammar is to say what combinations of logical and nonlogical symbols constitute a *sentence in the official idiom*. Just as the logical form of arguments expressed in English depends upon the pattern of simple sentences and propositional connectives in their argument descriptions, so does the logical form of arguments in official standard form depend on the pattern of sentence letters and logical constants.

To know which combinations of symbols are sentences of the official idiom is not, however, sufficient to determine under what conditions complex sentences are true or false. One cannot tell whether or not an argument in official standard form is valid until *a way of understanding* the sentence letters and, in particular, the logical constants is specified. Thus, in the second stage of development of the official idiom, the logical constants are given *interpretations*. An interpretation specifies how the logical constants function in the complex sentences of the official idiom in which they occur. Their interpretations are designed to ensure that they function in ways analogous to English propositional connectives, but, as we shall see, there are some important differences. The interpretations of the logical constants in the official idiom are the most important part of its *semantics*; they invest these symbols with precise meanings.

To create the official idiom, then, we specify a syntax and a (partial) semantics. The syntax gives the vocabulary and grammar of the official idiom, and the semantics includes interpretations for all the logical constants. The remainder of the semantics will be given in Chapter 3.

3.1 Exercises

In answering the following questions, you may find it helpful to refer to the summary of concepts and definitions introduced in this chapter on p. 169. Starred exercises are answered in Appendix III.

1. Explain in a brief paragraph the point of paraphrasing arguments into official standard form.
2. In what sense can an English argument in its natural habitat be said to have a logical form? Explain.
★3. What is the relation between paraphrase and logical form?
4. Is the following the correct way to distinguish between a natural language and a formal language? "A natural language is one that ordinary people speak, whereas a formal language is reserved for special occasions such as diplomatic negotiations." Why or why not? Explain.
5. What steps must be taken to create a language such as the official idiom? Explain.

4.

THE OFFICIAL IDIOM: SYNTAX

Here is a list of the items in the vocabulary of the official idiom and their most natural English analogues, or "readings," if any:

Name of Symbol	Symbol	Reading
1. The negation sign	~	'It is not the case that ____'
2. The conjunction sign	&	'. . . and ____'
3. The alternation sign	v	'. . . or ____'
4. The conditional sign	⊃	'If . . . , then ____'
5. The biconditional sign	≡	'. . . if and only if ____'
6. Left-hand parenthesis	(	
7. Right-hand parenthesis	)	
8. Sentence letters	p, q, r, with or without subscripts	

For the moment, attention will be concentrated on the propositional connectives, items 1 to 5, and their English readings. The connectives are given these readings because the special purpose of formalization is to enable us to tell whether or not arguments expressed in English are valid; therefore, we want to emphasize parallels between English and the official idiom when saying which sentences in the official idiom correspond to which English sentences.

It is important to understand correctly the relation between the connectives and their readings. They should not be thought of as being equivalent in meaning; it is best to regard readings as *clues* for finding the right paraphrase for English sentences. They call attention to features of English sentences (and arguments) that we want to preserve in paraphrase. Readings are useful guides for paraphrase because they perform approximately the same function in English sentences as do the logical constants in sentences in the official idiom.

The logical *constants* are so called because, unlike other expressions, such as sentence letters that abbreviate different sentences in different contexts, they never symbolize anything else. Whereas '*p*' and '*q*', for example, may abbreviate many different propositions in different contexts, '⊃', for example, always makes the same contribution to the complex sentences in which it occurs. In the preceding table of English readings for the connectives, the ellipses indicate positions where sen-tences occur; the two different styles of ellipsis indicate that differen

76

sentences *may* fill those spaces. The readings have the syntactical property that the result of replacing the ellipses with the appropriate number of sentences will always be an English sentence. Similarly, the corresponding propositional connectives form sentences out of sentences: Given the appropriate number of sentences in the official idiom, a new sentence in the official idiom can be created by their use. The negation sign, '~', for example, is a *unary* propositional connective similar to 'it is not the case that . . .'. The result of prefixing a sentence in the official idiom with the negation sign is also a sentence in the official idiom. For example, beginning with the simple sentence 'p', one can form the complex sentence '$\sim p$'. Since this, too, is a sentence in the official idiom, the same thing can be done again and again and the result is always a sentence: '$\sim\sim p$', for example. This corresponds to the grammar of the English reading of the negation sign. Beginning with the simple English sentence, 'Socrates is wise', one can form the complex sentence 'It is not the case that Socrates is wise'. Since this, too, is an English sentence, the same thing can be done again and the result is a new sentence: 'It is not the case that it is not the case that Socrates is wise'.

The other logical constants are all *binary* propositional connectives: Given any two sentences (not necessarily different), a new complex sentence can be created by means of the binary connectives. For example, given the simple sentences 'p' and 'q', one can form such sentences as '$p \lor q$', '$p \ \& \ q$', and so on. Given the complex sentences '$p \lor q$' and '$p \ \& \ q$', one can form sentences such as '$(p \lor q) \supset (p \ \& \ q)$', '$\sim(p \lor q) \ \& \ (p \ \& \ q)$', and so on. Again, this parallels English sentence construction: Given such English sentences as 'Grass is green' and 'The sky is blue', one can form the complex sentences 'If grass is green, then the sky is blue', 'It is not the case that grass is green and the sky is blue', and so on. The point is, given *any* two sentences in the official idiom, the result of joining them with a binary propositional connective is also a sentence in the official idiom.

Parentheses are used as punctuation; they prevent ambiguity. For example, an old joke relies on reading the following sentence in two different ways: 'Bring your wife or come stag and have a good time'. It might be taken to express the invitation either to bring one's wife or have a good time, but not both, or the quite different invitation to have a good time in either case. The sentence can be disambiguated in these two ways by the use of parentheses: (1) 'Bring your wife or (come stag and have a good time)' or (2) '(Bring your wife or come stag) and have a good time'.

Now we can give a precise characterization of the grammar of the official idiom. This amounts to defining the notion of *sentence in the official idiom* (SOI):

1. Any of the sentence letters p, q, r, with or without subscripts, is a *sentence in the official idiom.*
2. If A is any *sentence in the official idiom,* then $\sim A$ is a *sentence in the official idiom.*
3. If A and B are any two *sentences in the official idiom,* then
   (a) $(A \vee B)$
   (b) $(A \mathbin{\&} B)$
   (c) $(A \supset B)$
   (d) $(A \equiv B)$
   are *sentences in the official idiom.*
4. Nothing that is not the result of one of the clauses above is a *sentence in the official idiom.*[4]

Note that SOI employs the uppercase letters 'A' and 'B'. These symbols are not in the vocabulary of the official idiom. Therefore, neither they nor the complex forms in which they occur are sentences in the official idiom. Rather, they are used to talk about sentences in the official idiom. We have already made analogous use of these symbols in discussing the forms of English sentences, such as premises of the form of 'A or B'. Just as 'A or B' is not an English sentence itself but can be used to talk about the form of English sentences, '$A \vee B$' is used to talk about sentences of the official idiom. For example, when we say "If A is a sentence in the official idiom . . . ," we are using 'A' to designate *any* sentence in the official idiom, such as, for example, 'q', 'p', '$(p \supset q) \mathbin{\&} r$', and '$r \supset (r \supset (r \equiv q)) \mathbin{\&} (p \mathbin{\&} \sim p)$'. Symbols such as '$A$' and '$B$', which do not belong to the official idiom but are used to talk in this general way about expressions of the official idiom, are called *meta-variables.*

The logical constants appearing in SOI stand for themselves; they are used autonymously, to use a technical word common in logic. In clause (3b), for example, '$\&$' *is* the conjunction sign; in this occurrence it designates itself. Clause (3b) says that every result of replacing the meta-variable 'A' with a sentence in the official idiom, followed by '$\&$', followed by a replacement of the meta-variable 'B' by a sentence in the official idiom, is a sentence in the official idiom. The other clauses are to be understood in parallel fashion. Different meta-variables indicate that different sentences in the official idiom may be combined by means of each of the binary logical constants, but of course this is not required. It is a consequence of (3c), for example, that '$p \supset p$' is a sentence in the official idiom. This is because 'p' is a sentence in the official idiom, by

---

[4] For convenience we shall adopt the convention that the outermost parentheses of a sentence in the official idiom may be dropped. Thus '$((p \supset q) \vee r)$', for example, becomes '$(p \supset q) \vee r$'.

clause (1). Hence '*p*' is a sentence and '*p*' is a sentence [by a second application of clause (1)]. So, by clause (3c), '*p* ⊃ *p*' is a sentence in the official idiom.

To recapitulate: The sentence letters '*p*', '*q*', and '*r*' are used to paraphrase particular English sentences into the official idiom. The metavariables '*A*' and '*B*' (we shall also use '*C*' and '*D*' if necessary) are used to represent sentences in the official idiom, and the logical constants are used to represent themselves. Any sentence in the official idiom containing at least one logical constant is a *complex* sentence. Otherwise, it is a *simple* sentence.

4.1 Exercises

In answering the following questions, you may find it helpful to refer to the summary of concepts and definitions introduced in this chapter on p. 169. Starred exercises are answered in Appendix III.

1. Why are the propositional connectives of the official idiom said to be logical *constants*?
2. What is the relation between the logical constants and their English readings?
3. Which of the following are sentences in the official idiom and which are not? Defend your answers by citing the relevant clauses of SOI.

   a. *p* & *q* & *r*   b. *p* & *q*
   ★c. (*p* & *q*)   d. ~(~(~(*p*)))
   e. (~~*p*)   f. *p* ~ *p*
   g. ~~~*p*   ★h. *pq*
   i. (*A* ≡ *B*) & *C*   j. *p* & *q* ⊃ *r*
   ★k. *A* ≡ (*p* & ~*p*)   l. *p* ≡ *p*$_1$
   m. (*p* ∨ *p*$_2$) ⊃ ~*p*   n. *p*

   Which of these are simple sentences and which are complex sentences?
4. Is the official idiom as described in this section a language? If not, what else would one have to do to make it a language?
5. Consider the sentence '((*p* & *q*) & *r*)'. Is '&' a tertiary (i.e., three-place) propositional connective here? Why or why not?
6. Explain the difference in meaning between the following two sentences:
   a. If '*p*' is a sentence in the official idiom and '*q*' is a sentence in the official idiom, then '*p* & *q*' is a sentence in the official idiom.
   b. If *A* is a sentence in the official idiom and *B* is a sentence in the official idiom, then *A* & *B* is a sentence in the official idiom.

5.

THE OFFICIAL IDIOM: SEMANTICS

Relative to a scheme of abbreviation one may think of the sentence letters as expressing propositions. If, for example, '*p*' is the abbreviation for 'Grass is green', then one may think of it as expressing the proposition that grass is green. Since this proposition is true, '*p*' is true in that context. When a sentence in English or in the official idiom is true, we shall say that it has truth as its *truth value* (the reason for this locution will become apparent later). If '*p*' abbreviates a false proposition, it has falsity as its truth value. Every proposition is either true or false, and no proposition is both. Hence, on any given occasion of paraphrase, a sentence letter will have one or the other truth value (but never both).

Complex sentences express (complex) propositions; so they too must have truth values. In English and in the official idiom alike, the truth value of a complex sentence depends on two things: first, the truth values of the embedded simple sentences, and second, the *contribution* made by the contained propositional connectives to the truth value of the entire sentence.

This contribution is already fixed in English by the meanings of the English propositional connectives. That is, because we already understand the English propositional connectives, we are able in certain standard cases to determine the truth value of the complex sentences in which they occur once we know the truth values of the embedded simple sentences. In the case of the propositional connectives of the official idiom, *we* have to *specify* what contributions they are to make to the truth values of the complex sentences of the official idiom in which they occur. To make this specification is to *interpret* them. Logical constants of the official idiom do not stand for or express anything; their job is only to make certain systematic contributions to the truth value of complex sentences containing them. Yet they are still to be thought of as *propositional* connectives. Just like the English propositional connectives that are their readings, the logical constants "connect" propositions expressed by embedded sentence letters. Thus they also contribute to the truth values of the complex sentences in which they occur. By making this sort of systematic contribution to the truth values of complex sentences, the logical constants actually determine the relations among propositions expressed by the embedded simple sentences of the official idiom upon which an argument's validity or invalidity depends.

Knowing how the connectives are to be interpreted is crucial to the enterprise of paraphrase. One cannot tell whether the paraphrase of an

English sentence into one in the official idiom is correct unless one understands both sentences. The situation is similar to translating from German, say, into English. As anyone who has ever learned a foreign language is aware, one can know well enough that a given sentence is grammatically correct (that it is *a sentence in German,* say) but not know what it means. Then whether or not a given English sentence is an accurate translation, as may be claimed, cannot be determined. Our goal is to interpret the connectives in a manner ensuring that their contributions to the truth values of the complex sentences of the official idiom corresponds, in selected standard cases, to the contributions that their readings make to the truth values of English sentences in which they occur.

The nature of the correspondence between connectives in the official idiom and their English readings, then, is this: They are not equivalent in meaning, but they make equivalent contributions to the truth values of the complex sentences in which they occur. Since validity is defined partly in terms of truth, this correspondence is exactly what paraphrase into official standard form elucidates. The contribution made by a propositional connective, either of English or of the official idiom, is revealed in what are called the *truth conditions*[5] of the complex sentences containing them. The truth conditions of a complex sentence in the official idiom are given by one or more rules determining its truth value relative to every possible combination of the truth values of its embedded simple sentences. It is easiest to understand the concept of truth conditions in concrete cases; so let us proceed to the first connective, negation.

First, notice that the English reading of the negation sign has the function of negating English sentences. If 'Tom is tall' is true, then the result of prefixing 'it is not the case that . . .', to it, that is, 'It is not the case that Tom is tall', is false. Conversely, if 'Tom is tall' is false, 'It is not the case that Tom is tall' is true. Thus the contribution of 'it is not the case that . . .' is to change the truth value of sentences in which it occurs. We can represent the matter thus:

---

[5] Two sentences, either of English or the official idiom (or a mixture of the two) are said to have the same truth conditions if they are true (false) together under exactly the same "circumstances." In the most elementary case the circumstances in question are the all possible combinations of truth values of their component simple sentences (if any). In the more complex case, more is involved in the similarity of circumstances under which two sentences are true and false together. In any case, a common way of expressing the fact that two sentences are true and false together under all the same circumstances is to say they are *logically equivalent.* We shall defer discussion of logical equivalence until we have developed the necessary technical notions in Chapter 3 to make this notion more precise.

Tom is tall	It is not the case that Tom is tall
T	F
F	T

This chart shows what the truth value of 'It is not the case that Tom is tall' is *under the condition that* the embedded simple sentence is true or false, respectively. The complex sentence has the truth conditions it has because of the contribution of 'it is not the case that . . .' to the truth value of the whole sentence relative to alternative truth values of the embedded sentence.

The logical interpretation of the negation sign is fixed to make its contribution to complex sentences of the official idiom correspond to that of the English reading:

For any *sentence A in the official idiom, ~A is true if and only if A is false. Otherwise, ~A is false.*

The logical interpretation of the negation sign may be "graphed" in the following "truth table,"[6] clearly showing its contribution to complex sentences of the official idiom containing it to be exactly parallel to that of 'it is not the case that . . .':

A	$\sim A$
T	F
F	T

Truth tables have a dual purpose. In this section they are used to display graphically the truth conditions of sentences (and forms of sentences). In Appendix II they will also be used as devices to facilitate the evaluation of arguments.

It is worth reemphasizing that the interpretations of the logical connectives only approximate the *meanings* possessed by the English readings in their usual contexts. This is permissible because that *part* of the meaning which determines the truth conditions of sentences in which English propositional connectives occur is captured by the logical interpretations. This amounts to the requirement that nothing relevant to validity be left out, since that notion is defined partly in terms of truth. On the other hand, it is equally important to ignore features of English propositional connectives that are irrelevant to validity.

---

[6] If this truth table is not immediately comprehensible, consult the detailed discussion of truth tables in the beginning sections of Appendix II.

The logical sign for conjunction, '&', is a binary connective used to paraphrase English sentences having the logical form of conjunctions. Let us now develop an interpretation for '&' according sufficiently well with the English connective '. . . and ____'. We do not, of course, know the actual truth values of 'Tom is tall' and 'George is short', for example, but we know what the possibilities are. Both could be true, both false, the first true and the second false, and vice versa. Let us ask, then, under what conditions the compound sentence 'Tom is tall and George is short' would be true and under which it would be false. A moment's reflection will show that the conjunction of these sentences is true if and only if both simple sentences are true. We then fix the logical interpretation for '&' in the same manner as for '~', by stipulating:

For any sentences A, B in the official idiom, A & B is true if and only if A is true and B is true. Otherwise, A & B is false.

The graph for conjunction is as follows:

A	B	A & B
T	T	T
T	F	F
F	T	F
F	F	F

A and *B* are called "conjuncts" in *A* & *B*.

The alternation sign, 'v', is interpreted as follows:

For any sentences A, B in the official idiom, A v B is true if and only if A is true or B is true, or both. Otherwise, A v B is false.

The graph for alternation is

A	B	A v B
T	T	T
T	F	T
F	T	T
F	F	F

The alternation sign is so called because of the alternate ways *A* v *B* can be made true. The two alternated sentences, *A* and *B*, are called "alternants." The foregoing provides a good example of an interpretation capturing only a part of the meaning of its corresponding English read-ing, for it fixes the contribution of '. . . or _____' in only one of its two common English uses. The divergence between the two uses of the English connective has to do with its contribution to the alternation of two true sentences. In most contexts we should regard an alternation such as 'Grass is green or the sky is blue' true because both alternants are true. So, there is at least this *inclusive* use of '. . . or _____' in English, in accordance with our interpretation of 'v'. It is often thought, how-ever, that there is another use of '. . . or _____' in which an alternation containing such an occurrence is false if both alternants are true. This is called the *exclusive* use of '. . . or _____'. For example, if President Carter were to announce, "Either the Soviet Union will respect the Universal Declaration of the Rights of Man or the United States will withdraw from the Strategic Arms Limitation Talks (SALT)," he would certainly be taken to be disingenuous if the Soviet Union did respect the Declaration and the United States proceeded to withdraw from SALT anyway. In other words, if Carter's sentence is regarded as true, one of the alter-nants must be regarded as false. Similarly, when a mother says, "You may have cake or you may have ice cream," she normally intends to rule out her child's taking both.

The decision to interpet 'v' in accordance with only the inclusive use of '. . . or _____' conforms to our goal of constructing a means of para-phrasing arguments into official standard form in a manner preserving only what is essential to validity. As will be seen in Section 7, this decision does not prevent us from paraphrasing arguments in which the exclusive use of '. . . or _____' is involved, for the effect of the exclusive use can be achieved by paraphrases using 'v' together with other connectives.

The fourth connective is the conditional, '⊃'. It is used to paraphrase sentences of the form 'If A, then B'. Such sentences are said to be "con-ditionals" because B is asserted *on the condition* that A is true. A is called the *antecedent* and B the *consequent*. The interpretation of the conditional sign diverges more from the meaning of its reading, the colloquial 'if . . . , then _____', perhaps, than does any other connective's interpreta-tion from the meaning of its reading. We shall begin by specifying the interpretation for '⊃'; then we shall briefly discuss a few uses of 'if . . . , then _____' in which it agrees with the desired interpretation, reserving discussion of uses in which it does not agree until Sections 7 and 8 of this chapter.

This is the interpretation of the conditional sign:

For any sentences A, B of the official idiom, $A \supset B$ is true if and only if A is false or B is true, or both. Otherwise, $A \supset B$ is false.

Graphing this interpretation onto a truth table is left as an exercise for the reader. Now, one of these truth conditions is noncontroversial, namely, the condition under which a sentence of the form $A \supset B$ is false. Consider the following sentence: 'If San Francisco is in California, then San Francisco is east of New York'. Everyone would agree that this sentence is false, because its antecedent, 'San Francisco is in California', is true and its consequent, 'San Francisco is east of New York', is false. In this case, 'if . . . , then ____' makes exactly the same contribution to the truth value of the whole as that specified by the interpretation of the conditional sign when the antecedent of a sentence of the official idiom of the form $A \supset B$ is true and its consequent is false.

It may be more difficult to see why the other truth conditions for conditional sentences are appropriate. Let us proceed by examining a couple of familiar arguments from Chapter 1 in which the English conditional is used in the specified way. Recall Roscoe Frostbite's scrape with Apassionata L'amour. Roscoe made the inference recorded by:

A (1) *If I tell Crustacea that the meeting with Apassionata was strictly professional, then Crustacea will believe the worst.*
(2) *If I do not tell Crustacea that the meeting with Apassionata was strictly professional, then Crustacea will believe the worst.*
(3) *Therefore, Crustacea will believe the worst.*

Intuitively, **A** is valid, and since we may suppose Roscoe to know his wife's psychology, it is sound. Therefore, the conclusion is true. Now the conclusion sentence appears as consequent in both (1) and (2), so we have two true conditionals that happen to have true consequents. Yet their antecedents are incompatible—Roscoe cannot both tell and not tell Crustacea that the meeting was strictly professional—so one antecedent is true and the other false. Therefore, one conditional is true when it has a false antecedent and a true consequent, while the other is true when it has a true antecedent and a true consequent. Both these uses of the English conditional sign agree with the specified interpretation of '$\supset$'.

Now look at the second argument:

B (1) *If Roscoe murdered Crustacea, then he was home between midnight and 2:00* A.M. *Tuesday.*
(2) *It is not the case that Roscoe was home between midnight and 2:00* A.M. *Tuesday.*
(3) *Therefore, it is not the case that Roscoe murdered Crustacea.*

Argument **B** is intuitively valid and it is easy to imagine it to be sound, as in the story about Roscoe. If (2) is true, the embedded sentence

'Roscoe was home between midnight and 2:00 A.M. Tuesday' must be false given our understanding of the English propositional connective 'it is not the case that . . . '. Similarly, if (3) is true, the contained sentence 'Roscoe murdered Crustacea' must be false. These two sentences are the consequent and antecedent, respectively, of (1). Thus (1) involves a use of 'if . . . , then ____' which accords with the final truth condition of sentences of the form $A \supset B$—that the conditional is true when antecedent and consequent are both false.

The foregoing arguments involve natural uses of 'if . . . , then ____' which agree with the truth conditions for conditional sentences of the official idiom. In other words, these English conditionals were true when their antecedents were false or their consequents true (or both). The other truth condition, that conditionals are false if their antecedents are true and consequents false, as in the case of 'If San Francisco is in California, then San Francisco is east of New York', is obvious.

There are, however, many uses of 'if . . . then ____' that do not agree with the interpretation for '$\supset$'. Some of these will be discussed in Sections 7 and 8 of this chapter. We ignore them here because our goal in interpretation is to clarify only those uses of the conditional that are relevant to the validity of English arguments, and this interpretation is most suitable for arguments of the sort with which we are concerned in this book.

The last connective to be interpreted is '$\equiv$'. Consider the sentence 'The picnic will be canceled if and only if it rains'. Under what conditions would we regard this sentence to be true or false? It seems clear that if a person believed this sentence to be true and it did not rain, then he would show up expecting the picnic to be held. In other words, if we thought this sentence true and the embedded sentence 'It rains' to be false, then we would expect the other embedded sentence, 'The picnic will be canceled', to be false also. Conversely, if it *does* rain we would expect the picnic to be canceled. Now suppose that we find out that the picnic is canceled, that the sentence 'The picnic will be canceled' is true. If we supposed the biconditional to be true, we should immediately conclude that it is raining, because the biconditional specifies the *only* condition under which the picnic will be canceled. Similarly, were we to discover that the picnic is not canceled, we would know that it is not raining. We have now specified the conditions under which 'The picnic will be canceled if and only if it rains' is true. What would make it false? It would be false just in case the conditions for its truth fail to hold. A moment's reflection on the foregoing description of conditions under which it would be true shows that it is true in all those cases in which the embedded sentences have the same truth values. So, it will be false just in case the truth values of the embedded sentences are not the same. The interpretation of the biconditional, then, is

> For any sentences A, B of the official idiom, $A \equiv B$ is true if and only if A is true and B is true, or A is false and B is false (but not both). Otherwise, $A \equiv B$ is false.

The relevant truth table is

A	B	$A \equiv B$
T	T	T
T	F	F
F	T	F
F	F	T

5.1 Exercises

In answering the following questions, you may find it helpful to refer to the summary of concepts and definitions introduced in this chapter on p. 169. Starred exercises are answered in Appendix III.

1. Upon what does the truth value of a simple sentence in the official idiom depend?
2. Upon what does the truth value of a complex sentence in the official idiom depend?
3. What does it mean to given an interpretation for one of the propositional connectives of the official idiom? Are the readings of the logical constants given interpretations? Explain.
4. What does the following statement mean?
   a. 'It is not the case that Tom is tall' has the same truth conditions as '~p'.
★5. Under what circumstances will it be the case that 'It is not the case that Tom is tall' has the same truth value as '~p'? In general, what is the difference between the truth conditions for a sentence (either of English or of the official idiom) and its truth value?
6. What is the difference between the inclusive and exclusive senses of the English propositional connective '. . . or ____'?
7. Give the truth-table "graph" of the interpretation specified for the conditional sign on p. 85.
8. What, if anything, do the propositional connectives stand for? Explain.

9. Are the following statements true or false?
   a. An interpretation of a propositional connective that does not capture the precise meaning of the corresponding English reading is inadequate.
   b. An interpretation of a propositional connective has no connection whatsoever with the meaning of the corresponding English reading.
   Explain fully.

6.
PARAPHRASE OF SENTENCES INTO THE OFFICIAL IDIOM

Learning to paraphrase sentences into the official idiom is a little like learning to translate from one natural language into another. One tries in both cases to represent certain information in the second language originally expressed in the first. In paraphrase into the official idiom, the only information one tries to preserve is the logical form of the original propositions and arguments. Because this form is imposed on them by argument descriptions, we speak, derivatively, of the logical form of sentences and argument descriptions. One ignores aspects of the meanings of English phrases that do not matter to the validity or invalidity of arguments. What is crucial in paraphrase is *preservation of the truth conditions* of the original sentences; for to say that two sentences have the same logical form is, in part, to say that they have the same truth conditions. Although some paraphrases may be more nearly perfect than others, we shall consider any paraphrase of an English sentence into the official idiom that preserves the truth conditions of the original to be *adequate*. Like translation from one natural language into another, paraphrase takes sensitivity and skill, because *there are no mechanical rules* for paraphrase. Although some rules of thumb will be given, none is foolproof; in the end only a great deal of practice will ensure development of the necessary skills. We shall begin with a few straightforward cases and then proceed to more difficult cases in the next section.

First, we shall introduce the notion of a *standard occurrence* of a reading of one of the propositional connectives in the official idiom. We shall say that a reading has a standard occurrence in a complex English sentence if and only if it makes the same contribution to the truth value of the whole sentence as that specified by the interpretation of its corresponding logical constant for sentences of the official idiom. In Section 5 the propositional connectives were interpreted in the light of certain models involving standard occurrences of their readings, so the paraphrases of these sentences is easy. Here are some examples which came up in that discussion; each involves a standard occurrence of an English propositional connective:

(1) *It is not the case that Roscoe murdered Crustacea.*
(2) *Tom is tall or George is short.*
(3) *Tom is tall and George is short.*

89

(4) If San Francisco is in California, then San Francisco is east of New York.

(5) The picnic will be canceled if and only if it rains.

To paraphrase these sentences into the official idiom, we

a. Identify the embedded simple sentences.
b. Identify the propositional connective and determine that it does indeed make the same contribution to the truth value of the whole as specified by the interpretation of its corresponding connective to complex sentences of the official idiom.
c. Choose a scheme of abbreviation.

This is sufficient for finding a complex sentence of the official idiom having the same truth conditions as the original English sentence.

Now (1) as a whole is true if and only if the embedded simple sentence 'Roscoe murdered Crustacea' is false. Otherwise, it is false. Thus the English connective 'it is not the case that . . . ' does in this context make the same contribution to the truth value of (1) as does '~' to sentences in the official idiom of the form $\sim A$. Let 'p' be the abbreviation of 'Roscoe murdered Crustacea'. Then the correct paraphrase of (1), having the form $\sim A$, is '$\sim p$'.

Example (2) is true if and only if either or both embedded simple sentences are true. It is false otherwise. Thus the connective '. . . or ____' in this context makes the same contribution to the truth value of (2) as '∨' makes to sentences in the official idiom of the form of $A \vee B$. Let 'p' be the abbreviation of 'Tom is tall', and 'q' be the abbreviation of 'George is short'. Then the correct paraphrase of (2) into the official idiom is '$p \vee q$'.

Example (3) is true if and only if both embedded sentences are true; otherwise it is false. So, '. . . and ____' makes the appropriate contribution to the truth value of the sentence. Thus its paraphrase is into a sentence of the form $A \& B$. On the same scheme of abbreviation as in the case of (2), it is '$p \& q$'.

Example (4) involves a standard use of 'if . . . then ____' in which the whole is true unless the antecedent is true and the consequent false. Since this is the contribution of '⊃' to sentences in the official idiom, the sentence should be paraphrased as '$p \supset q$', where 'p' is 'San Francisco is in California' and 'q' is 'San Francisco is east of New York'.

Example (5) involves a standard use of '. . . if and only if ____', so abbreviating 'The picnic will be canceled' as 'p' and 'It rains' as 'q', the correct paraphrase is $p \equiv q$.

These five sentences in the official idiom reveal the logical forms of their English counterparts. (1) has the form of a negation (namely, $\sim A$), (2) of an alternation (namely, $A \lor B$), (3) of a conjunction (namely, A & B), (4) of a conditional (namely, $A \supset B$), and (5) has the form of a biconditional (namely, $A \equiv B$). Paraphrase into the official idiom makes the truth conditions of each original English sentence explicit because, if correct, it has the same truth conditions as the original, and the truth conditions of sentences in the official idiom are made completely precise by the interpretations of the connectives. Note that sentences in the official idiom of many different forms have the same truth conditions. For example, '(It is not the case that San Francisco is in California) or (San Francisco is east of New York)' has the same truth conditions as sentence (4) above. It can be seen, in fact, that all sentences of the forms $A \supset B$ and $\sim A \lor B$ have the same truth conditions. Simply inspect the interpretations of $A \supset B$, $\sim A$, and $\sim A \lor B$. The results of such an examination might be represented as in the following truth table:

		I	II	III
A	B	$A \supset B$	$\sim A$	$\sim A \lor B$
T	T	T	F	T
T	F	F	F	F
F	T	T	T	T
F	F	T	T	T

As columns I and III show, sentences of the forms $A \supset B$ and $\sim A \lor B$ are false just when A is true and B false; otherwise, they are true.

Let us return to sentence (4). If we bear in mind the original scheme of abbreviation, the table shows that '$p \supset q$' and '$\sim p \lor q$' have the same truth conditions, but '$\sim p \lor q$', strictly speaking, would not be a correct paraphrase of 'Is San Francisco is in California, then San Francisco is east of New York' because the latter English sentence is conditional, whereas '$\sim p \lor q$' is not. Further, the latter sentence contains the negation of one alternant, whereas there is no negation in the original English sentence. A more extreme case will help to drive home the point: Another sentence in the official idiom with the same truth conditions as '$p \supset q$' is '$\sim(\sim(p \supset \sim p)) \lor (q \ \& \ (\sim q \supset q))$', but no one would be apt to regard this as a correct paraphrase of 'If San Francisco is in California, then San Francisco is east of New York' (on the same scheme of abbreviation). Ideally, correctness of paraphrase and preservation of logical form involves more than preservation of the truth conditions of the sentence in question. Unfortunately, however, it is not always clear what the logical form, strictly speaking, of an English sentence is. So some latitude in this respect prevails in the paraphrase. To date, no satisfactory theory of the logical form of English sentences exists that would enable one to say what are necessary and *sufficient* conditions for the correctness of paraphrase. Indeed, no such theory may be possible, as we have said. This is why we distinguish between *correctness* of paraphrase and *adequacy* of paraphrase. A paraphrase that preserves truth conditions is *adequate* for our purposes because such a paraphrase of an argument will always be equivalent in validity (or soundness) or invalidity (or unsoundness) to the original argument. So, for the purposes of evaluating arguments, absolute correctness in this sense is not required. Again the analogy of translation from one natural language to another is useful here; it is easier to tell what makes a translation wrong than it is to say exactly under what conditions it would be right. Nevertheless, such theoretical difficulties as the lack of a sufficient condition for correctness of translation do not make it appreciably more difficult to accomplish correct translations from one natural language to another. The same holds of paraphrase from English into the official idiom: It should be emphasized that this *theoretical* difficulty does not interfere with the *practical* accomplishment of the task for which the technique of paraphrase is introduced. Even though the paraphrase of an argument into the official idiom may not capture everything involved in the logical form of the original argument, enough is preserved to enable accurate determination of validity or invalidity. What is essential for this is only that the truth conditions of all the sentences comprising the argument description are preserved by a correct paraphrase.

In the next two sections we shall discuss more difficult cases of paraphrase. They involve the paraphrase of complex English sentences containing propositional connectives other than readings of the propositional connectives of the official idiom and paraphrases involving nonstandard occurrences of the readings.

6.1 Exercises

In answering the following questions, you may find it helpful to refer to the summary of concepts and definitions introduced in this chapter on p. 169. Starred exercises are answered in Appendix III.

1. Why is preservation of truth conditions of English sentences the goal of paraphrase into the official idiom?
2. What does it mean to say that '. . . and ____' has a standard occurrence in the sentence 'California is a state and San Francisco is a city'?
★3. Let 'p' abbreviate 'San Francisco is in California' and 'q' abbreviate 'San Francisco is in Nevada'. Now consider the following three putative

paraphrases of the sentence '(It is not the case that San Francisco is in California) and San Francisco is in Nevada':

a. ~(p & q)

b. p v q

c. ~p & q

Do these putative paraphrases differ in respect of *correctness* of paraphrase? If so, how?

Do they differ in respect of *adequacy* of paraphrase? If so, how?

4. Paraphrase the sentences below as well as possible, using the scheme of abbreviation given:

'p': 'John will pass the course'.

'q': 'John studies'.

'r': 'John plays poker'.

's': 'Someone helps John'.

   a. If John studies, then John will pass the course.
   b. If someone helps John, then John will pass the course.
   c. John will pass the course if and only if John studies and someone helps him.
   d. If John plays poker and it is not the case that someone helps him, then he will not pass the course.
★e. If John does not study and someone helps him, then he will pass the course only if he does not play poker.
   f. If John plays poker he won't pass, and if he doesn't play poker he won't pass, and if he studies he won't pass either.
   g. Someone will help John if and only if he doesn't play poker.

7.
STYLISTIC VARIANCE[7]

There are many more English connectives than those designated as readings of the logical constants. For example, '. . . unless ____', '. . . but ____', and '. . . provided that ____' are propositional connectives, but they are not readings of any logical constant. This does not mean that complex English sentences containing such connectives cannot be paraphrased into the official idiom. To accomplish such paraphrases, we need only reflect on the fact that someone who uses one of these English connectives may well be saying the same thing as would be asserted by means of one of the readings. That is, in a particular use, one of these connectives may make the same contribution to the truth value of the complex sentence in which it is contained as is made by one or more of the readings of the logical constants. In that case the sentence is paraphrased into the official idiom with the logical constant making the appropriate contribution to sentences of the official idiom. This procedure reflects the fact that we often choose propositional connectives other than the readings not to assert something different but only to make our style less monotonous: hence the expression "stylistic variant."

To be precise: A complex English sentence containing one or more propositional connectives other than readings of the logical constants is a *stylistic variant* of another English sentence containing no propositional connectives other than readings of logical constants if and only if they have the same truth conditions.

The point of paraphrasing stylistic variants is, of course, exactly the same as for sentences containing occurrences of the readings: It is to match an English sentence with a sentence in the official idiom having the same truth conditions. We shall not attempt to account for every conceivable sort of stylistic variance but shall content ourselves with illustrating the procedure in some especially clear cases.

Consider the sentence

(1) *The picnic will be canceled if it rains.*

(1) seems clearly to be a complex sentence, the result of replacing the ellipses in '. . . if ____' with the simple sentences 'The picnic will be

---

[7] The term 'stylistic variance' comes from R. Montague and D. Kalish, *Techniques of Formal Reasoning* (New York: Harcourt Brace Jovanovich, Inc., 1964). The term is used in a more restrictive sense in the present text.

canceled' and 'It rains', but '. . . . if _____' is not a reading of one of the logical constants. Nevertheless, (1) is quite similar to a sentence that results from such an operation on one of the readings, namely,

(2) *If it rains, then the picnic will be canceled.*

(1) is a stylistic variant of (2) if and only if they have the same truth conditions. Indeed, it seems that this is so, because '. . . if _____' makes just the same contribution to the truth value of (1), given the reversed order of simple sentences, as is made by 'if . . . then _____' in (2). Both (1) and (2) are true if and only if it does not rain or the picnic is canceled (or both). Otherwise, they are false. These are the truth conditions for sentences of the form $A \supset B$, so the correct paraphrase of (1) into the official idiom is

(3) $p \supset q$

Scheme of abbreviation—p: 'It rains'; q: 'It pours'. Note that '$q \supset p$' would not give the right truth conditions in this scheme of abbreviation.

Recall the example in Section 5 of Carter's warning on human rights. It involved the exclusive sense of '. . . or _____':

(1) *Either the Soviet Union will respect human rights or the United States will withdraw from SALT.*

This sentence is *false* if both alternants are true or if both are false (otherwise, it is true). Thus it is not paraphrasable into a sentence of the official idiom having the form $A \vee B$ because sentences of this form are true when both alternants are true. Nor is there any other single connective that makes the same contribution to complex sentences as the exclusive '. . . or _____'. One can, however, construct an appropriate complex sentence of the official idiom using more than one connective. Think, for a moment, of another way of putting the point of (1):

(2) *Either the Soviet Union will respect human rights or the United States will withdraw from SALT, and not both.*

This makes the intended truth conditions of (1) more explicit. The correct paraphrase of (1), then, will be whatever is the paraphrase of (2), namely, a sentence of the form $(A \vee B) \mathbin{\&} \sim(A \mathbin{\&} B)$. One can easily verify that a sentence of this form does have the appropriate truth conditions by using a truth table.

A	B	A ∨ B	A & B	~(A & B)	(A ∨ B) & ~(A & B)
T	T	T	T	F	F
T	F	T	F	T	T
F	T	T	F	T	T
F	F	F	F	T	F

The last column shows that $(A \lor B)$ & $\sim(A$ & $B)$ is true when A is true or B is true but is false when A and B are both true or both false. These are the truth conditions of (1), so this is the right paraphrase of (1):

(3) $(p \lor q)$ & $\sim(p$ & $q)$
    Scheme of abbreviation:
        p: 'The Soviet Union will respect human rights'.
        q: 'The United States will withdraw from SALT'.

Now consider a more difficult case, which illustrates, incidentally, how context may help determine which of two or more possible paraphrases is probably the best. Ordinarily, sentences containing '. . . but ____' are stylistic variants of those containing ' . . . and ____'. For example, in

(1) *Julian was a biologist, but Aldous became a writer.*

'. . . but ____' makes the same contribution to the truth value of the whole as '. . . and ____'. So (1) should be paraphrased as '*p & q*' (in the obvious scheme of abbreviation. This is not so clear in the case of

(2) *Jones is poor but honest.* [8]

First, one has to see that '. . . but ____' is indeed a propositional connective. This is obscured by the fact that the sentence following it is largely deleted. Nevertheless, anyone who understood (2) would take it to have the same truth conditions as

(3) *Jones is poor but Jones is honest.*

The second difficulty is that in ordinary English '. . . but ____' carries the flavor of some sort of *contrast* drawn by conjoining two sentences. Someone who said that Jones is poor but honest might well be supposed

---

[8] This example is due to H. P. Grice, "The Causal Theory of Perception," *Proceedings of the Aristotelian Society Supplement,* Vol. 35, 1961.

to think that poor people are not usually honest (i.e., that there is some kind of conflict between poverty and honesty), or at least that *Jones's* honesty may be expected not to hold up under the burden of poverty. Even so, the truth conditions of what is said are not affected by these nuances; (2) is true just in case it is true both that Jones is poor and that Jones is honest. These are the truth conditions for sentences in the official idiom of the form $A \ \& \ B$. Thus in the obvious scheme of abbreviation (2) should be paraphrased as

(4) $p \ \& \ q$

Contrast the foregoing use of '. . . but ____' with one in which it is again a propositional connective but does not express conjunction:

(1) *It never rains but it pours.*

Normally, it would be ludicrous to read (1) as a conjunction like 'It never rains and it pours', because the original, although hackneyed, may be true, whereas the conjunction is self-contradictory. One has here to realize that (1) (taken rather literally) would be uttered during a downpour by someone feeling the cosmic injustice involved in his never being caught in a mere drizzle without an umbrella. What is meant is that it never rains (on him) *without* pouring. What, then, are the truth conditions for (1)? In the normal literal context use it would probably be regarded as true unless it rained and did not pour. Let 'p' abbreviate 'It rains', 'q' abbreviate 'It pours'. Then (1) should be paraphrased by means of whatever logical constant relates 'p' and 'q' such that the complex sentence is false if 'p' is true and 'q' false and is otherwise true. These are the truth conditions for sentences of the form $A \supset B$, so (1) becomes

(2) $p \supset q$

This paraphrase takes '. . . but ____' in this context to express the conditional, a fairly uncommon use of that connective. Usually, it is used to express conjunctions, but it is important to consider such relatively rare uses because they help one to understand the considerations involved in paraphrase of more usual cases.

A very troublesome English connective is '. . . unless ____'. In many contexts it is paraphrased as an alternation, as in

(1) *Lambert won't play golf unless it is sunny.*

Apparently, this would be true if it were sunny and Lambert refused to play on some other ground, as we would expect in the case of a genuine alternation. It could be, for example, that Lambert expected it not to be sunny and said that he wouldn't play unless it is sunny to provide himself with an excuse for avoiding Richardson, who is sure to beat him mercilessly; and when, contrary to his expectations, the day dawns bright, he may have to plead hacker's hip to get out of playing Richardson. Yet his previous statement would not be made *false* by this unsportsmanlike behavior. It seems that the *only* condition under which this sentence is actually false is when Lambert plays and it is not sunny.

A problem in paraphrasing this sentence has to do with the negation expressed by '. . . won't _____'. Clearly, it negates a sentence, but there are two possibilities, depending on the *scope* one takes negation to have. Using parentheses to indicate scope, they are

(1) *(It is not the case that (Lambert will play golf)) unless (it is sunny).*

and

(2) *It is not the case that ((Lambert will play golf) unless (it is sunny)).*

Ordinarily, negations have small scope, as in the first alternative, but the final decision depends on what is intended by the person who asserts the sentence. Now the second alternative, in which negation has the larger scope, says that it is not the case that (Lambert will play golf unless it is sunny), that is, that Lambert will not play and it will not be sunny. The more usual reading, and certainly the one intended in the story above, is given by the first alternative—that under certain conditions (i.e., if it is not sunny) Lambert will not play golf. This sentence has the same truth conditions as a sentence of the form $\sim A \lor B$, so it should be paraphrased as

(2) $\sim p \lor q$
     Scheme of abbreviation:
       '*p*': '*Lambert will play golf*'.
       '*q*': '*It is sunny*'.

There are, however, contexts in which '. . . unless _____' is not adequately paraphrased as an alternation or its equivalents. Consider

(1) *The picnic will be held unless it rains.*

Although this sentence superficially resembles 'Lambert won't play golf unless it is sunny', most people would take the two to have different truth conditions. Suppose that the picnic is held in the rain. Most people would regard (1) as false in such circumstances. Evidence for this is that if a notice were put up saying that the picnic will be held unless it rains and it began to look like rain on the day in question, everyone would expect the picnic not to be held. As the example about Carter's human rights warning illustrates, a sentence that exclusively alternates A and B is true if and only if A is true or B is true but not both. Thus (1) should be paraphrased as an exclusive alternation:

(2) $(p \vee q) \,\&\, \sim(p \,\&\, q)$
  Scheme of abbreviation:
  'p': 'The picnic will be held'.
  'q': 'It rains'.

This shows that sentences containing '. . . unless ___' can be stylistic variants of those containing '. . . or ___' in both uses of the latter reading. Only the inclusive '. . . or ___', however, corresponds to a logical constant under the interpretations we have specified for them, so the exclusive uses of '. . . unless ___' and '. . . or ___' alike must be paraphrased in terms of inclusive alternation, conjunction, and negation (or some other equivalent).

We shall briefly mention a few more examples of stylistic variance without completing the paraphrase.

1. *Concealment.* Often a sentence negation appears as a single word embedded in what appears to be a simple sentence, as in 'Tom is not tall', for example. Sometimes the negation of a sentence is expressed by a simple word prefix such as 'im-', 'un-', or 'in-'. 'Drunken driving is illegal (immoral, unacceptable, indecent, etc.)' is a stylistic variant of 'It is not the case that drunken driving is legal (moral, acceptable, decent, etc.)', and should be paraphrased into the official idiom as a sentence of the form $\sim A$. Note, however, that 'John is unenthusiastic' is *not* a stylistic variant of 'It is not the case that John is enthusiastic'. The latter would be true when John is neither enthusiastic or particularly lethargic (he is just in an ambivalent mood, perhaps), whereas 'John is unenthusiastic' would be false under these circumstances. This case differs from the example involving drunken driving, for all actions of this sort are either legal or illegal, acceptable or unacceptable, and so on. Every pair consisting of a sentence A *in the official idiom* and its negation, $\sim A$, is such that one is true and the other false. If what *appears* to be the negation of an English sentence does not have this property, as in the pair, 'John is enthusiastic' and 'John is unenthusiastic', a paraphrase of the second sentence as a negation in the official idiom of the first would be inadequate. The paraphrases of 'John is enthusiastic' and 'John is unen-

thusiastic' are in *each* case treated as simple sentences (i.e., represented by the sentence letters 'p' and 'q', say).

A second sort of concealment occurs when an English propositional connective, one of the readings or otherwise, occurs in what appears to be a simple sentence. An example is the sentence analyzed above: 'Jones is poor but honest'. One has to see that '. . . but ____' really relates two sentences, only one of which appears in its entirety. A similar example is 'John and George bought new cars', which is really the conjunction, 'John bought a new car and George bought a new car'.

Finally, relative pronouns often introduce clauses that should be paraphrased as sentences. For example, in 'Nixon, who was the first president of the United States to resign, still has many supporters in southern California, where he now lives', '. . . who ____' and '. . . where ____' conjoin relative clauses to the principal clause. This sentence says the same thing as 'Nixon was the first president of the United States to resign and Nixon still has many supporters in southern California and Nixon now lives in southern California', and should be paraphrased into a sentence of the form $((A \, \& \, B) \, \& \, C)$.

2. Sentences containing '. . . when ____' can also be stylistic variants of conditionals or even of biconditionals. Examples of each follow. Consider, 'When the government resorts to illegal actions, it is the individual's right to engage in civil disobedience', which would be true or false in most contexts under the same conditions as 'If the government resorts to illegal actions, then it is the individual's right to engage in civil disobedience'. Hence it is paraphrased as a sentence of the form of $A \supset B$. On the other hand, 'Triangle A is equilateral when it is equiangular' would usually be taken to imply not only that equilateral triangles are equiangular, but the converse as well. If this is what is intended, then the sentence should be paraphrased as a sentence of the form $A \equiv B$.

3. Sentences containing 'neither . . . nor ____' are stylistic variants of those containing negation and alternation. 'The lilies of the field toil not, neither do they spin', for example, is paraphrased as a sentence of the form $\sim(A \lor B)$.

4. A rather confusing case of stylistic variance involves such words as 'since' and 'because', which can express the conditional, merely introduce premises as conversational modifiers, serve as illative particles, or all three in the same context. Consider the sentence 'Since Roscoe was not home between 12 and 2 A.M. Tuesday, he did not murder Crustacea', which seems to encapsulate an entire argument. 'Since' marks 'Roscoe was not home between 12 and 2 A.M. Tuesday' as a premise, but it also indicates that 'Roscoe did not murder Crustacea' is true on the condition that the other premise is also true. The combination of 'since' and the comma break in the sentence locates the position of an illative particle,

although 'since' does not actually occur there. The argument could be reexpressed in English as follows:

(1) *Roscoe was not at home between 12 and 2* A.M. *Tuesday.*
(2) *If Roscoe was not at home between 12 and 2* A.M. *Tuesday, then he did not murder Crustacea.*
(3) *Therefore, Roscoe did not murder Crustacea.*

Here '. . . since _____' is replaced by the conditional in premise (2), and 'therefore' prefixes the conclusion. The final paraphrase into the official idiom is obvious.

Rules of Thumb   As we have often declared, there are no mechanical rules for paraphrase. Nevertheless, one can give some rules of thumb for paraphrasing into the official idiom sentences that contain the more troublesome English propositional connectives. One should always think of these rules of thumb first, remembering that the final test of adequacy of paraphrase is preservation of truth conditions. If the use of one of these rules results in a paraphrase not preserving the truth conditions of the original, then another paraphrase must be found.

Stylistic variants for English sentences of the grammatical form 'A and B' often include:

A although B
A but B
A while B
A whereas B

Further, many sentences containing 'who', 'which', and 'where' are also paraphrasable as sentences of the form A & B.

Stylistic variants for English sentences of the grammatical form 'If A, then B' often include:

It is not the case that A without its being the case that B.
A only if B
B if A
B provided that A
B given that A
B on the condition that A
B assuming that A

Further, many sentences of the grammatical form of 'A's being the case is a sufficient condition for B's being the case' and 'B's being the case is a necessary condition for A's being the case' are stylistic variants of 'If A, then B'.

Common stylistic variants for sentences of the grammatical form 'A if and only if B' include:

A when and only when B
A is equivalent to B
A just in case B
A exactly on the condition that B

Also, 'A's holding is a necessary and sufficient condition for B's holding' is a stylistic variant of 'A if and only if B'.

Common stylistic variants of sentences of the grammatical form 'A or B' include:

A unless B
Either A or B

It cannot be emphasized too frequently that although the preceding rules of thumb are usually reliable, they are not foolproof. Even in contexts in which the various stylistic variants do conform to the rules of thumb, the relevant connectives are in some sense apt to be "richer" than the logical constants that normally paraphrase them. The case of 'Jones is poor but honest' is a perfect example. Here '. . . but ____' does express conjunction, but there is also the *suggestion*, lacking in 'Jones is poor and Jones is honest', that in general, poverty and honesty are somehow in conflict. This nuance is probably due to the *meaning* of '. . . but ____' but has nothing to do with that *part* of the meaning having to do with determining the truth conditions of the sentences in which it occurs, and for this reason the nuance is irrelevant to our concerns. We are interested only in validity, and the validity or invalidity of an argument depends only on whether its form guarantees that there are no conditions under which the premises are jointly true and the conclusion false. Any nuance of the meanings of propositional connectives not affecting validity can be ignored. For example, suppose that we are concerned with an argument in gross standard form such as:

(1) *Jones is poor but honest.*
(2) *All poor people are gaunt.*
(3) *Therefore, Jones is gaunt.*

Determination of validity or invalidity would have nothing to do with the nuance in premise (1) that poverty may be incompatible with honesty. Suppose that it *is*. Nevertheless, the argument is valid because there are no conditions under which Jones *is* poor but honest (suppose, if you like, poverty and honesty to be incompatible in general) and all poor people are gaunt yet Jones isn't.

7.1 Exercises

In answering the following questions, you may find it helpful to refer to the summary of concepts and definitions introduced in this chapter on p. 169. Starred exercises are answered in Appendix III.

1. What does it mean to say that two English sentences are stylistic variants of one another? According to the characterization of stylistic variance given in this section, can two different propositional connectives, such as '. . . and ____' and 'if . . . , then ____, also be stylistic variants of one another?
2. Explain why each of the following pairs of sentences are stylistic variants of one another.
    a. The picnic will be canceled only if it rains.
       If the picnic is canceled, then it rains.
    b. John is tall and blond.
       John is tall and John is blond.
    c. We'll have no dinner unless someone goes to the store.
       Either someone goes to the store or we'll have no dinner.
    d. If demand increases, then prices rise.
       Prices rise provided that demand increases.
    e. Prices rise if and only if demand increases.
       That demand increases is a necessary and sufficient condition of prices rising.
    f. San Francisco, which is north of Los Angeles, is nicer.
       San Francisco is north of Los Angeles and San Francisco is nicer than Los Angeles.
3. Explain why the following pairs of sentences are not stylistic variants of one another.
    a. Demand increases only if prices rise.
       If prices rise, then demand increases.
    b. Demand increases if prices rise.
       If demand increases, then prices rise.
    c. John is unkind to Sally.
       It is not the case that John is kind to Sally.
    d. You will pass this course unless you fail the final.
       You will pass this course or you fail the final.
    e. All countries but Switzerland signed the treaty.
       All countries signed the treaty and Switzerland signed the treaty.

4. Paraphrase each of the following sentences into the official idiom, giving a scheme of abbreviation. Example:

    1. 'It is not true that ice cream is cheaper than steak,' '~p' (p: 'Ice cream is cheaper than steak'.)

    2. It is false that the moon is made of green cheese.

  ★3. It is hardly the case that you should take logic.

    4. I don't think truth is beauty.

    5. No one believes that capital punishment is humane anymore.

  ★6. Norman Mailer is illiterate.

    7. Norman Mailer is not a dentist.

    8. Virtue is unteachable.

    9. The missing portions of the tapes are far from unintelligible.

  10. Picasso is a painter and a sculptor.

  11. Nixon and Kissinger are both politicians.

  12. She was poor but honest.

  13. Roscoe Frostbite is a male chauvinist pig as well as an idiot.

  14. Whereas justice is a virtue, injustice is a vice.

  15. Even though recklessness is the opposite of cowardice, neither of them is a virtue.

  16. Marvin and Norman are cousins.

  17. Either the baby is awake or there is an intruder in the house.

  18. Erma is either sick or drunk.

  19. Either Carter or Brown will be the next President.

  20. We will hire Smith or Jones, but not both.

  21. The whole railroad system will wind up broke and/or nationalized.

  22. One of Tom, Dick, and Harry is thin.

  23. A cigar-store Indian is neither a cigar store nor an Indian.

  24. Tom can outrun Bill if Fred can.

 ★25. John can run for President provided he is over thirty-five.

  26. My car won't start only if there is no gas in the tank.

  27. Your doing all the homework is a sufficient condition for getting a "C" in this course.

  28. Having an informed electorate is necessary for having a successful democracy.

  29. There is only one possibility to save the U.S. troops from total annihilation: that is the honorable destruction of the encircled village.

  30. John comes to parties when and only when he thinks Mary will be there.

  31. A sentence is a logical truth just in case its denial is a logical falsehood.

  32. I'll catch the plane if I run.

33. When too many people lose their jobs, unemployment results. (Herbert Hoover)
34. Romance is the privilege of the rich, not the profession of the unemployed. (Oscar Wilde)
35. Colonel Merton lost his temper and his digestion in India. (Oscar Wilde)
36. Public opinion exists only where there are no ideas. (Oscar Wilde)
37. All men are mortal.
38. Only humans are capable of thought.

8.
DEVIANCE

In this section we shall discuss certain nonstandard occurrences of the readings of logical constants. A reading has a nonstandard occurrence in an English sentence when it fails to make the contribution to the truth value of the sentence in which it occurs specified by the interpretation of the corresponding logical constant for sentences of the official idiom. This can happen in at least three different ways:

1. The reading in question makes the contribution to the whole sentence normally made by some *other* reading.
2. The reading in question does not function as a propositional connective at all.
3. The reading does function as a propositional connective, but its contribution to the whole sentence is unlike that of any logical constant.

1. An example of the first type of nonstandard occurrence is 'Wreck my car and I will sue you', which seems clearly to be true unless you do wreck my car and I do not sue you (and it is false otherwise). Therefore, '. . . and ____' expresses the conditional rather than the conjunction (the logical relation that it *would* express in a standard occurrence), and the sentence should be paraphrased as one of the form $A \supset B$.

2. Now let us consider some occurrences of readings of logical constants in which they do not function as propositional connectives. In such cases one must not regard these as logical phrases. For example, the word 'and' is not always a binary propositional connective in English, and it would be wrong to paraphrase such an occurrence into the official idiom by means of '&', which *is* a binary propositional connective. Consider the sentence

(1) *Nixon and Carter talked for two hours.*

In this context 'and' is probably not a propositional connective; rather, it connects the names 'Nixon' and 'Carter' to form a compound subject. Were one to construe this occurrence of 'and' as an English propositional connective, one would misrepresent the truth conditions of (1). To see this, suppose that 'and' does express conjunction in (1) (i.e., that it is the connective '. . . and ____'). Then (1) would say the same thing as

(2) *Nixon talked for two hours and Carter talked for two hours.*

106

Since (2) is paraphrasable into a sentence of the official idiom having the form *A* & *B*, on this hypothesis (1) should be also. Both would become

(3) *p* & *q*
    Scheme of abbreviation:
      p: 'Nixon talked for two hours'.
      q: 'Carter talked for two hours'.

It is clear enough that (3) is the correct paraphrase of (2), but is it also the correct paraphrase of (1)? That it is *not* can be seen by imagining a situation in which their truth values differ. If this can be imagined, then they do not have the same truth conditions, so (3) cannot be the correct paraphrase. Such a situation is the following: Suppose that Carter talked for two hours to the United Nations and Nixon talked for two hours to the San Clemente Junior Chamber of Commerce. Then (2) and (3) would both be true, but (1) would be false. In normal contexts (1) implies that Nixon and Carter talked to *each other*. Thus 'and' here is not relating the propositions that Nixon talked for two hours and that Carter talked for two hours. Compare (1) with an earlier example of concealment:

(4) *John and George bought new cars.*

wherein '. . . and ____' is functioning as conjunction. Although (1) and (4) have the same superficial *grammatical* form, they have *different logical forms;* (4) has the logical form of a conjunction of two simple sentences, whereas (1) does not. They are shown to have different logical forms by the discovery of a context in which their truth conditions diverge [i.e., in which the truth value of the whole differs given certain specified truth values of the (putative) parts]. Because (1) does not have the form of a conjunction (or any other complex sentence in the official idiom), it must be paraphrased as a simple sentence. Despite the *appearance* of complexity, it must be paraphrased as a sentence letter. Thus the paraphrase of (1) into the official idiom is just its abbreviation:

(5) *p*

Similar points arise with other *apparent* stylistic variants of sentences that contain readings of logical constants:

(1) *Since John came to Laguna Beach, all he cares about is getting a suntan.*
(2) *He gave his regards when he got to Broadway.*

In neither case is 'since' or 'when' functioning as a propositional connective, so both sentences should be abbreviated using single sentence letters.

3. *Non-truth-functionality.* We just considered a case in which 'and' was not used as a binary propositional connective and so could not be paraphrased as '&'. There are other contexts in which the readings do function as propositional connectives but fail to make any comprehensible contribution to the truth value of the sentences in which they occur. Consider, for example,

(1) *John slipped on a banana peel and fell down.*

Here '. . . and _____' seems clearly to be functioning as a propositional connective, as in

(2) *John slipped on a banana peel and John fell down.*

Now the grammatical structure of (2) suggests that it should be paraphrased as a sentence of the official idiom having the form $A \& B$, but this turns out not to be so. Suppose that what really happened is that John fell down *first*, then got up again, then slipped on a banana peel but did not fall down this time. Then 'John slipped on a banana peel' and 'John fell down' would both be true, yet most of us would regard both (1) and (2) to be false in such circumstances. If (2) as a whole can be false in some contexts when both its component simple sentences are true, and true in other contexts in which its component simple sentences remain true, then something more than the truth values of the embedded simple sentences must be involved in determining the truth value of the whole sentence. The logical interpretation of '&' ignores whatever facet of the meaning of the English connective '. . . and _____' is responsible for this phenomenon because our interest is only in how the truth values of the simple sentences alone contribute to the truth value of the whole. The technical way of putting this is to say that the logical constants are all *truth-functional.* This means that the truth value of the whole sentence, simple or complex, is determined *solely* by the truth values of its (sententinal) parts.[9]

---

[9] A *function* is an association between two sets A and B such that to every member of A (called the *arguments* of the function) there corresponds exactly one member of B (called the *value* of the function for that argument). A telephone book describes a functional relationship between the set of owners of telephones and the set of phone numbers: To each person listed in the book there corresponds exactly one phone number. The converse relation is not a function, because people share phones—it is not the case that to each number listed in the book there corresponds exactly one person. A *truth-functional* relationship is a functional relation between the truth values of simple sentences and the truth value of the complex sentence in which they are embedded.

There are natural language contexts, such as those discussed above, in which the English readings of the logical constants are *not* truth-functional, so it would be wrong to paraphrase such sentences, even if they appear to be complex, as complex sentences in the official idiom. For example, in (2) the joint truth of 'John slipped on a banana peel' and 'John fell down' *alone* does not determine the truth value of their conjunction. The order in which the events took place must be right. If '. . . and ___' were truth-functional in (2), its truth value could not be affected by the order of these events given that the truth values of the parts are the same. We are concerned only with truth-functional uses of propositional connectives, so in cases of non-truth-functionality, whatever internal structure is possessed by the English sentence in question cannot be captured within the resources of the official idiom. In other words, the readings are not regarded as logical phrases and the sentences in which they occur are treated as simple sentences on a par with 'Socrates is wise'. Thus the proper paraphrase of (2) is by a sentence letter:

(3) p

where 'p' abbreviates the entire sentence.

There are many non-truth-functional uses of 'if . . . then ___.' One colloquial use is to assert that a *causal connection* holds between two events. For example, suppose that Cyrus Vance were to declare before a large gathering of foreign policy experts,

(1) *If I snap my fingers, then Idi Amin will be deposed.*

It is easy to see that the connection asserted to hold between antecedent and consequent in most plausible contexts of the use of (1) would not be truth-functional. For if the truth conditions of (1) were those of a sentence of the form $A \supset B$, then its truth value would depend on nothing more than the truth values of the embedded simple sentences. Such is not likely to be the case. Suppose that Vance does not snap his fingers; then it would not *follow*, in the sort of context imagined, that (1) as a whole is true. It might be or it might not be. That it might be taken to be true is shown by the rapt *attention* paid to Vance's remarks even though it were evident that he would not snap his fingers (to avoid creating an international incident). In most imaginable contexts, such as this, the truth value of (1) would not depend solely on the truth values of the component sentences, but would depend, rather, on whether or not Vance had some sort of "power" to set Amin's fall from power into motion. It is important that the truth of the complex sentence depends on his having this power, or being able to *cause* deposition, and not upon the falsity of the antecedent. If such is the case, then 'if . . . then ____' does not mark a truth-functional relationship between the embedded sentences in (1). So it would be wrong to attempt to paraphrase (1) into the official idiom by means of any of our logical constants because all of them are truth-functional. In other words, we must treat (1) as a simple sentence from the standpoint of the official idiom, even though it is a complex English sentence. For our purposes, it might be regarded as a simple sentence because it does not have the logical form of a complex sentence in the official idiom. Thus (1) is to be paraphrased as

(2) *p*

where '*p*' abbreviates the entire sentence.

The last examples of non-truth-functionality we will consider concern '. . . when ____'. In

(1) *You get a free copy of* Zen and the Art of Motorcycle Maintenance *when you buy a new BMW.*

'. . . when ____' seems to function as a propositional connective. (1) appears to be a stylistic variant of 'If you buy a new BMW, then you get a free copy of *Zen and the Art of Motorcycle Maintenance*', but a moment's reflection casts doubt on this reading. Would (1) be true if you bought a BMW today from Jones and tomorrow your aunt sent you a copy of *Zen* for your birthday? This is doubtful. The truth of (1) seems to require that the events described in the component sentences, if they occur, be closely connected to one another. Thus the correct paraphrase of (1) is, again,

(2) *p*

where '*p*' abbreviates the entire sentence. A similar example involves the noted climber of El Capitan:

(3) *Sibylle was embarrassed when she fell down the stairs.*

Here it is evident that the truth of (3) requires her to fall down the stairs to *cause* the embarrassment. If she were embarrassed first, by some *other* event, say, and then fell down the stairs, (3) would probably be thought false. It is the fact that (3) could be either true or false when its component sentences do not change in truth value that shows '. . . when ____' to be non-truth-functional.

Two cautions: Perhaps one can imagine a context for every complex

English sentence in which it is non-truth-functional. The point is not that some sentences are always truth-functional and others never truth-functional. One has, as always, to see what is meant in a given context by the speaker. Second, even if a sentence might plausibly be taken to be non-truth-functional in a given context, it might also be best to take it to be truth-functional in another context. For example, someone who asserted any one of the preceding examples *might* have intended only to assert a truth-functional relationship between the propositions expressed by the embedded sentences. If so, then it would be proper to paraphrase the sentences as complex sentences in the official idiom.

8.1 Exercises

In answering the following questions, you may find it helpful to refer to the summary of concepts and definitions introduced in this chapter on p. 169. Starred exercises are answered in Appendix III.

1. What is the difference between a variant occurrence of a propositional connective and a deviant occurrence?
2. How can the correct paraphrase into the official idiom of a complex English sentence be a sentence letter such as 'p'? Why should not all complex English sentences be paraphrased as complex sentences in the official idiom?
3. Each of the following pairs of sentences exemplifies a different type of deviance. In each case
   i. Identify the propositional connective involved.
   ii. Explain the nature of the deviance.
   iii. Paraphrase the sentence into the official idiom.
   a. I'll get some diet soda just in case Karen comes.
      I like beans as well as artichokes.
   b. With a copy of our new book you can make a lot of money on the stock market.
      Make another pun like that and I'll have you thrown out.
   c. The fox crouched, took a run, and jumped.
      If Gerald Ford had not been made President, he would still be a Congressman today.
4. Paraphrase the following sentences into the official idiom, giving a scheme of paraphrase.
   1. Jack and Jill went up the hill and Mary's little lamb was not far behind.
   2. I touch thee not yet I see thee still.
   3. When you're hot, you're hot; when you're not, you're not.

　　4. I like beans, as well as artichokes. (*Hint:* Note the placement of the comma.)

★5. Give us more funds and we'll improve the library.

　　6. 'And' has three letters but 'or' has only two.

　　7. If *A* is true and *B* is true, then *A* & *B* is true; otherwise, *A* & *B* is false.

　　8. Not only the Swiss are rich but so are the Arabs.

　　9. Only the brave deserve the fair.

　10. You can fool some of the people all of the time or all of the people some of the time, but you can't fool all of the people all of the time.

5. Why is it acceptable to paraphrase 'John will go to the store and the larder is empty' either as 'p & q' or as 'q & p' (p: 'John will go to the store'; q: 'The larder is empty'), whereas 'John will go to the store only if the larder is empty' cannot be paraphrased as either '$p \supset q$' or '$q \supset p$' (on the same scheme of abbreviation)?

Difficult

6. Identify the propositional connectives in the following sentences. Then determine which ones have non-truth-functional occurrences and which have truth-functional occurrences. Finally, paraphrase each of them into the official idiom. Defend your answers.

　　1. It is necessarily the case that the Pope will ascend to Heaven.

　　2. The Pope will, necessarily, ascend to Heaven.

　　3. It is not the case that the Pope will ascend to Heaven.

　　4. It is necessarily the case that the Pope will not ascend to Heaven.

　　5. Thales fell down a well and said "All is water."

★6. Bismark said that one could have guns or butter, but Johnson thought we could have both guns and butter.

　　7. Nero fiddled while Rome burned.

　　8. If guns are outlawed, only outlaws will have guns.

★9. If Gerald Ford were William Douglas, he would have had nothing but contempt for his attempt to impeach himself.

　10. It is necessary that boys will be boys.

　11. If Christine Jorgenson were a man, she would be a woman.

　12. Howard Hughes's phony will provided that large sums be given to a service station operator in Nevada.

9.
OFFICIAL STANDARD FORM

We have discussed most of the issues involved in the paraphrase of sentences. Now we use these techniques to clarify arguments. Consider, first, two different argument descriptions that actually express the same argument:

A (1) *If shale oil can be retrieved, then we will have sufficient oil.*
  (2) *Shale oil can be retrieved.*
  (3) *Therefore, we will have sufficient oil.*
B (1) *We will have sufficient oil provided that shale oil can be retrieved.*
  (2) *Shale oil can be retrieved.*
  (3) *Therefore, we will have sufficient oil.*

A and **B** are obviously quite similar, but the different literary styles of their first premise sentences may obscure the fact that **A** and **B** are, in fact, different gross standard formulations of exactly the same argument. They express the same argument because the simple sentences 'Shale oil can be retrieved' and 'We will have sufficient oil' express the same propositions in each context, and those propositions are related in the same way. They are related in the same way because premise (1) of **B** is a stylistic variant of premise (1) of **A**. In other words, **A** and **B** have exactly the same *logical form,* and the same propositions are expressed by the simple sentences occurring within them; so they express the same argument. In each case the correct paraphrase into the official idiom is

C (1) $p \supset q$
  (2) p
  (3) $\therefore q$
    Scheme of abbreviation:
    p: *'Shale oil can be retrieved'.*
    q: *'We will have sufficient oil'.*

When an argument is paraphrased into the official idiom, as just stated, it is in *official standard form.* As before, the scheme of abbreviation is an essential part of an argument in official standard form, for if one does not know what sentences the sentence letters abbreviate, then

113

he does not know what propositions they are to be thought of as expressing and, hence, what argument is being expressed in official standard
form. Omitting the scheme of abbreviation would never affect the validity of an argument, but it could affect its soundness. For example, suppose that '*p*' abbreviated any true proposition and '*q*' abbreviated any
false proposition. Then **C** would express an unsound argument.

In general, an argument is *in official standard form* if and only if

1. The premise sentences are listed in vertical order.
2. The conclusion sentence is listed last.
3. The conclusion sentence is prefixed by the illative particle ∴.
4. The premise sentences and conclusion sentence are all numbered.
5. The premise and conclusion sentences are all sentences in the
   official idiom.
6. A scheme of abbreviation is given.

9.1 Exercises

In answering the following questions, you may find it helpful to refer to the
summary of concepts and definitions introduced in this chapter on p. 169.
Starred exercises are answered in Appendix III.

1. How can the paraphrase of an argument into official standard form help
   to clarify it?
★2. Under what conditions is it correct to say that two arguments in gross
   standard form are the same?
3. Which of the following are arguments in official standard form relative
   to the scheme of abbreviation given and which are not? Defend your
   answers.
   Scheme of abbreviation:
       p: 'Prices rise'.
       q: 'Demand increases'.
       r: 'Shortages will occur'.

a. (1) $p \supset q$ d. (1) p
   (2) p (2) ∴r

b. (1) $A \supset B$ e. (1) $p \supset q$
   (2) A (2) p
   (3) ∴B (3) ∴q

c. (1) $p \equiv q$ (4) $r \supset s$
   (2) ∴q (5) r
                         (6) ∴s

10.
PARAPHRASE OF ARGUMENTS INTO OFFICIAL STANDARD FORM

We shall illustrate the paraphrase of arguments into official standard form by means of four examples. The first two are familiar arguments that we left in gross standard form in Section 2. The other two illustrate the entire process of paraphrase from natural habitat to official standard form.

EXAMPLE 1

Let us return to the argument concerning Earl Butz's money-saving hints. In gross standard form, it was

(1) *If in order to save money we should eat more fish, then fish is cheaper than meat.*
(2) *Meat is cheaper than fish.*
(3) *Therefore, it is not the case that in order to save money we should eat more fish.*

Sentence (1) already has the form of a conditional, but the antecedent itself seems to consist of two sentences that are somehow related: The first sentence is concealed in the noun clause 'in order to save money' and the second is 'We should eat more fish.' What relationship does Earl Butz's critic, who formulated the argument, think holds between the propositions expressed by the constituent sentences of (1)? This cannot be determined merely by staring at the argument in gross standard form; one must recall the context. The context was that Earl Butz had given a piece of advice to shoppers about how they could save money, a claim that Butz's critic disputes. Butz's idea was that in order to save money we should eat fish. What would make *Butz's claim* true or false? Evidently, it would be false only when one eats fish and does not save money. So *Butz's claim* is conditional in form and should be so paraphrased into the official idiom. Let us abbreviate the constituent sentences of this argument as follows:

p: 'We eat more fish'.
q: 'We will save money'.
r: 'Fish is cheaper than meat'.

Since Butz's claim is only part of (1), and since (1) is a premise offered not by Butz but by his critic, it is properly paraphrased as

(1) $(p \supset q) \supset r$

Sometimes paraphrasing complicated sentences into official standard form is made easier by "paraphrasing inward"[10] in intermediate steps. This was implicitly done above. The idea is first to represent the "largest" logical structure within the sentence to be paraphrased, then the next largest, and so on, by using parentheses and, if necessary, stylistic variants of the various sentences that may be embedded in the main sentence. For example, in the case of (1), one might first write:

'If (in order to save money we should eat more fish), then (fish is cheaper than meat).'

Having discerned that the antecedent of this sentence is complex, one might then write:

'If (if (we eat more fish), then (we save money)), then (fish is cheaper than meat).'

On this scheme of paraphrase, then, (1) becomes '$(p \supset q) \supset r$'.

Premise (2) requires a small but important change. Note that it is not explicitly a negation, although it is obvious that the speaker intends to deny the consequent of (1) by asserting that meat is cheaper than fish. Here we are interested in what *proposition* the speaker intended to assert, and it is clear from the context that he used sentence (2) to assert the negation of the proposition expressed by the consequent of (1). Thus (2) should be paraphrased as the negation of the consequent of (1):

(2') $\sim r$

Sentence (3) is just the negation of the antecedent of (1) and should be paraphrased as

(3') $\sim(p \supset q)$

---

[10] This technique is borrowed from W. V. Quine, *Methods of Logic* (New York: Holt, Rinehart and Winston, 1969), p. 44.

Fully paraphrased, then, the argument is this:

(1') $(p \supset q) \supset r$
(2') $\sim r$
(3') $\sim(p \supset q)$

Note that the paraphrase of (2) as (2') rather than as a new sentence letter, 'p_1', say, is, in effect, to take 'meat is cheaper than fish' to be a stylistic variant of 'It is not the case that fish is cheaper than meat.' This is an unusual case, for obvious reasons, but it seems justified by the criterion of obviousness. Here the criterion governs the inclusion of an unasserted premise in *official standard form*. That is, if (2) were paraphrased as 'p_1', then the argument in official standard form would be

(1') $(p \supset q) \supset r$
(2") p_1
(3') $\therefore \sim(p \supset q)$

Although we have not yet discussed validity in detail, one should be able to see that the first argument is valid and the second is not, for, in official standard form, premise (2") is utterly irrelevant to the argument. Thus the argument *requires* (2') for validity. Of course, we cannot add just any premise that makes an argument valid, for people do frequently give invalid arguments. We need to know, in addition, whether (2') is the *speaker's* premise. Indeed, it seems to be, for the context makes it *obvious* that it is not the case that fish is cheaper than meat.

Fully paraphrased, then, the argument is this:

(1) $(p \supset q) \supset r$
(2) $\sim r$
(3) $\therefore \sim(p \supset q)$
     Scheme of abbreviation:
       p: 'We eat more fish'.
       q: 'We will save money'.
       r: 'Fish is cheaper than meat'.

EXAMPLE 2

Recall the invalid argument in Chapter 1 given by the detective investigating Crustacea's death. In gross standard form it was

(1) *Roscoe didn't murder his wife unless he knows about poison.*

(2) *Roscoe knows about poison.*

(3) *Therefore, Roscoe murdered his wife.*

The first premise contains a negation, as is evident from the word 'didn't'. There are two possibilities with regard to paraphrasing (1), depending on the *scope* one takes negation to have. If we use parentheses to indicate scope, (1) might be read either as 'It is not the case that '(Roscoe murdered his wife unless he knows about poison)' or as '(It is not the case that (Roscoe murdered his wife)) unless (he knows about poison)'. The second choice is correct because, presumably, the detective thought that the only condition under which Roscoe would be *innocent* would be if he did not know about poison; he did not intend to deny that there is a *connection* between Roscoe's murdering his wife and knowing about poison, as is suggested by the first alternative.

What connection does (1) assert to obtain between 'It is not the case that Roscoe murdered his wife' and 'He knows about poison'? Note, first, that the question about the connection between the sentences 'It is not the case that Roscoe murdered his wife' and 'He knows about poison' presupposes that 'he' refers to Roscoe; indeed, for reasons of economy, the detective used the pronoun 'he' to refer to Roscoe. To keep this straight, 'he' will be replaced by Roscoe's name and the question rephrased: What connection has to hold between the embedded sentences in

(1') *(It is not the case that (Roscoe murdered his wife)) unless (Roscoe knows about poison).*

to make it true?

The rule of thumb for 'unless' suggests that (1') be paraphrased as an inclusive alternation. On this reading it would become:

(1") *(It is not the case that (Roscoe murdered his wife)) or (Roscoe knows about poison).*

If we abbreviate the constituent sentences in (1") as

p: 'Roscoe murdered his wife'.

q: 'Roscoe knows about poison'.

(1") goes into the official idiom as follows:

(1) $\sim p \lor q$

What would happen if (1) were (incorrectly) paraphrased as an exclusive alternation, as '$(\sim p \vee q) \mathrel{\&} \sim(\sim p \mathrel{\&} q)$'? Remembering what '$p$' and '$q$' abbreviate, we note that this proposed paraphrase says that either Roscoe did not murder his wife or he knows about poison, but *not both*. Since premise (2) says that he *does* know about poison, it follows from these two premises together that Roscoe murdered his wife. In other words, if 'unless' were paraphrased as an exclusive alternation, an obviously invalid argument would be paraphrased as a valid one.

Premise (2) of the detective's argument is just a simple subject–predicate sentence. The correct paraphrase is just the sentence letter 'q'. Similarly, the conclusion is 'p'. The official standard form of the detective's argument is thus:

(1) $\sim p \vee q$
(2) q
(3) $\therefore p$
     Scheme of abbreviation:
     p: 'Roscoe murdered Crustacea'.
     q: 'Roscoe knows about poisons'.

We shall now consider two examples that illustrate the entire process of paraphrasing arguments into official standard form. The first example is examined in detail; the second example gives a picture of the process in brief.

EXAMPLE 3

The first argument is taken from an interview with Professor Alexander Bickel of the Yale Law School:

Rampant pornography raises questions about the kind of society we live in. There are those who say we may not regulate pornography or any other conduct of consenting adults. This is absurd. Like all civilized societies we have long had many rules which attempt to set moral standards and regulate sexual conduct. Regulation of pornography is not different. It is more than coincidence that societies that have decayed collapsed—the Roman Empire is a perfect example—have generally done so in an atmosphere of steeply declining moral standards. [11]

[11] "Pornography, Censorship and Common Sense," an interview with Alexander Bickel by George Denison, *The Readers' Digest*, February 1974, p. 115.

First, does this passage contain an argument? If not, it is difficult to imagine what its point would be. It certainly seems to be more than unsupported ramblings on the topic of pornography. One signal that Bickel is not just rambling is the sentence, "This is absurd"; it indicates that he intends to refute the claim present in ". . . we may not regulate pornography or any other conduct of consenting adults." But this is not enough to make an argument. So far, all we have is the fact that Bickel disagrees with anyone who holds that ". . . we may not regulate pornography." To have an argument, some *reason* Bickel has for denying that we may not regulate pornography has to be identified. One of his reasons presumably is contained in the sentences "Like all civilized societies we have long had many rules which attempt to set moral standards and regulate sexual conduct. Regulation of pornography is not different." It seems, further, that the expression "more than coincidence" connecting the collapse of societies with declining moral standards is relevant to the argument.

So let us first determine exactly what Bickel's conclusion is. He does not deny the claim expressed in the entire sentence 'There are those who say that we may not regulate pornography or any other conduct of consenting adults' because then he would be denying his own assertion that there are people who say this. Actually, that there are people who say this is irrelevant to Bickel's argument—he is interested in *what* they say, not in the fact that they *say* it. Is his conclusion, then, the denial of the proposition expressed by the rest of his sentence, '. . . we may not regulate pornography or any other conduct of consenting adults'? Well, the sentence 'Regulation of pornography is not different' is one indication that he is interested *only* in pornography and not *other* behavior of consenting adults, but there is another reason why it would be mistaken to suppose that his conclusion is the denial of the proposition expressed by the larger sentence. Those Bickel disagrees with, according to him, say that we may not regulate pornography *or* any other conduct of consenting adults; that is, they say *both* that we may not regulate pornography and that we may not regulate any other behavior of consenting adults. To deny this it would be sufficient to show that there is *some* behavior of consenting adults which we may regulate. No one disagrees with this—certainly there is some behavior of some kind between consenting adults that we may regulate. If this conclusion were attributed to Bickel, his argument would be trivialized; he would be taken to be attacking a "straw man," that is, a nonexistent disputant. So one should suppose that he is really trying to establish the nontrivial conclusion that it is absurd to suppose that we may not regulate pornography. It is not charity alone that prompts our choice—the fact that he singles out pornography a few sentences later, as we suggested above, is contextual evidence that he is trying to establish the more interesting conclusion. Of course, we could be wrong; it is possible that he is trying to establish the trivial point that we may regulate some things. Attributing an argument to someone is always a little risky, but it should be pointed out that if a person is trying to persuade *us* to believe something, it is up to *him* to make his own argument clear. If we can narrow the range of possibilities, then we shall be in a position to decide whether or not some of the conclusions a person *might* be arguing for are worthy of consideration on the basis of the evidence he presents. For most purposes it matters less exactly what argument is intended than that one can tell which of those possible are worthy of consideration. In this case we limit ourselves to the interesting conclusion that Bickel is presumably promoting. The conclusion probably is

We may regulate pornography.

What are the premises? Evidently, they have to do with the fact, as Bickel sees it, that we, like all civilized societies, have long had rules regulating sexual conduct. So one premise probably should be

(1) *All societies have rules that regulate sexual conduct.*

Bickel seems to believe that, in the light of what he takes to be a connection between the decline of moral standards and the collapse of certain societies, the putative fact that all civilized societies have regulated sexual conduct *justifies* these rules. So the second premise should be

(2) *If all societies have rules that regulate sexual conduct, and decline of moral standards is connected with the collapse of society, then we may regulate sexual conduct.*

But, he says, the regulation of pornography is "not different" from the regulation of sexual conduct, so the third premise should be

(3) *If we may regulate sexual conduct, then we may regulate pornography.*

Finally, Bickel's citation of the Roman Empire makes it clear that he thinks the decline of moral standards is indeed connected with the collapse of society. So the fourth premise is

(4) *The decline of moral standards is connected with the collapse of society.*

The full argument, in gross standard form, is then:

(1) *All societies have rules that regulate sexual conduct.*
(2) *If all societies have rules that regulate sexual conduct and decline of moral standards is connected with the collapse of society, then we may regulate sexual conduct.*
(3) *If we may regulate sexual conduct, then we may regulate pornography.*
(4) *Decline of moral standards is connected with the collapse of society.*
(5) *Therefore, we may regulate pornography.*

Presumably, the force of 'may' in the preceding argument is 'it is morally permissible for us to' since if 'may' meant something like 'is physically possible for us to', then the argument would be ridiculous because premise (1) already says that all societies have such rules. In other words, if they *do* regulate sexual conduct, then, obviously, they *can* (physically) do it.

To paraphrase Bickel's argument into official standard form, the simple sentences comprising the premises have to be identified, the logical constants correctly paraphrasing the English connectives have to be determined, and, finally, the simple sentences have to be paraphrased as sentence letters in the official idiom. Thus "paraphrasing inward," first we take '. . . and ____' and 'if . . . , then ____' to have their usual paraphrases:

(1) *All societies have rules that regulate sexual conduct.*
(2) *((all societies have rules that regulate sexual conduct) & (decline of moral standards is connected with the collapse of society)) ⊃ (we may regulate sexual conduct).*
(3) *(we may regulate sexual conduct) ⊃ (we may regulate pornography).*
(4) *Decline of moral standards is connected with the collapse of society.*
(5) *Therefore, we may regulate pornography.*

Finally, Bickel's argument in official standard form is

(1) p
(2) $(p \ \& \ q) \supset r$
(3) $r \supset s$
(4) q
(5) $\therefore s$

      Scheme of abbreviation:
          p: *'All societies have rules that regulate sexual conduct'.*
          q: *'Decline of moral standards is connected with the collapse of society'.*

> *r:* 'We may regulate sexual conduct'.
> *s:* 'We may regulate pornography'.

Thus the probable form of Bickel's original argument in *The Reader's Digest* has been made explicit. In Chapter 3 we shall develop a way to *evaluate* arguments for validity based on explicit revelation of their logical form.

EXAMPLE 4

Consider the following argument:

It is an interesting question whether truth is important in poetry. This would be so provided that poetry attempts to describe the world. But no one who really understands poetry would suppose that it attempts to describe the world. So truth is not important to poetry.

In gross standard form the argument is

(1) *Truth is important in poetry provided that poetry attempts to describe the world.*
(2) *Poetry does not attempt to describe the world.*
(3) *So truth is not important to poetry.*

The rule of thumb for paraphrasing sentences containing '. . . provided that ____' suggests that we paraphrase (1) along the lines of:

(1') *(Poetry attempts to describe the world)* $\supset$ *(truth is important in poetry).*

This paraphrase of '. . . provided that ____' in (1) seems quite in order in the present context. If we abbreviate the simple sentences thus:

p: Poetry attempts to describe the world.
q: Truth is important in poetry.

Then, since the correct paraphrase of (2) is simply '$\sim p$' and of (3) is '$\sim q$', the argument in official standard form is

(1) $p \supset q$
(2) $\sim p$
(3) $\therefore \sim q$

10.1 Exercises

Retain your answers to this section; they will form the basis for future questions in Chapter 3. Starred exercises are answered in Appendix III.

1. The following arguments in gross standard form have appeared in various places in the text. Paraphrase them into official standard form.
   a. (1) Jones maintains that socialism is wrong.
      (2) Jones is a rich stockbroker.
      (3) If Jones is a rich stockbroker and maintains that socialism is wrong, then he is lying.
      (4) If Jones is lying, then socialism isn't wrong.
      (5) Therefore, socialism isn't wrong.
   b. (1) If I tell Crustacea that the meeting was strictly professional, then she will believe the worst.
      (2) If I don't tell Crustacea that the meeting was strictly professional, then she will believe the worst.
      (3) Therefore, Crustacea will believe the worst.
   c. (1) Roscoe didn't murder Crustacea unless he knows about poisons.
      (2) Roscoe knows about poisons.
      (3) Therefore, Roscoe murdered Crustacea.
   d. (1) If Roscoe murdered Crustacea, then he was home between 12 and 2 A.M.
      (2) Roscoe was not home between 12 and 2 A.M.
      (3) Therefore, Roscoe didn't murder Crustacea.
   e. (1) Light has mass.
      (2) If light has mass, then it is affected by gravity.
      (3) If light is affected by gravity, then if one observes Alpha Centauri at point *r*, it will appear to be at point *a*.
      (4) We do observe Alpha Centauri at point *r*.
      (5) Therefore, Alpha Centauri will appear to be at point *a*.
2. Paraphrase the following arguments first into gross standard form, then into official standard form:
   ★a. Unless you fish early in the morning or in the evening, you do not catch bass in August. So if you do not fish in the evening, but you catch bass in August, you fish early in the morning.
   b. If you are interested in history or scenery, then you will leave the main road. If you are not interested in history, then you won't leave the main road. Therefore, you are interested in history provided that you are interested in scenery.
   c. The instructor will be pleased if Anderson takes the test and passes. But if Anderson takes the test and writes illegibly, the instructor will not be pleased. In fact, Anderson will pass the test only if he writes illegibly. So Anderson won't both take the test and pass.

    d. Either their radiator is boiling over or their air conditioner is on. If their windows are up in this temperature, their air conditioner is on. Their windows are up. Therefore, their radiator isn't boiling over.

    e. It is not the case that man succeeds if and only if he has ability. A man has ability provided that he displays it once in a while. If a man displays his ability once in a while but does not succeed, then either he is unlucky or someone is against him. In case a man is unlucky, he cannot display his ability. Thus it is sufficient for a man's succeeding that he not have someone who is against him.

3. Refer to your answers to Exercise 5 in Section 2.1 of this chapter (p. 67). Paraphrase arguments a, c, d, ★e, f, g, ★h, j, k, l, m, p, s, and u from gross standard form into official standard form.

11.
EXPANSION OF THE OFFICIAL IDIOM: SYNTAX

Sometimes sentences are treated as simple despite the presence of quantificational structure. The sentence 'All societies have rules regulating sexual conduct', in Bickel's argument, is a case in point. For the purposes of clarifying and evaluating many arguments—Bickel's argument, for example—it is perfectly acceptable to paraphrase such sentences as simple sentences because the validity of the arguments in which they occur does not depend on any inner structure of the propositions expressed by those sentences. Rather it depends only on the external connections among these propositions. But there are many arguments the validity of which does depend on the internal structure of the constituent propositions, and this requires a deeper analysis of their logical form than that given so far.

Consider, for example, the following argument in gross standard form:

(1) *All men are mortal.*
(2) *Socrates is a man.*
(3) *Therefore, Socrates is mortal.*

It is certainly valid. But were we to paraphrase the premise and conclusion sentences as simple sentences in the official idiom, the paraphrased argument would be invalid. In official standard form the paraphrased argument would have the following form:

(1) *A*
(2) *B*
(3) *∴C*

Arguments of this form are obviously invalid because *A* and *B* can be replaced by true sentences and *C* by a false one.

The invalidity of the argument thus formalized in no way undoes the claim that the validity of the original argument depends upon its logical form. It shows instead that the paraphrase does not correctly reveal the logical form of the original. It happens that the validity of the original argument depends in part upon the inner structure of its constituent propositions, and this is not correctly represented by the paraphrase. In other words, 'All men are mortal' does not really have the form of a

126

simple sentence. The situation is analogous to our earlier discovery that 'If all men are mortal, then Socrates is mortal', say, is not a simple sentence either but has the form of a conditional.

Now we shall see that the antecedent of 'If all men are mortal, then Socrates is mortal' is also complex. The nineteenth-century mathematician and philosopher Gottlob Frege was one of the first[12] to notice that propositions expressed by sentences such as

(1) *All men are mortal.*

do not have the same logical form as those expressed by simple subject–predicate sentences such as

(2) *Socrates is a man.*

Note that (1) and (2) have the same *grammatical* form—both can be parsed into a subject and a predicate. Frege observed an interesting fact about the negations of such sentences. In the case of (2), it makes no difference whether the negation is placed before the entire sentence or just before the predicate. That is, the sentences

(3) *It is not the case that Socrates is a man.*

and

(4) *Socrates is not a man.*

are true or false under exactly the same conditions. The reason, in effect, is this: 'Socrates is a man' expresses a true proposition only when the entity referred to by the name 'Socrates' belongs to the set of things the predicate '___ is a man' is true of, namely, the set of men. Now if 'Socrates is a man' is not true, then it makes no difference whether we describe this state of affairs as its being the case that Socrates does not belong to the set of men or that Socrates belongs to the set of everything that is not a man. But in the case of 'All men are mortal', the two different ways of negating the sentence result in sentences with *different* truth conditions. That is,

(5) *It is not the case that all men are mortal.*

does not have the same truth conditions as

---

[12] "On Sense and Reference," *Translations from the Philosophical Writings of Gottlob Frege*, P. T. Geach and Max Black, eds. (Oxford: Basil Blackwell & Mott Ltd., 1958).

(6) *All men are not mortal.*

In particular, (5) will be true in a situation where some men are mortal and some are not, whereas (6) will be false in this situation. Frege suggested that the reason for this anomaly is that, appearances to the contrary, unlike 'Socrates' in 'Socrates is mortal', it is not the function of 'All men' in 'All men are mortal' to refer to anything at all. Because the truth of 'All men are mortal' does not depend on 'all men' referring to something that is asserted to belong to the set of mortals, then, he said, there is no reason to think that these two different ways of negating the sentence *should* have the same truth conditions. Frege suggested that 'All men are mortal' is really conditional in form—what it says is that *if* something belongs to the set of men, *then* it belongs to the set of mortals. In other words, 'All men are mortal' is true if and only if the set of men is a subset of the set of mortals. [13]

Note that 'all men' does not refer to the set of men, nor does the sentence 'All men are mortal' say that the set of men belongs to the set of mortals, because sets themselves are neither mortal nor immortal; only certain of their members can be mortal or immortal. Once one realizes that 'all men' functions in a very different way from 'Socrates' one can explain why the two ways of negating 'All men are mortal' have different truth conditions. 'It is not the case that all men are mortal' says that the set of men *is not* a subset of the set of mortals, whereas 'All men are not mortal' says that the set of men *is* a subset of the set of nonmortals. The two resultant sentences have different truth conditions just because it is not the same thing for the set of men not to be a subset of the set of mortals as it is for the set of men to be a subset of the set of nonmortals. Again, if some men are mortal and some men are not mortal, the set of men will not be a subset of the set of mortals. If this is the case, 'It is not the case that all men are mortal' is true. But in this circumstance the set of men will not be a subset of the set of nonmortals either, so 'All men are not mortal' will be false.

The upshot of this discussion is that to display correctly the logical form of arguments whose validity depends upon the inner structures of their constituent propositions, the official idiom must be expanded. In particular, we need to make the following additions to the vocabulary of the official idiom (which began in the table on p. 76):

We can best explain these additions by adverting again to the argument opening this section. Let us begin with premise (2): 'Socrates is a man'. Grammatically, this is a subject–predicate sentence: 'Socrates' is

---

[13] By definition, a set A is a subset of a second set, B, if and only if anything that is a member of A is a member of B.

| | | Readings | |
Name of Symbol	Symbol	Preferred	Alternate
9. Universal quantifiers	$(x), (y), (z)$	'Every entity t is such that . . . t . . .'	'Everything . . .' 'All . . .
10. Existential quantifiers	$(Ex), (Ey), (Ez)$	'There is an entity t such that . . . t . . .'	'Some . . .'
11. Subject letters (or ''names'')	a, b, c		
12. Variables	x, y, z		
13. Predicate letters	$F\_\_\_, \quad G\_\_\_, \quad H\_\_\_$ $F^2\_\_\_, \quad G^2\_\_\_, \quad H^2\_\_\_$ . . . . $F^n\_\_\_, \quad G^n\_\_\_, \quad H^n\_\_\_$		

All of these symbols may occur with or without subscripts.
In the readings for the quantifiers, 't' is a meta-variable.
'Every entity t is such that . . . t . . .', for example, designates the result of replacing t with whatever variable, 'x', 'y', or 'z', is in question.

the subject and '. . . is a man' is the predicate. '. . . is a man' is called a *one-place predicate* because a sentence results from putting one name or variable into the blank. Premise (2) itself is the result of putting 'Socrates' into the blank. If we were to put a variable into the blank, we would get something like 'x is a man'. We shall consider this to be a sentence, but it should be pointed out that if we do not know what 'x' refers to, then we have no way of knowing whether or not this sentence is true. Further, it is in the nature of variables that, in general, we do not know what they refer to, although we take them to refer to something or other. Such sentences are analogous to English sentences such as 'It is a man'. To mark this fact, we will call such sentences ''open sentences,'' following the logician W. V. Quine. Examples of *two-place predicates* are '. . . is a brother of ____', '. . . is east of ____', and so on. Two-place predicates are such that the result of completing both blanks with names of variables is a sentence.

The superscripts above the predicate letters indicate how many places each has. One-place predicates are said to stand for or ''express'' *properties* while two-place predicates are said to stand for or ''express'' *relations*.

Subject letters are self-explanatory. Examples of English subject terms include 'Socrates', 'Boston', 'The teacher of Plato', and so on. Each of these is to be paraphrased by means of the letters 'a', 'b', 'c', and so on. If we run out of names in the official idiom, we shall subscript those letters. For the sake of convenience we shall assume that every subject letter in the official idiom is used to stand for something, and, further, that everything is named by one of the subject letters in the official idiom. This assumption may seem strange in view of the fact that we could never *know* all these names, but as will be seen shortly, this assumption is quite harmless.

The correct way to paraphrase 'Socrates is a man' into the official idiom, then, is to choose a subject letter in the official idiom to stand for Socrates and to choose a predicate letter to stand for the property of being a man. Suppose that we choose 'a' and 'F ____', respectively. Then the correct paraphrase into the official idiom of 'Socrates is a man' is 'Fa'.

Quantifiers are logical constants, but their function is not the same as that of the propositional connectives. They are devices that make statements out of open sentences in the official idiom. Consider for a moment the analogous operation in English. A single predicate, such as '____ is brown' is not, of course, a sentence. It can be made into a sentence by the addition of any of a number of noun phrases, for example, 'Everything', 'Nothing', 'The Empire State Building', 'Socrates', 'This', and the pronouns 'He', 'She', and 'It'. 'It is brown' is an English sentence, but, as remarked above, whether it is true or false depends upon what 'it' is used to refer to. If 'it' refers to something that is brown, the sentence is true; otherwise, it is false. Ordinarily, no difficulty arises because a sentence such as 'It is brown' is uttered only in those contexts where it is obvious what is referred to. For example, a speaker might point to, say, a telephone pole, and say "It is brown." This sentence is true if the telephone pole is brown and false otherwise. Variables, for example, 'x', 'y', 'z', and pronouns have certain similarities and they share certain differences with names. Like names and pronouns, variables always refer to something or other. Like pronouns, but unlike names, one and the same variable can, on different occasions, refer to different things. But unlike both names and pronouns, it is usually not clear, on a given occasion, just *what* a variable refers to. For example, usually the truth value of 'It is brown' is known because 'it' is used to refer to a particular object that is clear from the context. But the truth value of 'x is brown' is undetermined because we have no idea to what 'x' refers. The only constraint we have placed on variables is that they refer to something.

To sum up the discussion so far, two ways of making an English sentence out of a predicate have analogues in the official idiom. *First*, if '____ is brown' is an English predicate, and 'Socrates' an English name, then 'Socrates is brown' is an English sentence. Similarly, since 'he,' 'she', 'it', and 'this' can replace English names, 'He is brown', 'It is brown', and so on, are also English sentences. In parallel fashion, if '*a*' is a subject term in the official idiom and '*F* ___' a predicate in the official idiom, then '*Fa*' is a sentence in the official idiom. Again, if '*x*' is a variable in the official idiom and '*F* ___' a predicate, then '*Fx*' is an *open* sentence in the official idiom and hence a sentence therein.

The *second* way to produce an English sentence is to complete the predicate, for example, '___ is brown', with a phrase such as 'Everything', 'Something', or 'Nothing'. Thus 'Everything is brown', like 'Socrates is brown' and 'It is brown', is a sentence. But, as Frege pointed out, a sentence such as 'Everything is brown' is really unlike 'It is brown'. The difference, it will be recalled, is in the different ways these two sentences are to be evaluated for truth. 'It is brown' is true if and only if the subject term, 'It', refers to an entity that belongs to the set of things the predicate '___ is brown' is true of (i.e., the set of brown things). The truth value of 'Everything is brown', on the other hand, is not determined by looking to see if 'everything' refers to something that belongs to the set of brown things. Thus what is really intended in a sentence such as 'Everything is brown' is this: "Whatever thing you choose, it belongs to the set of brown things." Another way of saying this is: "Consider the sentence 'It is brown'—now whatever you refer to with 'it' the sentence will be true."

This way of speaking is also paralleled in the official idiom. One can create a sentence in the official idiom by prefixing one of the quantifiers to an open sentence with one variable. This operation is a way of "closing" the sentence and the result of the operation is a *closed sentence* or *statement* with a definite truth value. Given some open sentence, say, '*Fx*', in the official idiom, '(*x*)*Fx*' is a sentence (to be read, "Every entity *x* is such that *x* is *F*") and '(*Ex*)*Fx*' is a sentence (to be read, "There is an entity *x* such that *x* is *F*"). The first sentence is said to be *universally quantified* and the second is said to be *existentially quantified*.

Premise (1) of the argument description opening this section is a universal sentence in English and should be paraphrased into the official idiom as such. Recall Frege's insight that a sentence such as 'All men are mortal' is really conditional in form—it says that every entity is such that if it is a man, then it is mortal. The correct way to paraphrase this sentence, then, is to choose predicate letters with which to abbreviate the English predicates. In paraphrasing premise (2), 'Socrates is a man', we already decided upon '*F* ___' as the abbreviation for '. . . is a man', so we must assign that predicate letter to '. . . is a man' consistently throughout the argument. Suppose that we choose '*G* ___' as the abbreviation for '. . . is mortal'; then the correct paraphrase of 'All men are mortal' into the official idiom is '(*x*)(*Fx* ⊃ *Gx*)'. Finally, the correct paraphrase of the conclusion of argument (2), 'Socrates is a mortal', is 'Ga'. Fully paraphrased into the expanded official idiom, the argument is

(1) $(x)(Fx \supset Gx)$
(2) Fa
(3) $\therefore Ga$

Thus its logical form is displayed, but demonstrations of its validity will be postponed until the development of the appropriate evaluation techniques in Chapter III. In (1) we say that the universal quantifier '(x)' *binds* the two occurrences of the variable 'x'. That is, the quantifier makes it unnecessary to ask what the variable stands for—whatever it stands for, that thing has the property expressed by 'G' if it has the property expressed by 'F'. An occurrence of a variable that is not bound is *free*. For example, '$Fx \supset Gx$' has two free occurrences of 'x'. An open sentence, then, is any sentence in the official idiom that has one or more occurrences of a free variable.

Now, we redefine precisely the notion of *sentence in the official idiom* (SOI):

1. If P^n is an n-place predicate and $t_1 \cdots t_n$ are subject letters or variables, then $P^n(t_1 \cdots t_n)$ is a sentence in the official idiom.
2. $p, q, r, \ldots$ are sentences in the official idiom.
3. If A is a sentence in the official idiom, then so is $\sim A$.
4. If A and B are sentences in the official idiom, then so are
    (a) $(A \vee B)$
    (b) $(A \& B)$
    (c) $(A \supset B)$
    (d) $(A \equiv B)$
5. If t is a variable and A is a sentence in the official idiom, then
    (a) $(t)A$
    (b) $(Et)A$
    are sentences in the official idiom.
6. Nothing that is not the result of the clauses listed above is a sentence in the official idiom.

11.1 Exercises

In answering the following questions, you may find it helpful to refer to the summary of concepts and definitions introduced in this chapter on p. 169. Starred exercises are answered in Appendix III.

1. According to the unextended official idiom, a sentence such as 'Bachelors are unmarried' was a simple sentence. Is this sentence simple according to the extended official idiom? Why or why not? Is 'It is necessary that bachelors are unmarried' simple or complex according to the extended official idiom? Why or why not?

2. Does the first argument in each of the following pairs have the same logical form as the second member of the pair?

   A   (1) Nothing is in my house.
        (2) Nothing is a dinosaur.
        (3) Therefore, a dinosaur is in my house.
        (1) John is in my house.
        (2) John is a man.
        (3) A man is in my house.

   B   (1) Someone is my cousin.
        (2) Someone is my neighbor.
        (3) Thus someone is my cousin and my neighbor.
        (1) John is my cousin.
        (2) John is my neighbor.
        (3) Thus John is my cousin and my neighbor.

   C   (1) John is in my house.
        (2) John is a man.
        (3) Thus a man is in my house.
        (1) John is in my car.
        (2) John is a man.
        (3) Thus a man is in my car.

   Explain your answers. What, if anything, do these examples show?

3. Both quantifiers and sentence connectives are among the logical constants in the extended official idiom. In what way do the quantifiers differ from the sentence connectives?

★4. According to English grammar, what sort of phrase is 'men' in the sentence 'Men are mortal'? What sort of phrase in the extended official idiom does 'men' correspond to? Is there any interesting difference between the two treatments of this phrase? Defend your answer.

5. How many ways can the following sentences be paraphrased into the extended official idiom? Give an example of each way.
   a. Ford loves English muffins.
   b. The White House is a large house.
   c. The White House is a white house.

6. Which of the following are sentences in the extended official idiom? Defend your answers.

   a. $(Ex)p$ b. $F(a \vee b)$
   c. $(Ex)(Fx \vee (x)(Fx))$ ★d. $(Ey)(Ex)(F^2xy)$
   e. $(y)(x)(F^2xy)$ f. $Fa \bigvee p$

g. $(x)(Ey)(xF^2xy)$

i. $(x)(Ey)(F^2xy)$

★k. $\sim(x) \sim F \vee G$

m. Fx

o. $(x)(x)(x)(F^2xx)$

★h. $(x)(Ex)(F^3xy)$

j. $(x)(Ex)(F^2x)$

l. Fa

n. Fd

p. F^2abz

7. Refer to Exercise 6:

a. Are all the occurrences of 'x' in (o) bound?

b. Is 'a' in (l) bound or free?

c. In '$(z)(Ex)(Fx \vee (y)(Fy \supset Gz))$', is 'z' bound or free?

12.
EXPANSION OF THE OFFICIAL IDIOM: SEMANTICS

To help interpret the other logical constants, we reflected on the truth conditions of English sentences constructed by means of their readings. The same strategy is employed in the interpretation of the quantifiers. For example, to interpret '(x)' in '$(x)Fx$', we shall consider sentences such as 'Everything is a mountain'. For were we to abbreviate '. . . is a mountain' by 'F ____', then '$(x)Fx$' would be the correct paraphrase of this sentence into the official idiom.

First, we need to introduce the notion of a *universe* of entities, sometimes called the *universe of discourse*. We cannot be certain of the truth value of a quantified sentence such as 'Everything is a mountain' until some specification of what the speaker is talking about is made: Is he talking about the set of peaks in the Alps, the set of famous points of scenic interest, the set of things on the earth's surface, or the set of entities in the physical universe? In the first case this sentence is true; in the second it is probably not true; and in the last two it is clearly false. Similarly, the truth value of quantified sentences in the official idiom, such as '$(x)Fx$', is relative to the specified universe of entities to be talked about in a given context. Of course, in different contexts, different universes may be specified.

Let us imagine a universe of objects, **U**, consisting of only three things. Suppose that they are three famous mountains: the Mönch, the Eiger, and the Jungfrau. Now we shall compare the conditions under which the following English sentences express true or false propositions:

(1) *The Mönch is a mountain.*
(2) *The Eiger is a mountain.*
(3) *The Jungfrau is a mountain.*
(4) *Everything is a mountain.*
(5) *Something is a mountain.*

Intuitively, the truth value of simple subject–predicate sentences such as those of (1) to (3) depends on three things:

a. The universe, **U**, that is chosen.
b. What entity e in **U** the subject term refers to.
c. Whether or not the predicate is true of that entity e.

135

The truth value of (1), for example, depends on whether 'the Mönch' refers to some entity in **U** that is a mountain. We have already decided, in this case, that **U** contains three mountains, so 'the Mönch' does refer to some entity *e* in **U** that is a mountain. Therefore, (1) is true relative to **U**; similarly with (2) and (3).

Suppose that we were to specify a different universe, **U'**, consisting of the Mönch, the Eiffel Tower, and the Mississippi River. Then (1) would be true, relative to **U'**, but (2) and (3) would be false. They would be false because the subject terms 'the Eiger' and 'the Jungfrau' would fail to refer to something in **U'** that is a mountain.

On the other hand, as we have already remarked, the truth value of (4) is not determined in this way. We do not look for an entity in **U** to which 'everything' refers to see whether or not it is a mountain. Rather, (4) is true, relative to **U** if and only if (1) to (3) are all true relative to **U**. Thus (4) is true just in case the following conjunction is true:

(4') *The Mönch is a mountain and the Eiger is a mountain and the Jungfrau is a mountain.*

Otherwise, (5) is false. Thus the truth conditions of (4) are the same as the truth conditions of the conjunction of (1) to (3).

Parallel considerations apply to (5). 'Something is a mountain' is true, relative to **U**, just in case at least one of the members of **U** is a mountain. Thus (5) is true relative to **U** just in case the following alternation is true relative to **U**:

(5') *The Mönch is a mountain or the Eiger is a mountain or the Jungfrau is a mountain.*

Otherwise, (5) is false. So the truth conditions of (5) are the same as the truth conditions of the alternation of (1) to (3).

Note that in a universe **U''**, having only one entity, (4) will be true if and only if (5) is. For example, suppose that **U''** contains only the Eiger. Then (4) is true if and only if

(2) *The Eiger is a mountain.*

while (5) is true if and only if

(2) *The Eiger is a mountain.*

Since (4) and (5) each are true if and only if (2) is true, it follows that (4) is true if and only if (5) is true, relative to this universe. That does not mean, however, that (4) and (5) mutually or separately *imply* one another—that an argument with either as premise and the other as conclusion would be valid. It is very important not to confuse the truth *values* that (4) and (5) have relative to a given universe with their truth *conditions*. In this case, (4) is true if and only if (5) is true relative to **U″**, but that does not mean they have the same truth *conditions*. The truth conditions of (4) and (5) are the ways their truth values are assessed relative to *any* universe of discourse, not just **U″**. Since the manner of assessing (4) and (5) differs, they have different truth conditions.

Based on these reflections, we are now in a position to fix the interpretations of the quantifiers. In our interpretations we will exploit the kind of relationships just explored. Suppose that every entity *e* belonging to **U** has a name in the official idiom and that every name in the official idiom names something in **U**. Then:

> *Where* **U** *is a given universe of discourse, and A is any open sentence in the official idiom containing free occurrences of the variable t,* *
>
> (1) *(t)A is true if and only if for every entity e in* **U** *the result of replacing all free occurrences of t in A by a name of e is a true statement.*
>
> (2) *(Et) A is true if and only if there is some e in* **U** *such that the result of replacing all free occurrence of t in A by a name of e is a true statement.*

---

* If *A* does *not* contain any free occurrences of *t*, then *(t)A* and *(Et)A,* respectively, are true if and only if *A* is true. Otherwise, *(t)A* and *(Et)A* are false.

Notice that '*t*' here is a meta-variable. It functions in much the same way as did the meta-variables '*A*' and '*B*' in previous definitions. '*(t)A*', for example, is read as "the result of prefixing any sentence *A* with the universal quantifier."

12.1 Exercises

In answering the following questions, you may find it helpful to refer to the summary of concepts and definitions introduced in this chapter on p. 169. Starred exercises are answered in Appendix III.

1. What is the difference between the truth value of a sentence and its truth conditions? In your answer, give examples of sentences from both the unextended official idiom and the extended official idiom.
2. Consider the following English sentences:
   ★a. Some numbers are even.
   b. Some numbers are odd.
   c. Seven is odd.
   d. It is not the case that there is a number between 4 and 7.

e. All numbers are odd.

f. 2 is even.

g. There is a number between 2 and 7.

h. Everything is a number.

What are truth *conditions* for each of these sentences? Relative to the universe $U' = \{1, 2, 4, 7\}$, which are true and which false? Relative to $U'' = \{4, 7, 9\}$, which are true and which false? Defend your answers.

3. Is '$(x)(p \& q)$' a sentence in the extended official idiom? What are its truth conditions?

4. For *every* open or closed sentence in the following list of the form $(t)A$ or $(Et)A$, write down A. Some sentences of one of these forms might be embedded in others. Examples:

$$\text{If } (t)A \text{ is } (x)(Fx \supset Gx) \text{ then } A \text{ is } (Fx \supset Gx).$$
$$\text{If } (Et)(t_1)A \text{ is } (Ex)(y)(Fxy) \text{ then } A' \text{ is } (y)Fxy \text{ and } A \text{ is } Fxy$$

a. $(x)Fx$

b. $(x)Fx \lor p$

c. $(x)Fx \lor (x)Gx$

d. $(x)(Fx \lor Gx)$

e. $(x)(Fx) \lor ((Ey)Gy)$

f. $(x)(Ey)((Fxy \lor Gy) \equiv p)$

g. $\sim(x)Fx$

Difficult

5. Consider a universe $U = \{$The Mississippi, The Hudson, The Rhine$\}$ and a scheme of abbreviation as follows:

$F\_$: '. . . is a river' a: 'The Mississippi'
$G\_$: '. . . is in the United States' b: 'The Hudson'
$F^2\_$: '. . . is longer than—' c: 'The Rhine'

Using the interpretative clauses for the quantifiers as well as those for the propositional connectives introduced in Section 5 of this chapter, give the truth value of each of the sentences below relative to U. (*Note:* The three rivers in order of descending length are as follows: The Mississippi, The Rhine, The Hudson.)

a. $(x)(Fx \supset Gx)$ b. $(x)(Gx \supset Fx)$

c. $(Ex)Fx$ d. $(Ex)Gx$

e. $(x)Fx$ f. $(x)Gx$

★g. $(Ex)Fx \lor (x)Gx$ h. $(Ex)(Fx \& \sim Gx)$

i. $(Ey)F^2cy$ j. $(x)F^2b$

k. $(Ex)(Ey)F^2xy$ l. F^2cb

m. $(x)(F^2xc \supset Gx)$

13.
PARAPHRASE OF SENTENCES INTO THE EXTENDED OFFICIAL IDIOM

The criterion for adequacy of paraphrase into the extended official idiom is exactly the same as for the unextended official idiom. The paraphrase of an English sentence into the official idiom is adequate just in case the two sentences have the same truth conditions (are logically equivalent). The actual process of paraphrase relies on our *understanding* of the quantifiers as interpreted in the previous section. As before, the readings of the quantifiers are to be used as *clues* for finding the right paraphrase. The readings are not always used in the same way as the corresponding quantifiers, so one must make sure in a particular case that the reading in question does have the use upon which the interpretation of the relevant quantifiers is based. Nevertheless, because the interpretations of the quantifiers are based on certain especially clear uses of the English readings, we can rely upon our understanding of these phrases to paraphrase into the official idiom in much the same way we rely on our understanding of two natural languages to translate from one to the other. The interpretations of the quantifiers are available to *check* a given paraphrase, but one should not have to continually make use of the interpretations to do the paraphrase. The same was true in nonquantificational paraphrase: Once the interpretations of the propositional connectives were learned, one could paraphrase from English into the official idiom without having to do it via the interpretations. Sometimes, in more complicated cases, the technique of "paraphrasing inward" (see p. 116) was used, partially to expose the logical form of the original before a scheme of abbreviation was introduced.

Because paraphrase into the official extended official idiom is, in general, more complicated than paraphrase into the unextended official idiom, we shall make greater use of paraphrasing inward. This requires using the readings of the quantifiers and other propositional connectives to expose as much logical form as possible before proceeding into the official idiom. When one has paraphrased inward as far as possible, then one needs only to ensure that the various readings of the relevant logical constants are used in a standard way, or, if they are not, then to determine the sort of stylistic variance or deviance involved. The final step involves little more than introducing a scheme of abbreviation and reexpressing in symbols what one has arrived at.

We shall begin by paraphrasing some of the sentences employed in the previous section, to help interpret the quantifiers:

139

(1) *The Eiger is a mountain.*
(2) *Everything is a mountain.*
(3) *Something is a mountain.*

Since (1) contains no quantifiers or propositional connectives, it is a simple sentence. Its truth value depends upon the truth value of the proposition expressed, but this, in turn, depends upon the internal structure of the sentence. In other words, (1) expresses a true proposition (and hence is true) just in case 'the Eiger' refers to an entity *e* in the selected universe **U**, which is a mountain. In our earlier treatment of simple sentences, it was said only that a sentence such as (1) is true (false) if and only if a true (false) proposition is expressed. The same is true here except that more structure is exposed in the sentence. So we have to consider what *makes* such a sentence express a true (false) proposition. In other words, we now analyze simple sentences previously left unanalyzed. Let us adopt the following scheme of abbreviation for (1) to (3):

> *a: 'The Eiger'*
> *F__: '. . . is a mountain'*

Then the correct paraphrase of (1) is

(1') Fa

Now (2), as we know, is true if and only if each entity in a given universe of discourse, **U**, is a mountain. In other words, paraphrasing inward,

(2') *Every entity x is such that x is a mountain.*

On the same scheme of abbreviation, '*x* is a mountain' becomes 'Fx', so the paraphrase of (2) is

(2") $(x)Fx$

The adequacy of this paraphrase can now be verified by invoking the interpretation of the universal quantifier. '$(x)Fx$' is true, with respect to **U**, if and only if for every *e* in **U** the result of replacing '*x*' in 'Fx' with a name of *e* is a true sentence. These results are all the sentences of the official idiom in which an element of **U** is referred to and said to be a mountain, and they are all *paraphrases into the official idiom* of the various English sentences, such as (1), in which a member *e* of **U** is referred to and said to be a mountain. Now (2') [and, as a consequence, (2)] is true if and only if all these English sentences are true. Any one of these English sentences is true if and only if its paraphrase into the official idiom is true. So it follows that (2″) is true if and only if (2) is true. Since **U** is an arbitrarily chosen universe, the same argument can be given for all universes. It follows that (2″) is true if and only if (2) is true for *every* universe **U′**. Therefore, (2) and (2″) have the same truth conditions. So (2″) is an adequate paraphrase into the official idiom of (2).

The first step in paraphrasing (3) is to bring the preferred reading of the existential quantifier into play:

(3′) *There is an entity x such that x is a mountain.*

The paraphrase, then, is

(3″) $(Ex)Fx$

As before, the paraphrase can be verified by reflecting on the truth conditions of (3) and (3″). Sentence (3) is true, with respect to a given universe **U** just in case there is at least one true English sentence in which a member *e* of **U** is referred to and said to be a mountain: for example, a sentence such as (1) above.

Similarly, (3″) is true with respect to **U** just in case at least one sentence in the official idiom, such as (1′) above, which results from replacing '*x*' in '*Fx*' with a name of some *e* in **U**, is true. Now one of these sentences in the official idiom [such as (1′)] will be true with respect to **U** if and only if the corresponding English sentence [such as (1), of which it is a paraphrase] is true. Since the same argument can be given for *every* universe **U′**, it follows that (3) and (3″) have the same truth conditions.

We shall briefly consider a few more complicated cases of quantificational paraphrase. The following sentences exemplify the familiar four "forms" of quantified sentences identified by Aristotle: universal affirmative, universal negative, particular affirmative, and particular negative:

(1) *All men are mortal.*
(2) *No men are mortal.*
(3) *Some men are mortal.*
(4) *Some men are not mortal.*

Let the scheme of abbreviation be

F__: '. . . *is a man*'.
G__: '. . . *is mortal*'.

As noted in Section 11, (1) is really conditional in form, a fact readily brought out by paraphrasing inward:

(1') *Every entity x is such that (if x is a man, then x is mortal)*.

Paraphrasing 'x is a man' and 'x is mortal' according to the scheme above, this becomes

(1") *(x)(if Fx, then Gx)*

and, finally,

(1''') $(x)(Fx \supset Gx)$

As before, the adequacy of this paraphrase may be verified by comparing the truth conditions of (1) and (1'''). Sentence (1''') is true, with respect to a given universe **U**, if and only if for every *e* in **U** the result of replacing each occurrence of 'x' in 'Fx $\supset$ Gx' by a name of *e* is a true sentence (of the official idiom). These results are all sentences in the official idiom, in which it is said of an element of the universe that *if* it is a man, *then* it is mortal, and they are all *paraphrases into the official idiom* of various English sentences. Now these English sentences are all true if and only if the set of men is a subset of the set of mortals. Sentence (1), in turn, is true if and only if the set of men is a subset of the set of mortals. Therefore, (1) is true for a given **U** if and only if (1''') is. Since **U** is an arbitrarily selected universe and the same argument can be given for all of them, (1) is true if and only if (1") is true, for all universes **U'**. Therefore, they have the same truth conditions.

To say that *no* men are mortal is to say that *every* man is *not* mortal. In other words.

(2') *Every entity x is such that (if x is a man, then x is not mortal)*.

Thus the paraphrase of (2) exactly parallels that of (1) except that the consequent must be negated. That is,

(2") $(x)(Fx \supset Gx)$.

Sentence (3) is paraphrased as follows. To say that some men are mortal is to say in part that something is mortal (i.e., that there is an entity that is mortal). But it is also to say that among these mortals are to be counted men, that is, that there is (at least one) entity that is *both* a man and is mortal. Thus

(3') *There is an entity x such that (x is a man and x is mortal).*

which becomes

(3") *(Ex)(x is a man and x is mortal)*

or

(3''') *(Ex)(Fx & Gx)*

Verification of the adequacy of these two paraphrases is left as an exercise for the reader. Notice, however, that (3) should not be paraphrased as

$(Ex)(Fx \supset Gx)$

The truth conditions for this sentence are as follows: It is true if and only if there is an entity e in **U** such that the result of replacing 'x' in '$Fx \supset Gx$' with a name of e is a true sentence. There will be such a replacement in a given universe **U** unless *everything* in **U** is a man and *nothing* is mortal. These are certainly not the truth conditions of (3). So this virtually empty assertion is not the right paraphrase.

Finally, (4) is paraphrased in parallel fashion to (3) except that the second conjunct of the quantified conjunction is negated. The four sentences correctly paraphrased, then, are respectively

(1) $(x)(Fx \supset Gx)$
(2) $(x)(Fx \supset \sim Gx)$
(3) $(Ex)(Fx \& Gx)$
(4) $(Ex)(Fx \& \sim Gx)$

A final word on the distinction between truth *conditions* and truth *values*. To paraphrase an English sentence into the official idiom is to preserve its truth conditions. That means that with respect to *any* universe **U**, one sentence will be true if and only if the other is. Thus correctly to paraphrase does not require any mention of a particular universe. But sometimes we might be interested in the actual truth value of a given sentence. Normally, this happens when contextual factors come into play. Suppose that someone says "Everything is a mountain" and we want to paraphrase this into the official idiom. The natural paraphrase is '$(Ex)Fx$'. Now, if this claim happens to be a premise of a valid argument, then the *soundness* of the argument may depend on the truth value of this sentence. Thus we would want to know what the universe should be. Normally, a particular universe of discourse is suggested by context. For example, it would be unusual for someone to assert that everything is a mountain and intend his universe of discourse to be the set of everything existing in the physical universe, because one normally intends to say something that is true, and this proposition is obviously false in such a case. On the other hand, it would also be odd for someone to assert that all men are mortal and intend his universe to be the set containing only, say, the Mönch, Jungfrau, and Eiger. In this case his assertion would be true, but it would be *vacuously* true because there are no men in this set. One does not normally intend to make vacuously true assertions; so this would not be the right universe. To avoid such unclarity, we shall in the future assume the universe of discourse for a paraphrase (if one is relevant to the task at hand) to be the set of all existing entities, *unless otherwise stated*.

The paraphrase of sentences containing relational predicates (i.e., those having two or more places) requires us to reflect on considerations similar to those that recently forced us to expand the official idiom. However, as the syntax and semantics of the expanded official idiom has been explained, such paraphrases will introduce no new difficulties. Consider:

A (1) *Guenièvre loves Lancelot.*
    (2) *Thus Guenièvre loves something.*

A is intuitively valid; it represents correct reasoning. Yet were we to attempt to paraphase **A** into official standard form using only one-place predicates, we would be unable to expose enough of its logical form to permit a demonstration of its validity. Suppose that we adopt the following scheme of abbreviation:

    a: 'Guenièvre'
  G__: '. . . loves something'.
  F__: '. . . loves Lancelot'.

Then (1) becomes

  (1') *Fa*

If we take '*G__*' to be the abbreviation of '. . . loves something', (2) becomes

  (2') *Ga*

The resultant argument,

B (1) Fa
     (2) $\therefore Ga$

is, however, invalid. For a counterexample, just replace 'a' with 'Jimmy Carter' '$F\_$' with '. . . is President', and '$G\_$' with '. . . is female'. This shows that the validity of **A** depends on logical form not revealed in **B**. If we represent '. . . loves' as a two-place predicate, however, the problem disappears. Let the new scheme of abbreviation be

     a: 'Guenièvre'
     b: 'Lancelot'
  $G^2\_$: '. . . loves ____'.

Premise (1) of **A** then becomes

(1″) G^2ab

The additional structure provided by the two-place predicate letter permits us to make use of our insight in Section 11 that 'something' is not a name and, hence, should be paraphrased as a quantifier rather than as a subject letter. That is, 'Guenièvre loves something' is true if and only if there is some e in the universe **U** such that Guenièvre loves e. In other words, if

There is some entity x such that (Guenièvre loves x).

which becomes

(2″) $(Ex)G^2ax$

An adequate, and indeed the most natural, paraphrase of argument **A** into official standard form, then, is

C (1) G^2ab
     (2) $\therefore (Ex)G^2ax$

C exposes the detailed logical form of **A** and enables us to show why **A** is valid. Its evaluation must be postponed, however, until we have developed the necessary techniques in Chapter 3, where this argument is evaluated as an illustration (p. 205). For now, the reader ought to see intuitively that **C** is valid.

We briefly illustrate a few more relational paraphrases:

(3) *Guenièvre loves Arthur.*
(4) *Lancelot loves Guenièvre.*
(5) *Arthur loves Guenièvre.*
(6) *Someone loves Guenièvre.*
(7) *Someone loves everyone.*
(8) *Everyone loves someone.*
(9) *Someone who is loved by everyone loves everyone.*

For the purposes of this discussion, let the universe **U** be the set of people, and let the scheme of abbreviation include the following addition:

c: *'Arthur'*

(3) to (5) are

(3') G^2ac
(4') G^2ba
(5') G^2ca

The only problem with (6) is to distinguish it from (2) in argument **C**, that is, $'(Ex)G^2ax'$. A first start would be

(6') *There is an entity x such that (x loves Guenièvre).*

which, finally, is

(6") $(Ex)G^2xa$

Note that the difference between (2) and (6") has to do with the "direction" of the predicate. The difference between $'G^2xy'$ and $'G^2xy'$ (relative to its abbreviating '. . . loves ___') is that for x to love y is not the same as for y to love x. Thus for $'G^2xa'$ to be true of something, that thing must love what $'a'$ names (i.e., Guenièvre), whereas for $'G^2ax'$ to be true of something, Guenièvre must love it.

The paraphrase of (7) is made clear by using the readings of the quantifiers,

(7') *There is an x such that (for every y, (x loves y)).*

Note that two different variables must be used. If we represented (7') as There is an x such that (for every x, (x loves x))', that would say that there is someone such that everyone loves himself. (7'), then, becomes.

(7'') $(Ex)(y)G^2xy$

Sentence (8) becomes

(8') *Every entity x is such that (there is an entity y such that (x loves y)).*

and, finally,

(8'') $(x)(Ey)G^2xy$

The last example, (9), involves only the additional problem of the relative clause, beginning with 'who. . .'. As noted in Section 7, this is generally the sign of conjunction:

(9') *There is an entity x such that (for every entity y, (y loves x) and (x loves y)).*

or

(9'') $(Ex)(y)(G^2yx \ \& \ G^2xy)$

Note in this case that the scope of the quantifiers is important. If (9) had been rendered, instead, as

(9''') $(Ex)(y)G^2yx \ \& \ (Ex)(y)G^2xy$

that would have said that there is somebody that everyone loves and there is somebody that loves everyone. But this could be true even if there is no *one* person who is loved by all and who loves all. The relative clause 'who . . .' determines that if the same person is being talked about in each case, and this has to be represented by binding the free variables in the open sentences 'G^2yx' and 'G^2xy' by the same quantifiers.

We have been presupposing that the universe is the set of people, so, assuming the legend of King Arthur to be true, (1) to (6) are true and (7) to (9), undoubtedly, are false. But if the universe is restricted to $U = \{$Arthur, Lancelot, Guenièvre$\}$, then (7) to (9) are true also.

13.1 Exercises

In answering the following questions, you may find it helpful to refer to the summary of concepts and definitions introduced in this chapter on p. 169. Starred exercises are answered in Appendix III.

1. What is the difference between a simple analyzed sentence and a simple unanalyzed sentence in the extended official idiom? Do they have different truth conditions? Explain.
2. Is the following argument valid?
   (1) All trespassers will be prosecuted.
   (2) Therefore, someone will be prosecuted.
   Explain.
3. According to the characterization of the official idiom given in Sections 11 and 12, which (if any) of the following sentences should be paraphrased as simple and which (if any) as complex? Defend your answers.
   a. All bachelors are male.
   b. All bachelors are unmarried males.
   c. It is necessarily the case that all bachelors are unmarried.
4. Paraphrase the following sentences into the extended official idiom, using the scheme of abbreviation provided.
   a. Not all gentlemen prefer blonds. (F__: 'is a gentleman', G__: '. . . prefers blonds')
   b. Fish are always cold-blooded. (F__: '. . . is a fish', G__: '. . . is cold-blooded')
   c. Some physicians are rich, though incompetent. (F__: '. . . is a physician', G__: '. . . is rich', H__: '. . . is competent')
   d. Gout sometimes afflicts the famous. (F__: '. . . is gout', G__: '. . . is famous', H^2__: '. . . afflicts ____')
   e. There's gold in them there hills. (F__: '. . . is gold', G__: '. . . is in them there hills')
   ★f. All that glitters is not gold. (F__: '. . . glitters', G__: '. . . is gold')
   g. Not every soldier was killed. (F__: '. . . is a soldier', G__: 'was killed')
   h. No soldier was killed. (F__: '. . . is a soldier', G__: 'was killed')
   i. No cautious driver had an accident. (F__: '. . . is a driver', G__: '. . . is cautious', H__: '. . . had an accident')
   j. If no soldier gets killed, everyone will be happy. (F__: '. . . is a soldier', G__: '. . . is happy', H__: '. . . is happy')

Use the following scheme of abbreviation for the remaining sentences.

a: 'Sigmund'
F^2__: '. . . despises ____'.
G__: '. . . is in Vienna'.

    k. Everyone despises Sigmund.

    l. Sigmund despises no one.

  ★m. There is someone that Sigmund despises in Vienna.

    n. There is not anyone that Sigmund despises.

    o. Sigmund does not despise anyone in Vienna.

    p. Sigmund does not despise everyone in Vienna.

5. Paraphrase the following sentences into the extended official idiom, providing your own scheme of abbreviation. Use only nonrelational predicate letters.

    a. There are round squares.

    b. A man is not ambiguous.

    c. Yes, we have no bananas.

    d. Nothing does not exist.

    e. All who blaspheme are wicked.

    f. Everything is either a substance or an attribute.

    g. The essence of a thing is either mixed throughout it or is at the core or puts down long roots.

  ★h. Everyone who knows both George and Mabel admires Mabel but hates George.

    i. John ate everything left on the table.

    j. Drunkards are not admitted.

    k. Some soldiers love war, but not all who love war are soldiers.

    l. Men and women who are over eighteen are permitted to vote.

    m. If only Republicans support the incumbent, and no Democrats support the candidate, then if anyone is a Democrat, someone supports neither the incumbent nor the candidate.

    n. There are men who are immortal.

    o. There are men and there are immortals.

Difficult

6. Which of the following are contradictories of 'All fat people are happy'? Defend your answers.

    a. No fat people are happy.

    b. There are no fat people who are happy.

    c. No happy people are fat.

    d. Not everyone who is fat is happy.

    e. Not everyone who is unhappy is not fat.

    f. Some fat people are unhappy.

    g. Happy people do not exist.

7. In which of the following pairs of sentences does the first imply the second?

a. $Fa \supset Ga$	b. $Fb \supset Gb$	c. $Ga \mathbin{\&} Fa$
$Fa \vee Ga$	$Fb \mathbin{\&} Gb$	$Fa \supset Ga$

    d. $(x)(Fx \supset Gx)$ e. $(x)(Fx \supset Gx)$ f. $(Ex)(Gx \ \& \ Fx)$
       $(x)(\sim Fx \ v \ Gx)$ $(Ex)(Fx \ \& \ Gx)$ $(x)(Fx \supset Gx)$

8. Suppose that we let 'I^2___' abbrevaite the nonlogical predicate '. . . is identical to ____'. Paraphrase the following sentences into the official idiom, giving a scheme of abbreviation.

    a. Guenièvre loves everyone except herself.
    b. Everyone except John can have a drink.
    c. At most one thing can be taller than Mont Blanc.
    d. If Guenièvre loves Mark but does not love the King, then Mark is not the King.

14.

MORE ON STYLISTIC VARIANCE AND DEVIANCE

When the material on stylistic variance in Section 7 has been mastered, cases involving the readings of the quantifiers should present no problems. Still, there are a few considerations of which one should be aware (some of which are only loosely related to stylistic variance proper).

1. Paraphrase of Names, Predicates, and Pronouns This question is not clearly one of stylistic variance because no readings of logical constants are involved. Nevertheless, it is important to remark in this connection that sometimes quite different names and predicates should be given the same abbreviation for paraphrase into the official idiom. Consider, for example, the following argument in gross standard form, which, we may imagine, was actually offered by someone, Roscoe Frostbite, perhaps:

A (1) *All men are rational.*
(2) *Crustacea is human.*
(3) *Therefore, Crustacea is rational.*

Now, if '. . . is a man' and '. . . is human' were given different abbreviations, the paraphrase of this argument in official standard form would be invalid. That is, given the scheme:

> a: 'Crustacea'.
> F __: '. . . is a man'.
> G __: '. . . is rational'.
> H __: '. . . is human'.

argument **A** in official standard form would be

B (1) $(x)(Fx \supset Gx)$
(2) Ha
(3) $\therefore Ga$

to which a counterexample can readily be found, as the reader may determine for himself. If we have the scheme

   a: '*Crustacea*'
F __ : '. . . *is a man*'.
G __ : '. . . *is human*'.
H __ : '. . . *is rational*'.

however, the paraphrase in official standard form is valid:

C   (1) $(x)(Fx \supset Gx)$
     (2) Fa
     (3) $\therefore Ga$

The question is, do we attribute argument **B** to Roscoe or argument **C**? To say that he intended **B** is to say that he gave an invalid argument, whereas to attribute **C** to him is to say that he gave a valid argument. ther, realizing that it would be difficult to see who was being excluded if a distinction between men and women were not intended, one factors. In most contexts **B** would probably be wrong because one who offered argument **A,** Roscoe in this case, would most likely not think that there is any relevant distinction to be drawn between men and humans. So, given the near identity in meaning between '. . . is human' and '. . . is a man', one should choose the second scheme of abbreviation, thus judging Roscoe's argument to have a valid form. This would not be the correct decision in all contexts, however. If one saw 'Only men are permitted to dine in this club' written on a sign, then, knowing that many clubs discriminate against females and further, realizing that it would be difficult to see who was being excluded if a distinction between men and women were not intended, then one would be entitled to conclude that '. . . is a man' is not to be taken as equivalent to '. . . is human' in this case.

Names are even more difficult. Whether or not to paraphrase two different names as the same subject letter also depends on the context, but the considerations involved are more difficult to assess. On the one hand, if a person uses two different names to designate the same object and it is obvious to him and his audience that the different names do designate the same object, then it may seem best to abbreviate them in the same way. Thus in the case of

   (1) *All men are rational.*
   (2) *Socrates is a man.*
   (3) *Therefore, the teacher of Plato is rational.*

the validity of the paraphrase in official standard form depends on abbreviating 'Socrates' and 'the teacher of Plato' by the same subject letter.

Now if the giver of this argument always seemed to use the phrases 'Socrates' and 'the teacher of Plato' interchangeably and his audience was well aware of that fact (and, perhaps, they did so also), then we should probably regard the person as having given a valid argument. In this case it would probably be best to abbreviate the two subject phrases by the same subject letter. On the other hand, if we are given reason to believe that a person does not know that the two names designate the same object, then it probably would not be correct to give them the same abbreviation.

Note that in neither case do these decisions make the validity of a certain argument in official standard form depend on what we know or on what is "obvious." The problem is to know under what conditions to *attribute* a certain proposition, and hence an argument of a certain form, to a person. All we are saying is that contextual features enter into this decision. The question is this: Given that we know that **B** above, for example, is an invalid possible representation of **A** and that **C** is a valid possible representation, what contextual factors should induce us to *attribute* **C** rather than **B** to the speaker as *his argument in official standard form?*

There are two referential uses of pronouns. The first is *direct*. In the direct referential use one employs the pronoun like a name, as a device for picking something out. If Caesar had not known Cassius's name, he might have said "He has a lean and hungry look," for example. In this case 'he' is just a substitute for 'Cassius', so it would be abbreviated in the same way. The second referential use is *anaphoric* (or reference backward). In anaphoric reference one employs a pronoun to refer a second time to an entity already referred to directly. For example, in 'Cassius has a lean and hungry look and he might cause trouble', 'he' refers to Cassius, not someone else. Thus 'he' is abbreviated in the same way as is 'Cassius'. Anaphoric reference most commonly occurs in quantificational contexts. When we bind a number of quantifiers and variables with the same quantifier, we do it to ensure that the various predicates involved are being predicated of the same things. For example, in 'Someone robbed the bank and he's now rich', that it is the same person who robbed the bank and is now rich is conveyed by employing the same variable and quantifiers: '$(Ex)(x$ robbed the bank and x is rich)'.

Finally, there are nonreferential uses of pronouns. In 'It is not the case that Aristotle lived in Hoboken', the 'it' does not, of course, refer to something of which '. . . is not the case that Aristotle lived in Hoboken' is predicated. Rather the phrase 'It is not the case that . . .' is taken as a unit and is paraphrased as the negation sign. Similarly, in 'The patriotic archbishop Stigand found it advisable to declare for [i.e., to side with] William', the phrase '. . . found it advisable ____' is just a conversational modifier and is not to be paraphrased into the official idiom at all. Thus this sentence becomes 'Stigand is the patriotic archbishop and Stigand declared for William'.

2. Common Variants of Sentences Containing Readings of the Quantifiers We list, without discussion, a few examples of variants of sentences discussed in Section 13:

a. Variants of 'Everything is a mountain' include: 'All things are mountains', 'Each and everything is a mountain', 'Any entity you care to pick is a mountain'.
b. Variants of 'Something is a mountain' include: 'There is a mountain', 'There are mountains', 'At least one thing is a mountain', 'At least one mountain exists'.
c. Variants of 'All men are mortal' include: 'If anything is a man, it is mortal', 'Every man is mortal', 'No men are nonmortal' (as explained in Section 13).
d. Variants of 'No men are mortal' include: 'All men are not mortal' (as explained in Section 13), 'All men are nonmortal'.
e. Variants of 'Some men are mortal' include: 'There are mortal men', 'There are men who are mortal', 'There are mortals who are men', 'At least one mortal is male,' 'At least one male is mortal'.

3. Deletion In many cases no reading of a quantifier is present, but one is understood. For example, 'Men are mortal' is to be understood as 'All men are mortal', 'Mountains exist' as 'There is a mountain,' 'Mountains are all there are' as 'Everything is a mountain'.

4. Deviance Sentences containing 'a' can be stylistic variants of those containing readings of either quantifier. 'A fish just swam by' is a variant of 'There is an entity such that it is a fish and it just swam by', whereas 'A fish is cold-blooded' would normally be taken as a variant of 'Every entity is such that if it is a fish, then it is cold-blooded'. (Of course, there are many cases where 'a' has nothing to do with quantification. In 'John is a man', for example, 'a' is part of the predicate '. . . is a man'.) Similarly, sentences containing 'something' are often deviant. 'Something which is a man is mortal' is a variant of 'All men are mortal', and 'Something that is an unmarried adult male is a bachelor' is a variant of 'Everything is such that if it is an unmarried adult male, then it is a bachelor'. In most contexts, however, sentences containing 'something' are variants of those containing readings of the existential quantifier.

5. "Compound" Quantifiers The phrases 'someone' and 'everyone' also behave as stylistic variants of quantifiers. 'Someone is a scoundrel' is a variant of 'There is an entity such that *it is a person* and it is a scoundrel'. [But note that 'Someone who is a fool is not a scoundrel' becomes '*Every* entity is such that (if (it is a person and it is a fool), then (it is not a scoundrel))'.]

6. Influence of Quantifiers on Complex Open Sentences Sometimes quantifiers (or deleted quantifiers) that are nondeviant themselves nevertheless induce a sort of deviance in the readings of the propositional connectives within their scope. Consider 'Only mad dogs and Englishmen go into the noonday sun'. The presence of the plural English subject 'mad dogs and Englishmen' indicates a deleted quantifier, and the 'only' indicates the presence of a conditional. One attempt to paraphrase this sentence, then, might be as 'Every entity is such that (if (it goes into the noonday sun), then ((it is a mad dog) and (it is an Englishman)))'. But notice that this sentence is not true for any normal universe of discourse, for if the antecedent is true, then the sentence will be false because nothing is both a mad dog and an Englishman. What is intended is that if something goes into the noonday sun, then *either* it is a mad dog *or* an Englishman, that is, 'Every entity is such that (if (it goes into the noonday sun), then ((it is a mad dog) or (it is an Englishman)))'. Thus '. . . and _____' in the original sentence performed as a propositional connective, but its contribution to the truth value of the whole was that of alternation. As a second example, consider 'All swans but Australian ones are white'. Here '. . . but _____' appears to do the work of conjunction, so the sentence seems to be a stylistic variant of a conjunction. But the presence of a quantificational structure introduces an additional complexity. The most straightforward start at paraphrasing would be 'Every entity is such that (if ((it is a swan) and (it is Australian)), then (it is white))', but obviously what is meant is this: 'Every entity is such that (if ((it is a swan) and (it is not the case that it is Australian)), then (it is white))'.

7. Interdefinability of the Quantifiers It can be shown on the basis of the interpretations we have given the quantifiers that every sentence containing one of the quantifiers has exactly the same truth conditions as a sentence containing the other quantifier. In particular, all sentences of the following form are equivalent in truth conditions:

1. $(x)A$ has the same truth conditions as $\sim(Ex)\sim A$.
2. $(Ex)A$ has the same truth conditions as $\sim(x)\sim A$.
3. $\sim(x)A$ has the same truth conditions as $(Ex)\sim A$.
4. $\sim(Ex)A$ has the same truth conditions as $(x)\sim A$.

For those who are interested, we now show that the first statement holds:

1. Suppose that $(x)A$ is true with respect to a given universe **U**.
2. Then, by the interpretation of the universal quantifier, for every e in **U** the result of replacing every free occurrence of 'x' in A with a name of e is a true sentence.
3. If *all* the results of replacing every free occurrence of 'x' in A with a name of some e in **U** are true, then the negations of all these sentences are false.
4. But if the negations of all these sentences are false, then it is not the case that there is an e in **U** such that the result of replacing every free occurrence of 'x' in $\sim A$ with a name of e is a true sentence.
5. But then $(Ex)\sim A$ is false.
6. So $\sim(Ex)\sim A$ is true.

This shows that *if* $(x)A$ is true with respect to any given universe, **U**, *then* $(Ex) A$ is true with respect to **U**. Now we must show that the converse is true also:

1. Suppose that $\sim(Ex)\sim A$ is true with respect to a given universe **U**.
2. Then $(Ex)\sim A$ is false.
3. Then it is not the case that there is an e in **U** such that the result of replacing every free occurrence of 'x' in $\sim A$ with a name of e is a true sentence.
4. If so, then all the results of replacing every free occurrence of 'x' in $\sim A$ with a name of some e in **U** are false.
5. But then all the results of replacing every free occurrence of 'x' in A with a name of some e in **U** is true.
6. But then $(x)A$ is true.

This shows that if $\sim(Ex)\sim A$ is true with respect to any given universe, **U**, then $(x)A$ is true. These two derivations taken together show that with respect to any given universe **U**, $(x)A$ is true if and only if $\sim(Ex)\sim A$ is true. This is what we wanted, for it follows that sentences of these forms have the same truth conditions.

Now given that the foregoing four equivalences hold, there are opportunities for liberalizing what is to count of as an *adequate* paraphrase into the official idiom. For example, returning to Subsection 2 above, we may also give the following sentences the same paraphrase, although they are not, strictly speaking, stylistic variants of one another:

a. 'Everything is a mountain', 'Nothing is not a mountain'; 'All men are mortal', 'No men are nonmortal'.
b. 'Something is a mountain', 'It is not the case that nothing is a mountain'; 'Some men are mortal', 'Not all men are nonmortal'.
c. 'Not everything is a mountain', 'Something is not a mountain'; 'Not all men are mortal', 'Some men are nonmortal'.

14.1 Exercises

In answering the following questions, you may find it helpful to refer to the summary of concepts and definitions introduced in this chapter on p. 169. Starred exercises are answered in Appendix III.

1. Paraphrase the following sentences into the official idiom, using nonrelational predicate letters, and giving a scheme of abbreviation.
    1. Only males can join.
    2. Truffles and cavier are expensive.
    3. Only he deserves his life and his freedom who seizes it anew each day. (Johann von Goethe)
    4. Only little old ladies and children drink tea.
    ★5. Women and children will be rescued first.
    6. Those whom the gods love grow young. (Oscar Wilde)
    7. Unless one is wealthy there is no use in being a clever fellow. (Oscar Wilde)
    8. Nothing that is worth knowing can be taught. (Oscar Wilde)
    9. When a truth becomes a fact it loses all its intellectual value. (Oscar Wilde)
    10. No crime is vulgar but all vulgarity is crime. (Oscar Wilde)
    11. Only the shallow know themselves. (Oscar Wilde)
    12. To be premature is to be perfect. (Oscar Wilde)
    13. Nothing that is not the result of one of the above clauses is a sentence in the official idiom.
    14. No one who hates children and dogs can be all bad. (W. C. Fields)
    15. Lawyers, provided that they are competent, should be permitted to advertise if and only if they are willing to donate time to the poor.
    16. If nuclear fusion is feasible, then if not all countries that need fuel use oil, then the energy crisis will be over.
    ★17. Americans like beer, but the Frenchman drinks wine.
    18. All mammals except porpoises and whales live on land.
    19. Some of the butter was rancid or moldy.
    20. If all philosophers are professors and some of them are poets, too, then some professors are poets.
    21. There is a lack of honest men.

22. There is no lack of wheat.
23. It's a strong man who will beat Ali.
24. Everyone voted to sustain a motion over some motion that everyone disagreed with.
25. Everyone has a father, but not everyone is a father.
26. Every number has a successor.
★27. No number succeeds every number.
28. Some number succeeds no number.

Difficult

2. Show that

a. (*Ex*)*A* has the same truth conditions as (*x*)~*A*.

3. Does the sentence 'No news is good news' imply the sentence 'No good news is news'? Defend your answer fully.

15.
PARAPHRASE OF QUANTIFICATIONAL ARGUMENTS INTO OFFICIAL STANDARD FORM

The following arguments must be paraphrased into the extended official idiom for evaluation. In this section we shall paraphrase two examples, first from their natural habitat into gross standard form and then into official standard form. Then we shall paraphrase one final example directly from gross standard form into official standard form. All will be evaluated in Chapter 3.

EXAMPLE 1

Imagine a conversation between two economists. One says to the other:

Your argument from the premise that mining stocks have fallen to the conclusion that no industrial metals are in high demand ignores several facts. Indeed, I can offer an argument for just the opposite conclusion: Anything in high demand is expensive unless it's abundant, we agree. Now some industrial metals are rare. Gold, as we all know, is both rare and expensive. Since, you will grant, gold is an industrial metal, my conclusion follows.

The first two sentences of the passage really belong to the natural habitat. They tell us that someone offered an argument for the conclusion that no industrial metals are in high demand and that the speaker is offering an argument for the "opposite" conclusion. This would probably be the contradictory of 'no industrial metals are in high demand', namely, 'There is at least one industrial metal in high demand'. It seems that they agree on one of the premises—that anything in high demand is expensive unless it is abundant. The other premises are obvious. Note that 'since' does not express a relation (or mark an inference) between the premise that gold is an industrial metal and the conclusion, but it does help to mark an inference between all the premises and the conclusion. It is one of the argument's two illative particles. The speaker has already stated his conclusion and it is only because he does not want to repeat it that he makes the comment, 'my conclusion follows'. This, of course, is not part of his argument but serves the same function as an

159

illative particle proper, so we shall count it as such (although it is redundant). In gross standard form, the argument is

(1) *Anything in high demand is expensive unless it is abundant.*
(2) *Gold is both rare and expensive.*
(3) *Gold is an industrial metal.*
(4) *Therefore, there is at least one industrial metal in high demand.*

The paraphrase into official standard form is fairly straightforward. Note that something is rare if and only if it is not abundant, so the same predicate letter should be used for each (being negated the second time). Another point concerns the paraphrase of 'gold'. Offhand, it looks as if premise (3), for example, is an instance of deleted quantification ['For every x ((if x is gold), then (x is an industrial metal))'] in the manner of 'Men are mortal', but there is a difference between these terms. Unlike the latter case, there is something in U that 'gold' can reasonably be taken to stand for, namely the object consisting of all the bits of gold in the world. Premises (2) and (3) say of this thing that it is rare (i.e., compared to other substances there is less of it), expensive, and used industrially. One could offer a more detailed paraphrase along the lines of 'For any x, (if (x is a *bit* of gold . . .))', and so on, but this is not really necessary. Let us adopt the following scheme of abbreviation:

a: 'gold'
$F\_\_$: '. . . is in high demand'.
$G\_\_$: '. . . is expensive'.
$H\_\_$: '. . . is an industrial metal'.
$F_1\_\_$: '. . . is abundant'.

The only difficult premise to paraphrase is the first, for the scope of '. . . unless ____' is unclear. That is, there are two possibilities:

(*q*)   (For all x) [(if (x is in high demand), then (x is expensive)) unless (x is abundant)].
(1')   (For all x) [if (x is in high demand)), then ((x is expensive) unless (x is abundant)].

That is,

(1) $(x)((Fx \supset Gx) \lor F_1x)$

or

(1') $(x)(Fx \supset (Gx \lor F_1x))$

It is rather difficult to tell which sentence is the more natural paraphrase of the first premise, but reflection on their truth conditions reveals that they are, in fact, equivalent.[14] Thus either paraphrase is adequate.

Let us choose (1') as the paraphrase of the first premise. Then the argument in official standard form is as follows:

(1) $(x)((Fx \supset Gx) \vee F_1x)$
(2) $\sim F_1a$ & Ga
(3) Ha
(4) $\therefore (Ex)(Hx$ & $Fx)$

EXAMPLE 2

Consider next an argument that cannot be adequately paraphrased into official standard form without the use of both quantifiers and relational predicate letters. In its natural habitat, it is

With respect to life sentences for murderers, it is important to realize that it is not true that all murderers will be paroled. In the first place, no one can be paroled unless the Parole Board is convinced that he is safe to release. And in case he is not rehabilitated, we rely on the good judgment

---

[14] That (1) and (1') have the same truth conditions may be shown in the following way. First, notice that (1) has the form $(t)A$, where A is '$(Fx \supset Gx) \vee F_1x$' and (1') has the form $(t)B$, where B is '$Fx \supset (Gx \vee F_1x)$'. Now (1) has the same truth conditions as (1') if and only if for every U, A is *true of* exactly the same things that B is *true of*. Notice that we do not say that A and B are simply *true* because they are open sentences and therefore are to be regarded in the same way as predicates. (In other words, there is here no interesting difference between a predicate such as 'Hx' and an open sentence such as '$Fx \supset Gx$'.) Thus all we need to do is to show that A is true of exactly the same things as B for an arbitrary universe U.

We argue in the following way. Suppose that A and B are *not* true of all the same things in U. Then there must be some e that A is true of which B is not true of, or vice versa. Consider the first possibility: A is true of some e and B is not true of e. Let us give e the following name: 'a'. Then:

(a) $(Fa \supset Ga) \vee F_1a$ is true.

and

(b) $(Fa \supset (Ga \vee F_1a))$ is false.

If (b) is false, then 'Fa' must be true and 'Ga' and 'F_1a' both must be false, as a consequence of the interpretation of the conditional and alternation signs. But if all this is so, then (a) is not true as we supposed, but false. For, if 'Fa' is true and 'Ga' is false, then '$Fa \supset Ga$' is false. But then the whole sentence is false. Thus it is not possible for (a) to be true and (b) to be false. Parallel reasoning shows that it is not possible for (b) to be true and (a) to be false. Thus (1) and (1') have the same truth conditions.

of the Parole Board, which has considered thousands of criminals, includ-
ing those murderers serving life terms. In fact, they have decided that
Charles Manson has not been rehabilitated.

Note that there are a number of conversational modifiers in this passage
which serve to narrow the context of the argument. The phrases 'with
respect to life sentences', and 'criminals, including those murderers serving life terms' are examples. It is unnecessary to include these phrases in
the paraphrase into gross standard form because they do not form part
of the evidence upon which the conclusion is based. Also, note that
there is a suppressed premise in the argument, which is that Charles
Manson is a murderer, it is assumed that everyone knows that Manson
is a murderer, so it is unnecessary in the natural habitat to say so. Its
inclusion in the gross standard form of the argument is sanctioned by
the criterion of belief. Everyone may be assumed to believe that Manson
is a murderer, and the premise is required for the validity of the argument. The argument, then, is

(1) *No one can be paroled unless the Parole Board is convinced that he is*
   safe to release.
(2) *If he has not been rehabilitated, then the Parole Board is not con-*
   vinced that he is safe to release.
(3) *Manson is a murderer.*
(4) *Manson has not been rehabilitated.*
(5) *Hence it is not true that all murderers will be paroled.*

The conclusion comes from the first sentence. Presumably, the argument
has been offered to allay the fears of those who think that everyone who
gets a life sentence is paroled. Premise (2) represents the claim concerning the good judgment of the Parole Board.

   To paraphrase this argument into official standard form, we need first
to decide on a scheme for abbreviation. First, we isolate the subject
terms. Obviously, 'Charles Manson' is one. So, too, is 'the Parole
Board'. Thus

   a: *'Charles Manson'*

and

   b: *'the Parole Board'*

The one-place predicates are '. . . is paroled', '. . . is rehabilitated',
and '. . . is a murderer'. Thus

F__: '. . . is paroled'.
G__: '. . . is rehabilitated'.
H__: '. . . is a murderer'.

Now we have to decide on 'convinced'. Evidently, it is not a one-place predicate, for the Parole Board is not merely "convinced"—they are convinced that something is the case, namely that someone or other is safe to release. So this predicate is relational. We will represent '. . . is convinced that . . . is safe to release', then, as F^2___. The paraphrase into the official idiom proceeds as follows: In (1) the pronoun 'he' indicates that anything said of people who are paroled is to be said of people the Parole Board is convinced are safe to be released. What (1) says is that either the Parole Board is convinced that a person is safe or he is not paroled. Alternatively, we can represent (1) as a conditional which says that if a person is paroled, then the Parole Board is convinced he is safe to release. Thus, paraphrasing inward, (1) becomes either

(a) *It is not the case that [(there is an x such that) ((x is paroled) and (It is not the case that the Parole Board is convinced x is safe to release))].*

or

(b) *(for all x) [If (x is paroled), then (the Parole Board is convinced that x is safe to release)].*

Let us choose (b) because, although it is equivalent to (a), it is less complex. Using the scheme of abbreviation introduced above, we get:

(1') $(x)(Fx \supset F^2bx)$

In (2) 'he' does not specifically refer back to anything mentioned in (1), so the variable that is the paraphrase for 'he' need not be bound by the quantifier in (1). Thus we can list (2) as a separate, universally quantified sentence:

(for all x) [(if (It is not the case that (x is rehabilitated)), then (it is not the case that the Parole Board is convinced that x is safe to release))].

Again, on the current scheme of abbreviation, (2) becomes

(2') $(x)(\sim Gx \supset \sim F^2bx)$

(3) becomes

(3') Ha

(4) is

(4') Ga

and (5) is

(5') $\sim(x)(Hx \supset Fx)$

Note that we could just as easily have represented (5) as

(5") $(Ex)(Hx \ \& \sim Fx)$

given the earlier account of the logical relations among four traditional forms of quantified sentences. That is, we know that '$(Ex)(Hx \ \& \sim Fx)$' is the contradictory of '$(x)(Hx \supset Fx)$', so if the negation of the second sentence is true, then the first sentence must be true as well.

Fully paraphrased, then, the argument under consideration is

(1') $(x)(Fx \supset F^2bx)$
(2') $(x)(\sim Gx \supset \sim F^2bx)$
(3') Ha
(4') Ga
(5') $\therefore \sim(x)(Hx \supset Fx)$

EXAMPLE 3

We shall briefly discuss one final example of paraphrase into the extended official idiom. Suppose that we have the following argument in gross standard form:

(1) *Every country is such that if it enters into nuclear war, then it will be a catastrophe for the world.*
(2) *Therefore, if there is a country that enters into nuclear war, then it will be a catastrophe for the world.*

First, the 'if' in the premise suggests that (1) is a conditional, but it is difficult to see what the antecedent and consequent of the conditional are. In particular, should the premise be read in either of the following ways?

> (a) *If (every country is such that it enters into nuclear war), then (it will be a catastrophe for the world).*

or

> (b) *Every country is such that (if (it enters into nuclear war), then (it will be a catastrophe for the world)).*

In other words, what is the scope of the quantifier in the premise? The first suggestion is implausible because what it says is true on the condition that *all* countries enter into nuclear war, whereas the original seems to say of *each* country that something is true if *it* enters into nuclear war. This is the scope indicated in (b); so we will adopt it as the correct rendition of the premise.

Another important point is that the second occurrence of the word 'it' in (b) does not function in the way the first occurrence does. The first occurrence is being used as an anaphoric pronoun to refer back to whatever is being talked about in the quantificational expression 'Every country', but the second occurrence of 'it' cannot be construed either as a subject term or as an anaphoric pronoun. The sentence 'it will be a catastrophe for the world' does not predicate '. . . will be a catastrophe for the world' of something referred to by 'it' *directly* because there is nothing plausible for 'it' to refer to. Similarly, it does not refer *anaphorically* because the only previous reference is in the open sentence '*x* is a country and *x* enters into nuclear war' (i.e., to countries). We are not predicating '. . . will be a catastrophe for the world' of a country (even as a relational predicate '. . . will be catastrophic for ____') because the intent is not to *limit* the catastrophe to the countries engaged in the war. So, given the following scheme of abbreviation:

$F\_\_$: '. . . is a country'.
$G\_\_$: '. . . into nuclear war'.
p: 'it will be a catastrophe for the world'.

premise (1) should be paraphrased as

(1') $(x)((Fx \, \& \, Gx) \supset p)$

The conclusion states that a certain thing is true on the condition that there is a country which enters into nuclear war, namely, the same thing mentioned in the premise, but notice that now the scope of the quantifier is only the antecedent. Thus the entire argument should be paraphrased as:

(1') $(x)((Fx \,\&\, Gx) \supset p)$
(2') $\therefore (Ex)(Fx \,\&\, Gx) \supset p$

15.1 Exercises

Retain your answers to this section; they will form the basis for exercises in Chapter 3. Starred exercises are answered in Appendix III.

1. Paraphrase the following arguments into the extended official idiom; use only one-place predicate letters.
   a. (1) All men are mortal.
      (2) Therefore, some men are mortal.
   b. (1) All dogs are animals.
      (2) All mammals are animals.
      (3) Therefore, all dogs are mammals.
   c. (1) Dogs are expensive if and only if they are pedigreed.
      (2) Therefore, if there is a dog, then something is expensive if and only if something is pedigreed.
   d. (1) All babies are illogical.
      (2) No one is despised who can manage a crocodile.
      (3) Illogical persons are despised.
      (4) Therefore, no babies can manage a crocodile.
      (Lewis Carroll, *Symbolic Logic*)
   e. (1) If John borrows money from Ted, he will cease to be Ted's friend.
      (2) If John remains Ted's friend, he will write Ted at least once a year.
      (3) Therefore, John will borrow money from Ted.
2. Paraphrase the following arguments into the extended official idiom; use only one-place predicates.
   a. (1) Only dogs who are quiet make good pets.
      (2) German shepherds are noisy.
      (3) Therefore, German shepherds do not make good pets.
   b. (1) Dogs who are quiet make good pets.
      (2) German shepherds are noisy.
      (3) Therefore, German shepherds do not make good pets.
   ★c. (1) Athletes are either dumb or rich.
      (2) Not all of them are dumb.
      (3) Therefore, some of them are rich.

    d. (1) No student who is absent or criticizes the professor will pass.
       (2) Therefore, no absent student will pass.
    e. (1) No king who is either stupid or tyrannical can rule.
       (2) Some kings are tyrannical.
       (3) Not all kings are intelligent.
       (4) Therefore, no king can rule.
    f. (1) Cats are either nice or crabby.
       (2) Cats are not all nice.
       (3) Therefore, there are crabby ones.
    g. (1) All communists are Marxists.
       (2) Some professors are communists.
       (3) Some Marxists are economists.
       (4) Therefore, some professors are economists.
    h. (1) All violinists are nimble-fingered.
       (2) Some conductors are not nimble-fingered.
       (3) Therefore, some conductors are not violinists.
    i. (1) No pilots are afraid of flying.
       (2) Some psychiatrists are afraid of flying.
       (3) Therefore, some psychiatrists are not pilots.
    j. (1) All climbers are crazy.
       (2) Some surfers are climbers.
       (3) Therefore, not all surfers are sane.
3. The following arguments were used in the text as illustrations at various points. Paraphrase them into the extended official idiom; use only one-place predicates.
    a. (1) Iron does not float on water.
       (2) My latch key is made of iron.
       (3) Therefore, my latch key does not float on water.
    b. (1) Anything that causes cancer is a public health menace.
       (2) Smoking causes cancer.
       (3) Therefore, smoking is a public health menace.
★c. (1) Anything that causes cancer is a public health menace.
       (2) Smoking is a public health menace.
       (3) Therefore, smoking causes cancer.
    d. (1) All humans have brain waves.
       (1) All fetuses have brain waves.
       (3) Therefore, all fetuses are humans.
    e. (1) All successful athletes eat Wheaties.
       (2) I eat Wheaties.
       (3) Therefore, I am successful.
    f. (1) Cats in a deep sleep phase always sleep on the backs of their heads.

   (2) My cat is in a deep sleep phase.
   (3) Therefore, my cat sleeps on the back of its head.
4. Refer to the exercises in Section 11.1 of this chapter (p. 133). Paraphrase the arguments from Exercise 2 into the extended official idiom.
5. Refer to your answers to Exercise 5 of Section 2.1 of this chapter (p. 67). Paraphrase arguments ⋆b, o, q, r, t, and v into the extended official idiom. Relational predicate letters may be necessary in some cases.

Difficult
6. Paraphrase the argument in Exercise 1(e) above, using the following scheme of abbreviation:

   a: 'John'
   b: 'Ted'
   F^3___: '. . . borrows ___ from . . .'.
   F^2___: '. . . remains a friend of ___'.
   F___: '. . . is money'.
   G^2___: '. . . will write ___ at least once a year'.

Do you think that the additional structure exposed affects the validity of this argument in official standard form? Explain.

16.
SUMMARY OF IMPORTANT DEFINITIONS AND CONCEPTS IN CHAPTER 2

1. An argument is *in gross standard form* if and only if
   (1) The sentences expressing its premises are listed vertically and the sentence expressing its conclusion is listed last.
   (2) Each sentence is numbered.
   (3) The conclusion sentence is prefixed by an illative particle.
2. Definition of *sentence in the official idiom* (SOI):
   (1) If P^n is an n-place predicate and $t_1, \ldots, t_n$ are subject terms or variables, then $P^n(t_1, \ldots, t_n)$ is a sentence in the official idiom.
   (2) $p, q, r, \ldots$, with or without subscripts, are sentences in the official idiom.
   (3) If A is a sentence in the official idiom, then so is $\sim A$.
   (4) If A and B are sentences in the official idiom, then so are:
       (a) $(A \vee B)$
       (b) $(A \mathbin{\&} B)$
       (c) $(A \supset B)$
       (3) $(A \equiv B)$
   (5) If t is a variable, and A is a sentence in the official idiom, then
       (a) $(t)A$
       (b) $(Et)A$
       are sentences in the official idiom.
   (6) Nothing that is not the result of the clauses listed above is a sentence in the official idiom.
3. A *simple sentence in the official idiom* is one that contains no logical constants or quantifiers.
4. A *complex sentence in the official idiom* is one that contains at least one logical constant or quantifier.
5. A complex English sentence containing one or more propositional connectives or quantifiers other than readings of items in the official idiom is a *stylistic variant* of another English sentence containing no propositional connectives or quantifiers other than readings of items in the official idiom if and only if they have the same truth conditions.
6. A *function* is a rule that associates with each entity in a given set (called the *arguments* of the function) one and only one entity from another set (called the *values* of the function).

169

7. A complex sentence is *truth-functional* if and only if its truth value is a function of the truth values of its constituent simple sentences.

8. An argument is *in official standard form* if and only if
   (1) The premise sentences are listed in vertical order.
   (2) The conclusion sentence is listed last.
   (3) The conclusion sentence is prefixed by the illative particle, ∴.
   (4) The premise sentences and conclusion sentence are all numbered.
   (5) The premise and conclusion sentences are all sentences in the official idiom.
   (6) A scheme of abbreviation is given.

CHAPTER

3

Evaluation of Arguments

1.
COUNTEREXAMPLES

We know from Chapter 1 that an argument **D** is a counterexample to an argument **A** if and only if **D** has the same logical form as **A**, and **D**'s premises are true and its conclusion false. Because the logical form of an argument is determined by the structure of its logical and nonlogical phrases, we were able to produce counterexamples to relatively simple invalid arguments merely by replacing the nonlogical phrases (simple sentences, subject terms, or predicate terms) in an argument description in a way that resulted in an argument description expressing a new argument with true premises and false conclusion. For example, a counterexample to

A (1) *If Roscoe murdered Crustacea, then Roscoe knows about poisons.*
(2) *Roscoe does know about poisons.*
(3) *Therefore, Roscoe murdered Crustacea.*

was produced in the following way. First, we exposed the form of the argument:

B (1) *If A, then B.*
(2) *B.*
(3) *Therefore, A.*

Then we replaced '*A*' and '*B*' with appropriate sentences to produce an argument description with true premises and false conclusion. In particular, replace '*A*' with '6 is an odd number' and '*B*' with '6 is a number'. The result is

A'   (1) *If 6 is an odd number, then 6 is a number.*
       (2) *6 is a number.*
       (3) *Therefore, 6 is an odd number.*

which expresses a counterexample.

Using the resources of the official idiom, we can make this procedure considerably more perspicuous. First, let us paraphrase the original argument into official standard form:

C   (1) $p \supset q$
     (2) q
     (3) $\therefore p$
         Scheme of abbreviation:
            p: *'Roscoe killed Crustacea'.*
            q: *'Roscoe knows about poisons'.*

Now the effect of replacing the nonlogical phrases, namely, simple sentences, in **A** to yield a counterexample can be achieved equally well by changing the scheme of abbreviation for **C** thus:

C'   (1) $p \supset q$
     (2) q
     (3) $\therefore p$
         Scheme of abbreviation:
            p: *'6 is an odd number'.*
            q: *'6 is a number'.*

The argument expressed by **C'** is a counterexample to that expressed by **C** because they have the same form and the premises of **C'** are true and its conclusion is false.

It is not important what sentences 'p' and 'q' abbreviate in **C'**. It matters only that 'p' abbreviate a sentence expressing some false proposition or other and that 'q' abbreviate a sentence expressing some true proposition or other. The interpretation of '$\supset$' guarantees that (1) will then express a true proposition. Then since (2) expresses a true proposition and (3) a false one, it follows that **C'** as a whole expresses a counterexample to argument **C**. This shows that there is a counterexample to argument **A**; so it is invalid.

An even less cumbersome way of looking at the matter is this: Instead of characterizing the difference between **C** and **C'** as consisting of a difference in schemes of abbreviation according to which 'p' and 'q' abbreviate sentences expressing different propositions in the two contexts, we can simply associate the sentence letters directly with propositions. To put the point in technical language, we can *assign* different propositions to the sentence letters '*p*' and '*q*'. In the first case we assign to '*p*' the proposition normally expressed by 'Roscoe killed Crustacea', and in the second case we assign it the proposition normally expressed by '6 is an odd number'. What matters most, however, is the truth value of the propositions assigned. Argument **C'** will express a counterexample to **A** *whatever* false proposition is assigned to '*p*' and whatever true one is assigned to '*q*'. This illustrates the point made in Chapter 1 that validity (or invalidity) is a *purely formal matter*; the actual or possible content of the argument as expressed in propositions is irrelevant.

Finally, whether the premises of argument **C'** are true or false depends not only on the truth values of the propositions *assigned* to '*p*' and '*q*', but also on the *interpretation* specified for '⊃', which is used to "construct" the complex proposition expressed by (1). In general, determining whether an argument is valid or invalid depends on

1. What is assigned to the nonlogical phrases.

and

2. The interpretations specified for the logical constants.

We turn now to extended discussions of these two concepts; they form the basis of our procedure for evaluating arguments, the goal of this chapter.

1.1 Exercises

In answering the following questions, you may find it helpful to refer to the summary of concepts and definitions introduced in this chapter on p. 109. Starred exercises are answered in Appendix III.

★1. Consider the following argument:
    A   (1) If demand increases, then prices rise.
        (2) Demand increases.
        (3) Therefore, prices rise.
    one of whose forms is
    B   (1) *A*.
        (2) *B*.
        (3) Therefore, *C*.
    Is argument **C,** below, a counterexample to **A,** given our present characterization of *counterexample?*

C (1) Iron is magnetic.
    (2) Wood floats.
    (3) Therefore, iron floats.
Explain fully.

2. Which of the arguments expressed by the following argument descriptions are counterexamples to argument **A** on p. 173 and which are not? Defend your answers. Explain fully.

D (1) If 6 is a number, then 6 is odd.
    (2) 6 is an odd.
    (3) Therefore, 6 is a number.

E (1) If the moon is made of cheese, then New York is east of Chicago.
    (2) New York is east of Chicago.
    (3) Therefore, the moon is made of cheese.

F (1) Either it is not the case that 6 is a number or 6 is odd.
    (2) 6 is a number.
    (3) Therefore, 6 is odd.

3. Suppose that argument **A** has true premises and false conclusion. How do you know it has a counterexample?

2.
ASSIGNMENTS

In Chapter 2 fixed interpretations were given to the propositional connectives of the official idiom and the quantifiers. The interpretations of the propositional connectives determined their contributions to the truth values of the complex sentences in which they occur. The interpretations of the universal and existential quantifiers were also explained partly in terms of the truth values of more simple sentences.

In contrast, the sentence letters in the official idiom were not given interpretations; they served simply as abbreviations for various English sentences. Although we could discuss the truth *conditions* of sentences such as, for example, '$p \supset q$' independently of a scheme of paraphrase, it was futile to ask after the actual truth *value* of such a sentence unless one knew what English sentences 'p' and 'q' abbreviate. Only after one determined in this way what propositions 'p' and 'q' were to be thought of as expressing could one determine their truth values and, hence, the truth value of '$p \supset q$'.

Henceforth we shall continue to use the sentence letters 'p' and 'q' to abbreviate English sentences when paraphrasing particular arguments into official standard form. But we shall also make use of assignments of different propositions to those sentence letters than are normally expressed by the sentences they abbreviate. The difference can be seen thus: Independently of a particular scheme of abbreviation, we cannot ask, for example, "What is the truth value of '$p \supset q$'?," but we can ask "What is the truth value of '$p \supset q$' when 'p' is assigned a true proposition and 'q' is assigned a false proposition?" Put this way, the question has a definite answer. In fact, it is "false."

For sentences of the unextended official idiom an assignment, **I**, is just an association of a true or false proposition to *every* sentence letter. Logicians sometimes speak of assignments as mathematical *functions*. Functions are like classifying machines. Classifying machines are constructed in such a way that what is put in the hopper on top gets spewed into a definite cubbyhole after processing. Think of a postal sorting machine, where a large mass of letters going into the hopper are sorted into cubbyholes representing the various states of destination. For each letter there is exactly one box in which it belongs and into which the machine sorts it. In the case of assignments to the *unextended* official idiom, the materials that go into the hopper of the assignment "machine" are just the sentence letters of the official idiom. There is an indefinitely large number of sentence letters, yet they all wind up in one of two cubbyholes, one designated 'true' and the other 'false'. There are only these two cubbyholes because we are interested only in the truth values of the propositions assigned, not in the propositions themselves. When one makes a different assignment to the sentence letters of the official idiom, he is simply installing a different assignment machine.[1]

In the case of sentences in the *extended* official idiom, an assignment involves two things: the universe, U, of discourse and the things and kinds of things in U to be assigned to the subject and predicate terms. Of course, U is familiar from Chapter 2. The universe U can be *any* set of existent entities; there is at least one inhabitant for each universe. Examples of possible universes other than the set of things existing in the physical universe, which includes every existent entity, are the set of people, the set of numbers, the set of things identical to the square root of 2, the set of cities in the United States, the set of cities in the world, and so on. All of the above are acceptable candidates for universes of assignments. The set of Greek gods, the set of round squares, and so on, do not qualify as possible universes for assignments because there exist no such entities.

An assignment I over the extended official idiom assigns to *all* sentence letters of the official idiom true or false propositions, to *all* subject terms of the official idiom various individuals in the given universe of the assignment, to *all* the predicate terms of the official idiom, *sets* of entities, or sets of pairs of entities, or sets of triples of entities, and so on, in U, depending on whether the predicate is one-place, two-place, three-place, and so on. Next, let us look into assignments in greater detail.

The nonlogical vocabulary of the extended official idiom consists of terms of belonging to various grammatical categories. There are sentence letters, 'p', 'q', 'r' (with or without subscripts); subject terms, 'a', 'b', 'c' (with or without subscripts); and predicate terms, '$F\_\_$', '$G\_\_$', '$H\_\_$' (with or without subscripts), '$F^2\_\_$', '$G^2\_\_$', '$H^2\_\_$' (with or without subscripts), and so on. Note that the vocabulary is unambiguous. One can tell by the shape of a given symbol to what grammatical category it belongs. For example, '$H^3_2\_\_$', can be seen to be a three-place predicate by the superscript and is distinguished from another three-place predicate, '$H^3_4\_\_$', by its subscript and 'p' can be seen to be a sentence letter and not, for example, a subject term. Now, the point of an assignment I is to associate an entity of a certain kind with each item of nonlogical vocabulary. Assignments are not made to any of the logical constants. Unlike the nonlogical phrases, they have interpretations that do not vary from context to context. An assignment

[1] A more technical definition of *function* is given at the end of Chapter 2.

I assigns a certain kind of entity to each sentence letter, another kind to each subject term, and yet another kind to each predicate. Two assignments I and I' might *differ* to varying extents. At one end of the scale they might not agree in their assignments to any of the nonlogical vocabulary of the official idiom. That is, although they are parallel because they assign items of the same kind to phrases of the same grammatical category, they may not assign in common any *particular* thing to a given phrase. At the other end of the scale, I and I' might make all the same assignments except that I assigns to $'p'$ the proposition that grass is green, whereas I' assigns to $'p'$ the proposition that iron floats in water. Although I and I' may agree in all the assignments they make to subject terms, predicates, and all the remaining sentence letters of the official idiom, they are still different assignments in virtue of there being at least one point where they do not agree. For two assignments I and I' to be different, it is required only that *some* symbol be assigned to a different object by I from that to which it is assigned by I'. It follows from this that if I and I' have different universes, U and U', respectively, they are different assignments. For, if U differs from U' they must contain different entities. Therefore, I must differ from I' at some point, so I must not be the same as I'. The converse, however, does not hold. Different assignments can have the same universe if what they assign in U differs for at least one symbol.

Let us consider an assignment I that has as its universe the set of objects existing in the physical universe. Then I assigns each *subject term* $'a'$, $'b'$, $'c'$ (with or without subscripts) an individual in U. For example, it may assign Socrates to $'a'$, the Eiger to $'b'$, and so on. A different assignment I' with the same universe may assign Socrates to $'b'$, the Eiger to $'a'$, and so on. If we think of $'a'$ as the *abbreviation* for 'Socrates' in a given context, then I corresponds to the real world and I' does not. This does not matter; there is no requirement that an assignment correspond to the real world. Indeed, if we are just considering the validity of an argument in official standard form, we may ignore the scheme of abbreviation. We should not want to be limited to assignments respecting an unknown scheme of abbreviation.

Assignments to *one-place predicates* are similar to those of subject letters but are a bit more complicated. The entities that I assigns to predicates are properties or relations holding between the individuals in U. For our purposes in this book, we can think of properties as *sets* of individuals in U (intuitively, those individuals having the property in question), and relations as sets of pairs (or triples, or n-tuples) of individuals in U (intuitively, those pairs, triples, or n-tuples of entities so related). Let us consider some illustrations.

Let U remain the same. Now, in U certain individuals, e, have the property of being red, for example. Ulrich's favorite shirt, numerous fire engines here and there, the bits of plastic covering various copies of *Quotations from Chairman Mao,* and so on, all have this property. We say that the English predicate '. . . is red' is *true of* each of these things, but '. . . is red' is also true of many other things that we have not mentioned. The property of being red is to be identified with the *set of* members u of **U** of which '. . . is red' is true (intuitively, the property of being red is what all the members of this set have in common, i.e., what each has if and only if it belongs to the set). Suppose that 'F__' is chosen as the abbreviation in the official idiom for '. . . is red'. Then there is an assignment **I** which assigns to 'F__' that subset of members of **U** of which '. . . is red' is true. Some other assignment **I'** might assign some entirely different subset of **U** to 'F__' (in which case the English predicate '. . . is red' would be false for each member of that subset). Assignment **I'** corresponds to the supposition that different things are red from those that happen to be red in the real world.

Assignments to *n-place predicates* (where n is greater than 1) are not of sets of individual members of **U**, but of sets of n-tuples of members of **U**. Suppose, for example, that 'F^2__' is the abbreviation of the two-place predicate '. . . is east of ____'. Now this English predicate is true not of individuals in **U** but of *ordered pairs* of individuals $\langle x, y \rangle$ such that x is east of y. Thus on the assignment **I** that corresponds to the real world, 'F^2__' is assigned the *set* of ordered pairs $\langle x, y \rangle$ such that x is east of y. For example, in the real world, $\langle$New York, Chicago$\rangle$ belongs to this set as well as $\langle$the Eiger, Japan$\rangle$. To say that these are *ordered* pairs, as distinct from sets containing two members, such as $\{$New York, Chicago$\}$, is to make clear that the arrangement of the elements is crucial. $\{$Chicago, New York$\}$ is the same *set* as $\{$New York, Chicago$\}$, but $\langle$Chicago, New York$\rangle$ is *not* the same ordered pair as $\langle$New York, Chicago$\rangle$. '. . . is east of ____' is true of New York and Chicago *in that order,* so $\langle$New York, Chicago$\rangle$ belongs to the set of ordered pairs **I** assigns to 'F^2__', but $\langle$Chicago, New York$\rangle$ does not. For three-place predicates such as '. . . is between ____ and ____', sets of ordered triples of members of **U** are the entities assigned. In general, for n-place predicates, n-tuples of elements of **U** are assigned.

2.1 Exercises

You may find it helpful to consult the list of definitions and concepts introduced in this chapter on p. 173. Starred exercises are answered in Appendix III.

1. Explain the difference between an assignment and an interpretation.

2. What is the difference between an assignment that assigns the proposition that 6 is a number to 'p' and a scheme of abbreviation according to which 'p' abbreviates the sentence '6 is a number'? Explain fully.

3. What if anything, does an assignment **I** assign to complex sentences such as '$p \supset q$', '$\sim p$', '$(p \& q) \equiv r$'? Explain fully.

★4. According to the Sherlock Holmes stories, he had an older brother. Is the set containing Sherlock and his brother the universe of any assignment? Why or why not?

5. Consider the universe **U** = $\{1, 2, 3, 6\}$. Relative to **U**, what is each of the following predicates true of?

    a. '. . . is odd'.
    b. '. . . is greater than 1'.
    c. '. ... is greater than ____'.
    d. '. . . is equal to the square of ____'.
    ★e. '. . . is between ____ and ____'.
    f. '. . . is an integer'.

6. In the left-hand column below is a list of symbols from the extended official idiom and in the right-hand column is a list of items for assignment. Match each item in the left-hand column with all the items in the right-hand column that various assignments *could* assign to it.

    a. 'a'
    b. 'F^3__' → 'F^3__'
    c. 'p'
    d. 'G__'
    e. 'b'
    f. $(x)Fx$
    ★g. A
    h. 'x'

    i. **U**
    ii. The set of men
    iii. George Washington
    iv. $\{\{1, 2, 3\}, \{2, 3, 4\}, \{7, 12, 16\}, \{0, 1, 3\}\}$
    v. The proposition that cats bark
    vi. $\{$Washington, Lincoln, Jefferson$\}$
    vii. This phrase is never assigned to anything.

3.
TRUTH UNDER AN ASSIGNMENT

Assignments are essential ingredients in the evaluation of the truth or falsity of a given sentence in the official idiom. One cannot tell whether a sentence is true or false until one knows what it stands for. The evaluation of truth or falsity of sentences in the official idiom, in turn, is essential to the determination of validity or invalidity. Recall that validity was defined in Chapter 1 partly in terms of the truth values of the premise and conclusion sentences of argument descriptions. The next task is to explicate the notion of truth under an assignment. Then we shall be able to give our final definition of validity.

Remember that the grammar of the official idiom is organized in such a way that the simple sentences are identified first, and then the complex sentences are delineated by means of rules showing how to produce them by means of the logical constants. We can also explain the notion of truth (falsity) under an assignment in parallel stages: first for the simple sentences and then for the complex sentences. Actually, the means for doing this are already available in the various rules for interpreting the logical constants explained in Chapter 2. In other words, we can define the notion of *truth under an assignment* as a product of the notion of *assignment* and the notion of an *interpretation* for the logical constants. We shall abbreviate the *definition of truth under an assignment* as *DTA*.

Consider first a sentence letter of the (extended) official idiom, say, '*p*'. This sentence will be true if and only if it expresses a true proposition, and false otherwise. So the first clause of DTA, the first evaluation rule, is a generalization of this idea:

1. If *A* is a sentence letter in the extended official idiom (OI), then *A* is true under an assignment **I** if and only if **I** assigns a true proposition to *A*. Otherwise, *A* is false under **I**.

Next, look at a simple "analyzed" sentence of OI, say, '*Fa*'. Intuitively, such a sentence will be true if the thing in the universe **U** of the assignment **I** that '*a*' stands for has the property (belongs to the set) '*F__*' stands for. If what **I** assigns to '*a*' does not belong to the set **I** assigns to '*F__*', then '*Fa*' will be false under **I**. For example, if **I** assigns the Eiger to '*a*' and the set of mountains to '*F__*', then '*Fa*' would be true under **I**. If **I** simultaneously assigns the Mississippi River to '*b*', then '*Fb*' will be false under **I** because the Mississippi does not belong to the set **I** assigns to 'F__' (i.e., the set of mountains). Generalizing this example to simple sentences containing n-place predicates, we get the second clause of DTA:

2. If P^n is an n-place predicate letter in OI and $t_1, \ldots, t_n$ are subject letters (but not variables) in OI, then $P^n(t_1, \ldots, t_n)$ is true under I if and only if the ordered n-tuple of things in U that I assigns to $t_1, \ldots, t_n$ belongs to the set of n-tuples of things in U that I assigns to P^n. Otherwise, $P^n(t_1, \ldots, t_n)$ is false under I.

Note that the symbol 'P^n' is a meta-variable used to stand for predicate letters in general just as, for example, 'A' stands for sentence letters generally. Similarly, 't' is a meta-variable for the subject letters and is used in other contexts to stand for variables generally (which one it is used to stand for is always explicit). The beginning phrase in clause 2, for example, is to be understood in the following way: "Any sentence in the official idiom which results from the placement of any n subject terms after any n-place predicate is true under I if and only if . . . ." This clause covers the case of one-place predicates for an "ordered 1-tuple" is just a member of U. Thus I assigns a subset of members of U to one-place predicates. This completes the evaluation rules for the simple sentences of the official idiom.

As we have seen before, complex sentences of the official idiom are constructed either by negating a simple sentence or joining together two simple sentences by means of a propositional connective or by quantifying a simple or complex sentence. The appropriate clauses in DTA for the evaluation of complex sentences of the official idiom are just a rehash of the interpretations given in Chapter 2. The reason those interpretations can do additional duty as evaluation rules is that they describe how the logical constants (propositional connectives and quantifiers) contribute to the truth value of sentences that contain them. So the motivation for the following clauses of DTA has already been given in Chapter 2:

3. Where A and B are open or closed sentences in the official idiom,
   (a) $\sim A$ is true under I if and only if A is false under I. Otherwise, $\sim A$ is false under I.
   (b) $A \lor B$ is true under I if and only if A is true under I or B is true under I. Otherwise, $A \lor B$ is false under I.
   (c) $A \& B$ is true under I if and only if A is true under I and B is true under I. Otherwise, $A \& B$ is false under I.
   (d) $A \supset B$ is true under I if and only if A is false under I or B is true under I. Otherwise, $A \supset B$ is false under I.

   (e) $A \equiv B$ is true under **I** if and only if A and B have the same
       truth value under **I**. Otherwise, $A \equiv B$ is false under **I**.
4. Where **U** is a given universe of discourse, and A contains one or
   more free occurrences of the variable t,*
   (a) $(t)A$ is true under **I** if and only if, for every e in **U**, the result
       of replacing every free occurrence of t in A by a name of e is
       true under **I**. Otherwise, $(t)A$ is false under **I**.
   (b) $(Et)A$ is true under **I** if and only if, for some e in **U**, the result
       of replacing every free occurrence of t in A by a name of e is
       true under **I**. Otherwise, $(Ex)A$ is false under **I**.

This completes the definition of truth under an assignment (DTA); DTA is reprinted at the end of this chapter. Note that DTA parallels SOI in the sense that for every clause of SOI showing how to construct a sentence of a certain logical form, DTA shows how to evaluate it for truth or falsity. This explains what is meant by the statement that in the official idiom, unlike English, there is no discrepancy between grammatical form and logical form, for *any two sentences of the official idiom that share a grammatical form are evaluated by the same evaluation rules of DTA.*

Finally, we are in a position to give a precise definition of validity and related notions. The definition of validity is a product of the notion of assignment and the interpretation of the logical constants, or, what is the same thing, the evaluation rules of DTA:

*Let **A** be an argument in official standard form. **A** is* valid *if and only if there is no assignment **I** (with universe **U**) of appropriate entities to the subject terms, predicate letters, and sentence letters of the official idiom such that the premise sentences of **A**'s written expression are true under **I** and the conclusion sentence is false under **I**.*

In other words, to say that an argument in official standard form is valid is to say that for all assignments of individuals to the subject terms of the official idiom, of sets of n-tuples to all the n-place predicate letters of the official idiom, and of propositions to the sentence letters the conclusion sentence is true under all assignments under which the premise sentences are jointly true. A counterexample to **A** is an argument of the same logical form, with true premises and a false conclusion. **A** *has* a counterexample just in case *there is* an assignment of the appropriate sort, to wit:

A has a counterexample *if and only if there is an assignment **I** (with universe **U**) of appropriate entities to the subject terms, predicate letters,*

---

* If A does not contain any free occurrences of t, then $(t)A$ and $(Et)A$, respectively, are true under **I** if and only if A is true under **I**. Otherwise, $(t)A$ and $(Et)A$ are false under **I**.

*and sentence letters of the official idiom such that the premise sentences of A's written expression are true under **I** and the conclusion sentence is false under **I**.*

To *give* a counterexample to **A** is to describe, or define, such an assignment **I**. Of course, an argrument expressed in *English* is valid (or has a counterexample) if and only if its *paraphrase* into official standard form is valid (or has a counterexample). From these definitions it is also clear that an argument is valid if and only if it or its paraphrase into official standard form has no counterexample and invalid if and only if it or its parphrase into official standard form has a counterexample. We now have all the requisite materials to evaluate arguments for validity or invalidity.

3.1 Exercises

You may find it helpful to consult the list of definitions and concepts introduced in this chapter on p. 193. Starred exercises are answered in Appendix III.

1. Let an assignment **I** assign the proposition that 1 is odd to 'p_1', the proposition that 2 is odd to 'p_2', the proposition that 3 is odd to 'p_3', and so on. What is the truth value of 'p_{27}' under **I**? Of 'p_{30}' under **I**? Defend your answers.
2. Imagine a language just like the official idiom except that the nonlogical vocabulary consists only of 'p', 'q', and 'r'. Give the truth values of the following sentences under each of the specified assignments.
   a. $p \lor q$
   b. r
   c. $p \supset (q \supset p)$
   ★d. $p \equiv \sim p$
   e. $r \& \sim r$
   f. $q \lor q$

   I_1: $I_1('p')$ = the proposition that iron floats in water.
   $I_1('q')$ = the proposition that grass is green.
   $I_1('r')$ = the proposition that the sky is blue.
   I_2: $I_2('p')$ = the proposition that the sky is blue.
   $I_2('q')$ = the proposition that iron floats in water.
   $I_2('r')$ = the proposition that grass is green.
   I_3: $I_3('p')$ = the proposition that grass is green.
   $I_3('q')$ = the proposition that the sky is blue.
   $I_3('r')$ = the proposition that iron floats in water.

3. Consider a language just like the extended official idiom but which contains only the following nonlogical vocabulary: 'F__', 'G__', and 'H²__' and 'a₁', 'a₂', 'a₃', ...
   Let assignment I be defined as follows:
   a. $U = \{1, 2, 3, 4\}$
   b. $I(t_k) = k$, where t is any subject letter and k any integer 1, 2, 3, . . .
   c. $I('F\_') = \{2, 3\}$
   d. $I('G\_') = \{1, 3\}$
   e. $I('H^2\_') = \{\langle x, y \rangle : x, y \in U$ and $x > y\}$, that is, the set of ordered pairs $\langle x, y \rangle$ of members of U such that x is larger than y
   What does I assign to 'a_5'?
   Does $\langle 3, 2 \rangle$ belong to $I('H^2\_')$?
   Does $\langle 50, 7 \rangle$ belong to $I('H^2\_')$?
   What are the truth values of the following sentences under I? Defend your answers by showing how the relevant clauses of DTA were used to obtain the answers.

   i. Fa_2
   ii. Ga_2
   iii. $(x)Fx$
   iv. $(Ex)Gx$
   v. $H^2a_2a_3$
   ★vi. $(x)(Ey)H^2xy$

   vii. $(Ex)(Ey)H^2xy$
   viii. $(x)Fx \supset Ga_{20}$
   ix. $(x)Fx \supset (Ex)Fx$
   x. $Ga_5 \equiv Fa_{10}$
   xi. $(Ex)Fx \equiv (Ex)Gx$
   xii. $(Ex)(Gx \supset \sim(Ey)H^2xy)$

4. In what ways is the definition of validity given in this section an improvement upon the earlier definition?
5. Consider a language just like the official idiom except that it contains only the following nonlogical vocabulary: 'p', 'q', 'a_1', 'a_2', 'a_3', 'F__' and 'G__' and the following invalid arguments in official standard form:

   A (1) $p \supset q$
      (2) $\sim p$
      (3) $\therefore \sim q$

   B (1) $(x)(Fx \supset Gx)$
      (2) Ga_1
      (3) $\therefore (Ex)Fx$

   C (1) $p \equiv q$
      (2) $(Ex)(Fx \equiv p)$
      (3) $\therefore q$

   Now which of the following assignments constitute counterexamples to which arguments? Explain fully.
   I_1: $I('p') =$ the proposition that bats swim
          $I('q') =$ the proposition that grass is green
   I_2: $U = \{1, 2, 3\}$
          $I('p') =$ the proposition that bats swim
          $I('q') =$ the proposition that grass is green
          $I('a_1') =$ Chicago
          $I('a_2') =$ New York

$I('a_3') =$ Boston

$I('F\_\_') = U$

$I('G\_\_') = U$

I_3: $U = \{1, 2, 3\}$

$I('p') =$ the proposition that iron floats

$I('q') =$ the proposition that grass is green

$I('a') = 1$

$I('a_2') = 2$

$I('a_3') = 3$

$I('F\_\_') = \{1, 3\}$

$I('G\_\_') = \{2\}$

I_4: $U = \{1, 2, 3\}$

$I('p') =$ the proposition that iron floats

$I('q') =$ the proposition that grass is green

$I('a_1') = 1$

$I('a_2') = 2$

$I('a_3') = 3$

$I('F\_\_') =$ the empty set

$I('G\_\_') = U$

I_5: $U = \{1, 2, 3\}$

$I('p') =$ the proposition that iron floats

$I('q') =$ the proposition that grass is blue

$I('a_1') = 1$

$I('a_2') = 2$

$I('a_3') = 3$

$I('F\_\_') =$ the empty set

$I('G\_\_') = U$

4.
INFORMAL EVALUATION PROCEDURE: PART I

The evaluation procedure gives an orderly method for determining whether or not an argument has a counterexample. If it does, then it is invalid. If it does not, then it is valid. We begin with two examples of arguments expressed in the unextended official idiom illustrating insights underlying the procedure, then introduce more precise details in subsequent discussion. To simplify the assignments we need to make, we shall imagine that the official idiom consists only of its unextended part. Because we can then restrict the notion of assignment only to sentence letters, we can ignore the more complicated features of an assignment. We shall take up the more complicated case in the next section. Suppose that

A   (1) p
     (2) $\therefore p \vee q$

is some argument or other in official standard form. As we have said, the evaluation procedure is designed for arguments in official standard form. Now, **A** is invalid if and only if it has a counterexample. Well, let us suppose that it does have a counterexample. Then, by definition of *has a counterexample*, there is some assignment, **I**, of propositions to all the sentence letters of the official idiom such that (1) is true under **I** and (2) is false under **I**. So our supposition is, at bottom, that (1) is true under **I** and (2) is false under **I** (for some assignment **I**). Because of the interpretation of '$\vee$', if (2) is false under **I** then 'p' is false under **I** and 'q' is false under **I**. But 'p' is the same as (1); so if 'p' is false under **I**, then (1) is also false under **I**. This contradicts our supposition that (1) is true under **I**, for, by definition, there is no assignment under which 'p' is both true and false. Therefore, there is no assignment **I** that both makes (1) true and (2) false. So **A** has no counterexample; it is valid.

Consider a second example:

B   (1) $p \vee q$
    (2) $\therefore q$

As before, suppose that **B** is invalid. Then there is an assignment, **I**, of propositions to all the subject letters of the unextended official idiom such that (1) is true under **I** and (2) is false under **I**. If **I** assigns a false proposition to *'p'*, then (2) is false under **I**, so suppose that **I** does this. But this assignment fails to determine any particular truth value for (1) as a whole because, consistent with the supposition that (2) is false under **I**, there are two possibilities for truth values of (1) under **I**, depending on what **I** assigns to *'p'*. If **I** assigns a false proposition to *'p'*, then (1) is false under **I** and if **I** assigns a true proposition to *'p'*, then (1) is true under **I**. Since this latter possibility exists, **B** has a counterexample. It has a counterexample because there is an assignment under which (1) is true and (2) is false—that **I** which assigns a true proposition to *'p'* and a false one to *'q'*. Therefore, **B** is invalid.

Each of these examples displays the general strategy of the evaluation procedure. First, it is *indirect;* it assumes the invalidity of an argument. If the argument assumed to be invalid really is valid, then its validity is made evident by showing the original assumption to be false. If the argument is really invalid, then its invalidity can be established by finding a counterexample to it which verifies the original assumption. One can find the counterexample by working through the implications of the assumption until one sees how it might be true, although this may take some insight. The evaluation procedure, informal as it is, establishes the validity of valid arguments by showing that they have no counterexamples, and it establishes the invalidity of invalid arguments by turning up assignments that give counterexamples. Now we need to make the procedure more precise by showing how to *justify* each step explicitly by appeal to some appropriate clause of DTA,[2] and how properly to give counterexamples.

Let us return to **A**. Argument **A** is valid if and only if there is no assignment **I** of propositions to all the vocabulary of the (unextended) official idiom under which (1) is true and (2) is false. So the first step in the evaluation procedure is to assume the opposite and to note its justification, namely, that it is an assumption for indirect evaluation:

STEP (1).   Suppose there is an assignment **I** such that *both*

(a) *'p' is true under* **I**.
(b) *'p ∨ q' is false under* **I**.

(*Assumption for indirect evaluation*)

Now we use DTA to help find such an **I** if there is one, by working back to see what assignments to sentence letters of the official idiom would make the assumption in step (1) true. First, let us examine (1b). If (1b) holds, as it must for the assumption to be true, then

---

[2] DTA is recapitulated concisely in the list of definitions for this chapter.

STEP (2). 'p' is false under **I** and 'q' is false under **I**.

[from step (1b), by DTA (3b)]

This, however, is incompatible with (1a). The assumption that **I** exists, together with DTA, implies that 'p' is both true and false under **I**:

STEP (3). But then 'p' is both true and false under **I**.

[from steps (1a) and (2)]

It follows that there is no assignment of appropriate propositions to the sentence letters of the unextended official idiom which makes **A**'s premise sentence, (1), true and **A**'s conclusion, (2), false. Hence argument **A** is valid:

STEP (4). There is no such **I** as described in (3).

STEP (5). Therefore, the assumption for indirect evaluation is false, and **A** is valid.

Here is the way the procedure looks without explanatory remarks:

Argument **A:** (1) p
(2) $\therefore p \vee q$

EVALUATION

STEP (1). Suppose that there is an assignment **I** such that *both*

(a) 'p' *is true under* **I**.
(b) '$p \vee q$' *is false under* **I**.

(*Assumption for indirect evaluation*)

STEP (2). Then 'p' is false under **I** and 'q' is false under *I*.

[from step (1b), by DTA (3b)]

STEP (3). But then 'p' is both true and false under **I**.

[from steps (1a) and (2)]

STEP (4). There is no such **I** as that described in step (3).

STEP (5). Therefore, the assumption for indirect evaluation is false, and **A** is valid.

Now we give the evaluation of argument **B,** without explanatory remarks:

Argument **B:**   *(1) p* ∨ *q*
                     (2) ∴*q*

EVALUATION

STEP (1).   Suppose that there is an assignment **I** such that *both*

(*a*) '*p* ∨ *q*' *is true under* **I.**
(*b*) '*q*' *is false under* **I.**

STEP (2).   Then, consistent with (1b), '*p* ∨ *q*' is true under *I* if and only if '*p*' is true under **I.**

[from steps (1a) and (1b) by DTA (3b)]

STEP (3).   But nothing in the previous steps is inconsistent with **I**'s assigning a true proposition to '*p*'.

STEP (4).   Suppose that **I** does assign a true proposition to '*p*'. Then the conditions of the assumption for indirect evaluation are verified, and **B** is invalid.

STEP (5).   Counterexample to **B:**

I('*p*') *is any true proposition.*
I('*q*') *is any false proposition.*

Where A is any sentence letter of the official idiom other than '*p*' *or* '*q*', *let* **I**(*A*) *be any arbitrarily selected proposition.*

Recall that to give a counterexample is to describe an assignment under which the premise sentences of a given argument description are true and the conclusion sentence is false. In step (5) we have done just this. The expression '**I**('*p*')' means 'The entity assignment **I** assigns to '*p*', this expression being analogous to the mathematical expression '(2)²' meaning 'the entity that is the square of 2.' Step (5) gives a *counterexample* to **B** by describing—that assignment **I** that assigns any true proposition to '*p*', any false proposition to '*q*', and any proposition you like to the rest of the sentence letters of the official idiom under which (1) is true and (2) is false. It is necessary to make an assignment to *every* item of the official idiom (restricted to the unextended official idiom) because an assignment is a function that assigns to every item of nonlogical vocabulary some entity or other. Strictly speaking, even though the validity or invalidity of **B** cannot be affected by what **I** assigns to, say, '*r*', every sentence letter must be assigned something.

Let us sum up before going on to Part 2 of the informal evaluation technique. The evaluation procedure has only two possible outcomes: Either the assumption for indirect evaluation leads to contradiction, showing the argument to be valid, or it does not. If it does not lead to contradiction, then one must construct an assignment **I** consistent with all the steps in the procedure, which verifies the assumption. Of course, this does not mean there is a mechanical way of achieving either result. In very complex valid arguments, the contradiction latent in the assumption for indirect evaluation may elude one; similarly, for invalid arguments, the assignment verifying the assumption may be difficult to ascertain. There *are* formal, and even mechanical, evaluation methods for a large class of arguments, although not for all, and some of these techniques are explained in Appendix II. The reader may proceed directly to Appendix II, omitting the remainder of this chapter if only mechanical evaluation techniques are of interest. In either case, the following point should be insisted upon: Although our informal evaluation procedure is, in some ways, more difficult to perform than the methods of Appendix II, it is far more valuable to know. First, it applies to a larger class of arguments than does any mechanical method. Second, the character of the important reasoning in more advanced logic courses more closely resembles the informal procedure than the mechanical procedures. Although the use of one's head in logic can be staved off to some degree at elementary levels by using mechanical evaluation procedures, it cannot be avoided forever. Practice with informal evaluation, therefore, will prove valuable in the long run, and in the short run it is much more conducive to a deeper understanding of the fundamental concepts involved in evaluation than are the mechanized methods of Appendix II.

4.1 Exercises

You may find it helpful to consult the list of definitions and concepts introduced in this chapter on p. 193. Starred exercises are answered in Appendix III.

1. Refer to your answers to Exercise 1, Section 10.1 of Chapter 2 (p. 124). There you paraphrased several arguments from gross standard form into official standard form. Now evaluate them. Arguments a, b, d, and e are valid, so you should find that the assumption for indirect evaluation

leads to a contradiction. Argument c is invalid, so your evaluation should result in a counterexample.

★2. Refer to your answers to Exercise 2, Section 10.1 of Chapter 2 (p. 124), where you paraphrased some arguments from gross standard form into official standard form. Now evaluate them.

More Difficult

★3. Return to your answers to Exercise 3, Section 10.1 of Chapter 2 (p. 124) and evaluate these arguments.

5.
INFORMAL EVALUATION PROCEDURE: PART 2

Suppose the following argument in the *extended* official idiom:

A (1) $(Ex)Fx$
  (2) $\therefore(x)Fx$

The first step in **A**'s evaluation, the assumption for indirect evaluation is exactly as before, but since we are now considering a different language, the assumption has to be complicated somewhat. Recall that assignments to the extended official idiom require a universe, **U**. Therefore, the assumption now is that there is an assignment *with a universe* **U** under which the premise sentence is true and the conclusion sentence is false.

STEP (1).   Suppose that there is an assignment **I** (with universe **U**) such that *both*

  (a) '$(Ex)Fx$' *is true under* **I**
  (b) '$(x)Fx$' *is false under* **I**.

(Assumption for indirect evaluation)

Next, one applies the relevant evaluation rule of DTA to (a) or (b) above. It makes no real difference where one begins, although normally it is more convenient to begin with the least complicated part of the assumption. Let us begin with (a):

STEP (2).   There is some *e* in **U** such that the result of replacing 'x' in 'Fx' with a name of *e* is true under **I**.

[from step (1a) by DTA (4b)]

At this point we introduce a convention to facilitate writing down the steps in the evaluation. We want to avoid the cumbersome locution "the result of replacing 'x' in 'Fx' by a name of some *e* in **U** . . . ." every time we want to talk about a sentence of the official idiom that is the result of performing this operation (or the analogous operation for the universally quantified sentences).

Convention C: *Let an n-place predicate letter from the official idiom followed by n meta-variables* $(t_1, \ldots, t_n)$ *for subject*

194

letters designate the result of appending n subject let-
ters to that predicate letter.

In this case we want to talk about a sentence that is the result of replacing *'x'* in *'Fx'* with a name of some *e* in **U**. Applying convention C to
step (2), then, we get:

STEP (3).   *Ft* is true under **I**, for some *t*.

[from step (2) by (C)]

In this case *'Ft'* designates the result of appending some subject letter
t (we do not know which) from the official idiom to the predicate letter
'F__'. The sentence is *'Fa'* or *'Fb'* or *'Fc'* or . . . . Convention *C* is only an
abbreviatory device; it can be omitted altogether in favor of writing
down in English the result of applying evaluation rules DTA (4a) or (4b)
to whatever step of the evaluation is in question; but this would be
rather unwieldy. All step (3) says is that there is some sentence of the
official idiom, the result of writing a subject term after *'F__'*, which is
true under **I**. We have now reached the level of simple (analyzed)
sentences of the official idiom for (1a), so we may begin part (1b).

STEP (4).   *It is not the case that* for *every e* in **U** the result of replacing *'x'*
in *'Fx'* by a name of *e* is true under **I**.

[from step (1b) by DTA (4a)]

STEP (5).   *There is* an *e* in **U** such that the result of replacing *'x'* in *'Fx'*
by a name of *e* is *false* under **I**.

[from step (4)]

Then, by application of *C* to step (5), we get

STEP (6). Ft_1 is false under **I** for some t_1 [t_1 may be different from the
subject letter *t* mentioned in step (3)].

[from step (5) by *C*]

We have now reached via DTA the level of simple sentences throughout,
so the procedure ends. The question now is whether or not steps (3) and
(6) can both be true. If so, then the argument is invalid. Such could be
shown by constructing a counterexample verifying the supposition in
steps (1a) and (1b). On the other hand, if (3) and (6) cannot both be true,
then the argument is valid. If so, this can be shown by showing that (3)
and (6) lead to contradiction.

First, let us investigate the hypothesis that (3) and (6) are contradictory. That means that it cannot be the case both that there is some sentence Ft which is true under **I** and some sentence Ft_1 which is false under **I**. But there is no contradiction in this at all. Suppose that t is 'a' and t_1 is 'b'. Then (3) would say that 'Fa' is true under **I** and (6) would say that 'Fb' is false under **I**. These two sentences can easily be true together. Just consider a universe **U** consisting of the set {Socrates, Plato, Napoleon}. Let **I** assign 'F__' the set {Socrates, Plato} (intuitively, this might correspond to abbreviating '. . . is a philosopher' as 'F__'). Then let **I** assign Socrates to 'a' and Napoleon to 'b'. Relative to **I**, 'Fa' is true because the entity assigned to 'a' (Socrates) belongs to the subset of **U** that **I** assigns to 'F__' (i.e., {Socrates, Plato}). And 'Fb' is false under **I** because the entity **I** assigns to 'b' (Napoleon) does not belong to {Socrates, Plato}. This shows that 'Fa' is true and 'Fb' false under **I** so defined, but we have not yet completed **I**. **I** is not yet an assignment because we have not yet said what all the subject letters, predicate letters, and sentence letters of the official idiom designate. These assignments are arbitrary because they cannot affect the counterexample we have already discovered, but they must be made because, by definition, an assignment must assign something to *every* item of nonlogical vocabulary. Thus

STEP (6).   Counterexample to **A**:

U *is the set* {*Socrates, Plato, Napoleon*}.
I('F__') *is the set* {*Socrates, Plato*}.
I('a') *is Socrates.*
I('b') *is Napoleon.*

For every name t other than 'a' *or* 'b', *let* **I**(t) *be Plato.*

For every n-place predicate P^n__, let **I**(P^n__) *be arbitrary sets of n-tuples of members of* **U**.

For every sentence letter A, let **I**(A) *be an arbitrarily chosen proposition.*

Let us show that **I** verifies the assumption for indirect evaluation and therefore gives a genuine counterexample by showing that it makes both steps (3) and (6) true. Ft is true for some t, namely 'a', because 'Fa' is true under **I**. 'Fa' is true under **I** because **I**('a') belongs to **I**('F__'). **I**('a') is Socrates and **I**('F__') is {Socrates, Plato}. Evidently, Socrates belongs to {Socrates, Plato}; so 'Fa' is true under **I**. By DTA (4a) it follows that '$(Ex)Fx$' is true under **I**. FT_1 is false for some t, namely 'b', because 'Fb' is false under **I**. 'Fb' is false under **I** because **I**('b') does not belong to **I**('F__'). **I**('b') is Napoleon, and **I**('F__'), as before, is {Socrates, Plato}.

Evidently, Napoleon does not belong to {Socrates, Plato}. So '*Fb*' is false under **I**. It follows from this that '(*x*)*Fx*' is false under **I** because there is at least one result of replacing '*x*' in '*Fx*' with a name of some *e* in **U**, which sentence is false under **I**. Then, **I** does give a genuine counterexample to **A**, for it is an assignment under which **A**'s premise sentence is true and conclusion sentence is false.

Having gone through this example in full detail, we shall now suggest a short cut. Strictly speaking, as we have said, an assignment must associate *every* sentence letter, subject letter, and predicate letter in the official idiom with an appropriate entity, but clearly not all such associations are required to describe a counterexample. A counterexample is *sufficient* if the associations it makes are confined to those items of the nonlogical vocabulary of the official idiom included in the premise sentences and the conclusion sentence. Hereafter, we shall require of a counterexample only that it be sufficient.

We shall recapitulate the preceding application of the evaluation procedure to **A** by presenting it in the short-cut way without explanatory remarks:

Argument **A:** (1) (*Ex*)*Fx*
      (2) ∴(*x*)*Fx*

EVALUATION

STEP (1).   Suppose that there is an assignment **I** (with **U**), such that *both*

(a) '(*Ex*)*Fx*' *is true under* **I**.
(b) '(*x*)*Fx*' *is false under* **I**.

              (*Assumption for indirect evaluation*)

STEP (2).   Then there is some *e* in **U** such that the result of replacing '*x*' in '*Fx*' by a name of *e* is true under **I**.

              [from step (1a) by DTA (4b)]

STEP (3).   Then *Ft* is true under **I,** for some *t*.

              [from step (2) by *C*]

STEP (4).   It is not the case that for every *e* in **U** the result of replacing '*x*' in '*Fx*' by a name of *e* is true under **I**.

              [from step (1b) by DTA (4a)]

STEP (5).   There is an e in **U** such that the result of replacing 'x' in 'Fx' by a name of e is false under **I**.

[from step (4)]

STEP (6).   Then Ft_1 is false under **I** for some t_1.

[from step (5) by C]

STEP (7).   Counterexample to **A**:

Let **U** be the set {Socrates, Plato, Napoleon}.
I('$F\underline{\quad}$') is the set {Socrates, Plato}.
I('a') is Socrates.
I('b') is Napoleon.

Ft is true under **I** for some t, and Ft_1 is false under **I** for some t_1. Hence '$(Ex)Fx$' is true under **I**, and '$(x)Fx$' is false under **I**, so **A** is invalid.

We shall complete the chapter by evaluating more of the arguments that served, in Chapter 2, as illustrations of the formalization procedure.

EXAMPLE 1

Recall the argument concerning Mr. Butz's inestimable advice. In official standard form, it was, on p. 117:

(1) $(p \supset q) \supset r$
(2) $\sim r$
(3) $\therefore \sim (p \supset q)$

Because we are concerned here only with evaluating the argument for validity, we may omit the scheme of abbreviation.

EVALUATION

STEP (1).   Suppose there is an assignment **I** such that all of the following obtain:

(a) '$(p \supset q) \supset r$' is true under **I**.
(b) '$\sim r$' is true under **I**.
(c) '$\sim (p \supset q)$' is false under **I**.

(*Assumption for indirect evaluation*)

STEP (2).   So 'r' is false under **I**.

[from step (1b) by DTA (3a)]

STEP (3).   And '$p \supset q$' is false under **I**.

[from steps (1a) and (2) by DTA (3d)]

STEP (4).   But '$p \supset q$' is true under **I**.

[from step (1c) by DTA (3a)]

STEP (5).   But steps (3) and (4) contradict each other. Therefore, there is no such **I** and the argument is valid.

EXAMPLE 2

Consider now the argument about truth in poetry on p. 123. If we omit the scheme of abbreviation, it was

(1) $p \supset q$
(2) $\sim p$
(3) $\therefore \sim q$

EVALUATION

STEP (1).   Suppose that there is an **I** such that all of the following hold:

(a) '$p \supset q$' *is true under* **I**.
(b) '$\sim p$' *is true under* **I**.
(c) '$\sim q$' *is false under* **I**.

STEP (2).   'p' is false under **I**.

[from step (1b), by DTA (3a)]

STEP (3).   'q' is true under **I**.

[from step (1c), by DTA (3a)]

STEP (4).   Counterexample:

I('p') *is a false proposition.*
I('q') *is a true proposition.*

'$p \supset q$' and '$\sim p$' are true under **I** and '$\sim q$' is false under **I**, so the argument is invalid.

EXAMPLE 3

Let us now turn to Bickel's views on pornography. In official standard form his argument (on p. 122) is

(1) p
(2) $(p \mathbin{\&} q) \supset r$
(3) $r \supset s$
(4) q
(5) $\therefore s$

EVALUATION

STEP (1).   Suppose there is an assignment **I** such that all of the following obtain:

(a) 'p' is true under **I**
(b) '$(p \mathbin{\&} q) \supset r$' is true under **I**.
(c) '$r \supset s$' is true under **I**.
(d) 'q' is true under **I**.
(e) 's' is false under **I**.

(Assumption for indirect evaluation)

STEP (2).   'r' is false under **I**.

[from steps (1c) and (1e) by DTA (3d)]

STEP (3).   '$p \mathbin{\&} q$' is false under **I**.

[from steps (1b) and (2) by DTA (3d)]

STEP (4).   So 'p' is false under **I** or 'q' is false under **I**.

[from step (3) by DTA (3c)]

STEP (5).   But 'p' is true under **I** and 'q' is true under **I**.

[from steps (1a) and (1d)]

STEP (6).   Steps (4) and (5) contradict each other, so there is no such **I** and the argument is valid.

As these examples illustrate again, the indirect evaluation procedure shows an argument to be valid by showing that the assumption that it has a counterexample leads, by means of DTA, to a contradiction. It is important to notice the additional detail that for some arguments, such an assumption can be effected in more than one way. In such cases the assumption for indirect evaluation, in effect, compresses several assumptions—a separate one for each way an assignment could make all the premises true and the conclusion false—and each of these possibilities must be shown to lead to contradiction. For example, consider arguments of the following form:

(1) $A \lor B$
(2) $\therefore A \& B$

Let us begin as usual (using meta-variables for greater generality):

STEP (1).   Suppose there is an assignment **I** such that both:

(a) $A \lor B$ *is true under* **I.**
(b) $A \& B$ *is false under* **I.**

                (Assumption for indirect evaluation)

STEP (2).   Then A is true under **I** or B is true under **I** or both.

        [from step (1a) by DTA (3b)]

CASE I

STEP (3).   *Suppose* that step (2) holds because both A and B are true under **I.** Then

STEP (4). A is true under **I.**

        [from step (3)]

STEP (5). A is false under **I.**

        [from step (1b) and DTA (3c)]

STEP (6).   Steps (4) and (5) contradict each other.

Now one should not leap to the conclusion that there is *no* **I** under which the premise is true and the conclusion false, because we have made the additional supposition in step (2) that the **I** *we were considering* made $A \lor B$ true in virtue of making both A and B true. There are two other ways of making $A \lor B$ true, and these must be considered. *Each* way of making the premise sentences true and the conclusion sentence false must be tested until each leads to a contradiction or a counterexample is found. Thus far we are entitled to say only the following:

STEP (7).   Therefore, there is no assignment **I** *as described in step* (3).

So *suppose*, then, that **I** makes *A* true and *B* false. It is easily discerned that *this* supposition yields a counterexample.

CASE II

STEP (8). Suppose that step (2) holds because *A* is true under **I** and *B* is false under **I**. Then

STEP (9). Counterexample:

A is true under **I.**
B is false under **I.**

There *is* a counterexample, so the argument is invalid. This reemphasizes the fact that although it is necessary to examine all the possible ways of making the premise sentences true and the conclusion sentence false (to show an argument to be valid), a single counterexample is sufficient to show it to be invalid.

Finally, we turn to the quantificational arguments in the final section of Chapter 2.

EXAMPLE 4

Recall the argument that originally forced us to expand the official idiom (see p. 152):

(1) *All men are mortal.*
(2) *Socrates is a man.*
(3) *Therefore, Socrates is mortal.*

On the most obvious scheme of abbreviation, this is

(1) $(x)(Fx \supset Gx)$
(2) Fa
(3) $\therefore Ga$

in official standard form.

EVALUATION

STEP (1). Suppose that there is an assignment **I,** with universe **U,** such that:

(a) '(x)(Fx ⊃ Gx) *is true under* **I**.
(b) 'Fa' *is true under* **I**.
(c) 'Ga' *is false under* **I**.

STEP (2).   Then, for every e in **U**, the result of replacing each occurrence of 'x' in 'Fx ⊃ Gx' with a name of e is true under **I**.

[from step (1a) by DTA (4a)]

STEP (3).   Thus 'Fa ⊃ Ga' is true under **I**.

[from step (2), letting t be 'a']

STEP (4).   But then 'Fa' is false under **I**.

[from step (1c) and (3) by DTA (3d)]

STEP (5).   Step (4) contradicts (1b), so there is no assignment **I** as described in the assumption for the indirect evaluation. Therefore, the argument is valid.

This shows how the greater expressiveness of the extended official idiom, together with the additional technical concepts we have developed, permits us to show that this argument is indeed valid.

EXAMPLE 5

Now consider the argument about nuclear war. On p. 166 it was represented in official standard form as:

(1) (x)((Fx & Gx) ⊃ p)
(2) ∴(Ex)(Fx & Gx) ⊃ p

EVALUATION

STEP (1).   Suppose there is an assignment **I**, with universe **U**, such that both

(a) '(x)((Fx & Gx) ⊃ p)' *is true under* **I**.
(b) '(Ex)(Fx & Gx) ⊃ p' *false under* **I**.
                    (*Assumption for indirect evaluation*)

STEP (2).   Then, for all e in **U**, the result of replacing 'x' in '(Fx & Gx) ⊃ p' by a name of e is true under **I**.

[from step (1a) by DTA (4a)]

STEP (3).   So '$(Ft$ & $Gt) \supset p'$ is true under **I** no matter what subject letter t is.

[from step (2) by C]

STEP (4).   (a) '$(Ex)(Fx$ & $Gx)'$ is true under **I,** and
(b) 'p' is false under **I.**

[from step (1b) by DTA (3d)]

STEP (5).   Then, for some e in **U,** the result of replacing 'x' in 'Fx & Gx' by a name of e is true under **I.**

[from step (4a) by DTA (4b)]

STEP (6).   'Ft_1 & Gt_1' is true under **I** from some t_1.

[from step (5) by C]

STEP (7). Ft & Gt is false under **I** for *all* t.

[from steps (3) and (4b) by DTA (3d)]

STEP (8).   But the subject letter t, mentioned in step (6), is the same as one of the other subject letters, t, mentioned in step (7). Thus Ft will be the same sentence as some Ft_1 and Gt will be the same as some Gt_1. Then Ft & Gt will be the same as some Ft_1 & Gt_1. But, by (6) and (7), this sentence is both true and false under **I.** There is no assignment **I** under which a sentence is both true and false, so the supposition in (1) is false and the argument is valid.

EXAMPLE 6

For another example of evaluation of argument in the extended official idiom, we turn to the argument concerning the relation between supply and demand of industrial metals. In official standard form it was (p. 161)

(1) $(x)(Fx \supset Gx) \lor F_1x)$
(2) $\sim F_1a$ & Ga
(3) Ha
(4) $\therefore (Ex)(Hx$ & $Fx)$

EVALUATION

STEP (1).   Suppose there is an assignment **I,** with universe **U,** such that all of the following:

(a) '$(x)((Fx \supset Gx) \vee F_1x)$' is true under **I**.
(b) '$\sim F_1a$ & Ga' is true under **I**.
(c) 'Ha' is true under **I**.
(d) '$(Ex)(Hx$ & $Fx)$' is false under **I**.

STEP (2). For no e in **U** is the result of replacing 'x' in 'Hx & Fx' true under **I**.

[from step (1d) and DTA (4b)]

STEP (3). Ht & Ft is false under **I**, for all t.

[from step (2) by C]

STEP (4). For every e in **U** the result of replacing 'x' in '$(Fx \supset Gx) \vee F_1x$' is true under **I**.

[from step (1a) by DTA (4a)]

STEP (5). $(Ft_1 \supset Gt_1) \vee F_1t_1$ is true under **I**, for all t_1.

[from step (4) by DTA (4a)]

STEP (6). *Counterexample:*

> **U** is $\{1, 2, 3\}$
> **I**('a') is 1
> **I**('H__') is $\{1\}$
> **I**('F_1__') is the empty set
> **I**('G__') is **U**
> **I**('F__') is the empty set

EXAMPLE 7

Now recall the argument for which we had to introduce relational predicates (cf. p. 146):

(1) *Guenièvre loves Lancelot.*
(2) *Therefore, Guenièvre loves someone.*

which, in the obvious scheme of paraphrase, is

(1) G^2ab
(2) $\therefore(Ex)(Gax)$

EVALUATION

STEP (1).   Suppose there is an assignment **I**, with universe **U**, such that both:

(a) 'F^2ab' is true under **I**.
(b) '$(Ex)(F^2ax)$' is false under **I**.

(*Assumption for indirect evaluation*)

STEP (2).   Then it is not the case that there is an e in **U** such that the result of replacing every occurrence of 'x' in 'F^2ax' by a name of e is true under **I**.

[from step (1b) by DTA (4b)]

STEP (3).   But (2) contradicts (1a) because 'F^2ab' is the result of replacing 'x' in 'F^2ax' with 'b'. Therefore, there is no assignment as described in step (1) and the argument is valid.

EXAMPLE 8

For our final example, look at the argument about paroling murderers. In official standard form, on p. 164, it is

(1) $(x)(Fx \supset F^2bx)$
(2) $(x)(\sim Gx \supset \sim F^2bx)$
(3) Ha
(4) $\sim Ga$
(5) $\therefore \sim(x)(Hx \supset Fx)$

EVALUATION

STEP (1).   Suppose there is an assignment **I**, with universe **U**, such that all of the following obtain:

(a) '$(x)(Fx \supset F^2bx)$' is true under **I**.
(b) '$(x)(\sim Gx \supset \sim F^2bx)$' is true under **I**.
(c) 'Ha' is true under **I**.
(d) '$\sim Ga$' is true under **I**.
(e) '$\sim((x)(Hx \supset Fx))$' is false under **I**.

(*Assumption for indirect evaluation*)

STEP (2).   For every e in **U** the result of replacing 'x' in '$Fx \supset F^2bx$' with a name of e is true under **I**.

[from step (1a) by DTA (4a)]

STEP (3).   So $Ft \supset F^2bt$ is true under **I** for all t.

[from step (2) by **C**]

STEP (4).   For every e in **U** the result of replacing 'x' in '$\sim Gx \supset \sim F^2bx$' with a name of e is true under **I**.

[from step (1b) by DTA (4a)]

STEP (5).   So $\sim Gt_1 \supset \sim F^2bt_1$ is true under **I** for all t_1.

[from step (4) by C]

STEP (6).   For all e in **U**, the result of replacing 'x' in '$Hx \supset Fx$' with a name of e is true under **I**.

[from step (1e) by DTA (3a) and DTA (4a)]

STEP (7).   So $Ht_2 \supset Ft_2$ is true under **I** for all t_2.

[from step (6) by C]

STEP (8).   '$Ha \supset Fa$' is true under **I**.

[from step (7) by C, where t_2 is 'a']

STEP (9).   'Fa' is true under **I**.

[from step (1c) and (8) by DTA (3d)]

STEP (10).   '$Fa \supset F^2ba$' is true under **I**.

[from step (3) by C, where t is 'a']

STEP (11).   So 'F^2ba' is true under **I**.

[from step (9) and (10) by DTA (3d)]

STEP (12).   '$\sim Ga \supset \sim F^2ba$' is true under **I**.

[from step (5) by C, where t_1 is 'a']

STEP (13).   '$\sim F^2ba$' is false under **I**.

[from step (11) by DTA (3a)]

STEP (14).   So '~Ga' is false under **I**.

[from steps (12) and (13) by DTA (3d)]

STEP (15).   But step (14) contradicts step (1d), so the argument is valid.

5.1 Exercises

You may find it helpful to consult the list of definitions and concepts introduced in this chapter on p. 193. Starred exercises are answered in Appendix III.

All of the following exercises are based on those of Section 15 in Chapter 2 (pp. 166–168).

  1. Evaluate the arguments for Exercise 1.
★2. Evaluate the arguments for Exercise 2.
★3. Evaluate the arguments for Exercise 3.
  4. Evaluate the arguments for Exercise 4.
★5. Evaluate the arguments for Exercise 5.

Difficult
  6. Evaluate the arguments for Exercise 6.

6.
SUMMARY OF IMPORTANT DEFINITIONS AND CONCEPTS IN CHAPTER 3

1. A *universe,* **U** (of discourse), is any nonempty set of existing entities.
2. A *property* may be identified with any subset of entities from **U.**
3. An *n-place relation* (where n is greater than 1) may be identified with any set of n-tuples of entities from **U.** (Properties are just a special case of relations.)
4. An *assignment* is a function associating an entity with each item of nonlogical vocabulary in the official idiom.
   a. An assignment to the unextended official idiom associates a true or false proposition with every sentence letter.
   b. An assignment to the extended official idiom associates with each subject letter of the official idiom an entity from the universe **U,** with each n-place predicate letter a set of n-tuples of members of **U** and with each sentence letter a true or false proposition.
5. *Truth Under an Assignment* (DTA)
   1. If A is a sentence letter of OI, then A is true under **I** if and only if **I** assigns a true proposition to A. Otherwise, A is false under **I.**
   2. If P^n is an n-place predicate letter in OI and $t_1, \ldots, t_n$ are subject letters in OI, then $P^n (t_1, \ldots, t_n)$ is true under I if and only if the n-tuple of things in **U** that **I** assigns to $t_1, \ldots, t_n$ belongs to the set of n-tuples of things in **U** that **I** assigns to P^n. Otherwise, $P^n (t_1, \ldots, t_n)$ is false under **I.**
   3. If A, B are sentences of OI, t a *variable,* then
      (a) $\sim A$ is true under **I** if and only if A is false under **I.** Otherwise, $\sim A$ is false under **I.**
      (b) $A \vee B$ is true under **I** if and only if A is true under **I** or B is true under **I.** Otherwise, $A \vee B$ is false under **I.**
      (c) $A \& B$ is true under **I** if and only if A is true under **I** and B is true under **I.** Otherwise, $A \& B$ is false under **I.**
      (d) $A \supset B$ is true under **I** if and only if A is false under **I** or B is true under **I.** Otherwise, $A \supset B$ is false under **I.**
      (e) $A \equiv B$ is true under **I** if and only if A is true under **I** and B is true under **I** or A is false under **I** and B is false under **I.** Otherwise, $A \equiv B$ is false under **I.**

4. Where **U** is a given universe of discourse and A contains one or more free occurrences of t^*, then

   (a) $(t)A$ is true under **I** if and only if for every e in **U**, the result of replacing all free occurrences of t in A by a name of e is true under **I**. Otherwise, $(t)A$ is false under **I**.

   (b) $(Et)A$ is true under **I** if and only if for some e in **U**, the result of replacing all free occurrences of t in A by a name of e is true under **I**. Otherwise, $(Et)A$ is false under **I**.

6. An argument **A** (in official standard form) is *valid* if and only if there is no assignment **I** (with universe **U**) of appropriate entities to the subject letters, predicate letters, and sentence letters of the official idiom such that the premise sentences of **A**'s written expression are true under **I** and the conclusion sentence is false under **I**.

7. **A** *has a counterexample* if and only if there is an assignment **I** (with universe **U**) of appropriate entities to the subject terms, predicate letters, and sentence letters of the official idiom such that the premise sentences of **A**'s written expression are true under **I** and the conclusion sentence is false under **I**.

8. A *counterexample* to argument **A** is another argument **D** such that **D** has the same logical form as **A** and **D** has true premises and a false conclusion.

9. To *give a counterexample* to **A** is to describe an assignment **I** with universe **U**, of appropriate entities to the subject terms, predicate letters, and sentence letters of the official idiom such that the premise sentences of **A**'s written expression are true under **I** and the conclusion sentence is false under **I**.

10. The *indirect evaluation procedure* is a way of establishing the validity of an argument by assuming the invalidity of that argument and demonstrating on the basis of DTA that the assumption is false.

11. Convention *C:*   Let an n-place predicate letter followed by n meta-variables $(t_1, \ldots, t_n)$ for subject letters designate the result of appending n subject letters to that predicate letter.

---

* If A does not contain any free occurrences of t, then $(t)A$ and $(Et)A$, respectively, are true under **I** if and only if A is true under **I**. Otherwise, $(t)A$ and $(Et)A$ are false under **I**.

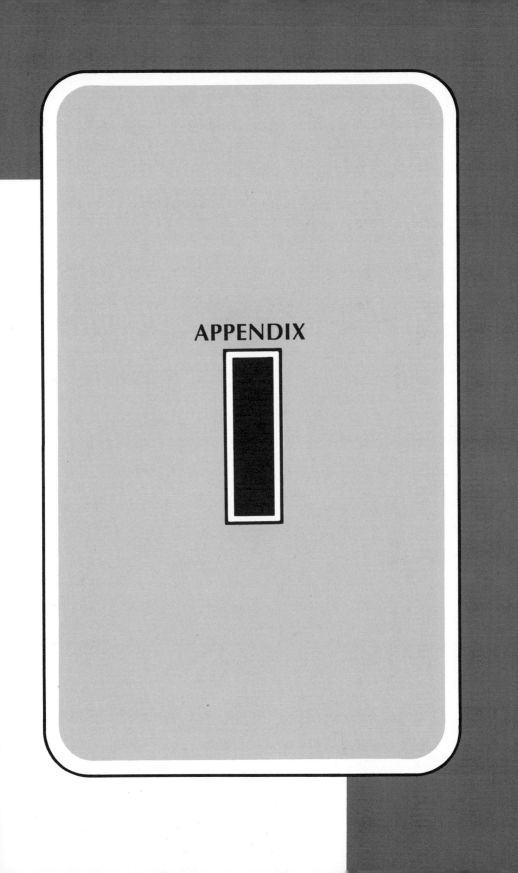

APPENDIX

I

Deduction and Induction

All of the arguments discussed in this book, both valid and invalid, have been deductive arguments. A deductive argument represents correct deductive reasoning if and only if it is valid. Further, we have stipulated that if an argument is valid, it is deductive. If an argument is invalid, however, it does not follow that it is deductive.

Many logicians think that there is an important species of argument not intended to be deductive, but which may nevertheless record correct inferences. Such arguments are called "inductive," as are the inferences they represent. An inductive argument is one in which the premises do not imply the conclusion but provide some *evidence* for the truth of the conclusion. We use such arguments every day. For example, if one hears that another person is going to jump off the Golden Gate Bridge, one may reasonably conclude that he will be killed on the grounds that all or nearly all of the preceding 590 jumpers were killed. In gross standard form the argument recording the inference in question would be as follows:

(1) *All or nearly all of the 590 people who have jumped off the Golden Gate Bridge to date were killed.*
(2) *Jones is going to jump off the Golden Gate Bridge.*
(3) *Therefore, Jones will be killed.*

Clearly, this argument is not valid; the reader is invited to supply a counterexample. Still many logicians have thought that the inference it records is correct; a person who believed the premises of this argument but thought that there was absolutely no reason to believe that Jones will be killed would be thought mad. Although inductive arguments are never valid, there is a distinction between good ones and bad ones. A correct inductive argument is one such that were the premises true, the conclusion would probably be true. (Some logicians have called correct inductive arguments in which the premises are true and the conclusion true, "reliable" inductive arguments.) There is a great deal of disagreement about how to determine whether a given inductive argument is correct. The problem is how to decide when the premises of an inductive argument make probable the truth of the conclusion. We need not discuss the details of this issue here. It will suffice to point out that the foregoing inductive argument, for example, is correct because, intuitively, the sample of cases investigated is large and, further, there is a background of highly confirmed scientific laws concerning the distressing effects on human bodies of falls from great heights.

Some inductive arguments contain statements of a statistical or probabilistic character; that is, they contain statements that report percentages or proportions or probabilities of something or other. For example, one might argue that 99 percent of new cars have no safety defects on the ground that out of a certain fair sample of new cars 99 percent had no defects. It is often thought that inductive arguments *must* contain statements of a statistical or probabilistic character, but this is mistaken. Let us suppose that it is true that all persons who have a certain disease D have a high pulse rate, high blood pressure, severe pains in the respiratory tract, and a high fever. Further let us suppose that poor Jones has all these symptoms. It would not be unusual for the physician examining Jones to conclude that he has disease D. This is an inductive inference, but it contains no statements of a statistical or probabilistic sort.

Another old and cherished account of the character of inductive arguments is found in many contemporary scientific textbooks. According to this account, a deductive argument differs from an inductive argument because a deductive argument proceeds from general premises to a particular conclusion, whereas an inductive argument proceeds from particular premises to a general conclusion. But this is incorrect. Recall the example just mentioned of an inductive argument that has the statement 'Jones has disease D' as the conclusion. That argument does not contain a general statement as conclusion; so in this case we have an inductive argument that does not go from particular premises to general conclusion. Again, recall Roscoe Frostbite's dilemma on p. 32. Remember that the premises of that deductive argument were not general. They were about Roscoe and Crustacea, and the conclusion was about Crustacea only. Since this argument does not go from general to particular, the old and cherished account is wrong for deductive arguments, too. It is not always the case that in a deductive argument the conclusion is a particular statement and the premises are general, or that even some of the premises are general.

The crucial distinction between correct deductive arguments and correct inductive arguments lies in the *connection* between premises and conclusion in the different kinds of argument. In a correct deductive argument the premises, if true, establish the conclusion conclusively, but in a correct inductive argument the premises only provide probable support for the conclusion. Consider a deductive argument used to test the hypothesis that learning is a continuous process. By this is meant that learning is a continuous process in which the correct response slowly and steadily prevails over competing but incorrect responses. The psychologist, in testing this hypothesis, may hope to show that the role of "insight" in learning is less important than continuous reinforcement of the correct response. So he may devise the following experiment. He measures the learning time for a certain group learning a specified response, say, going to the left in a T-maze. Then with another group he reverses what the correct response will be—going to the right in the T-maze—during the course of training. He expects learning to be retarded in this second group. Here is the argument that he might use to test his hypothesis:

(1) *Learning is a continuous process.*
(2) *If learning is a continuous process and the learning situation is reversed, then learning will be retarded.*
(3) *The learning situation is reversed.*
(4) *Therefore, learning will be retarded.*

This is a valid argument, as the reader may determine for himself. So if the conclusion turns out to be false, the psychologist will be able to conclude that one of his premises is false. Premise (2) is known to be true simply on the basis of what the psychologist means by "continuous process," and he makes (3) true by performing the experiment; so (1) would be the only premise left to be false. Thus, if the conclusion turns out to be false, he can conclude that his hypothesis, namely (1), is false.

If the conclusion is true, however, the psychologist cannot properly conclude that his hypothesis is true, because a valid argument with a true conclusion can have false premises. Nevertheless, if his conclusion is true, that *supports* the hypothesis to some extent because it rules out one way the hypothesis might have been false. The reason that this supports his hypothesis is that we can construct an inductive argument from the various propositions occurring in the preceding deductive argument. To make the situation clearer, let us suppose that the psychologist has run the experiment many times without ever having a result falsifying the conclusion. Then he can argue inductively as follows:

(1) *In case 1, the learning situation is reversed and learning was retarded.*
(2) *In case 2, the learning situation is reversed and learning was retarded.*
(3) *In case 3, the learning situation is reversed and learning was retarded.*

.
.
.

(n) *In case n, the learning situation is reversed and learning was retarded.*
(n + 1) *Therefore, every time the learning situation is reversed learning will be retarded.*

The conclusion of this argument, in effect, expresses the psychologist's original hypothesis that learning is a continuous process. This argument is not valid, as the reader can determine, for it has the form

(1) A_1
(2) A_2
(3) A_3

.
.
.

(n) A_n
(n + 1) $\therefore (x)Ax$

There is a second interesting contrast between this argument and the corresponding deductive argument. Whereas the inference that the deductive argument was used to record was *not* a means of establishing a belief in what the conclusion expresses (that argument was used to test the hypothesis), in the case of the inductive argument discussed above the inductive inference that it records *is* used to support a belief in what the conclusion expresses.

The hypothesis that appears as the conclusion in the argument above was supported by that argument, but there is nothing in the argument which suggests how it was discovered. Once a scientist arrives at a hypothesis, however it occurs to him, he may use both deductive and inductive arguments to test it. But is there a special kind of argument that helps us discover scientific hypotheses? Some philosophers have thought so. An American philosopher, Charles

Saunders Pierce, suggested that there may be a third kind of argument, which he called "abductive." Here is an example of an abductive argument: Let us imagine two psychologists, A and B, to be discussing a famous stimulus transfer experiment. Psychologist A says, "Now you will recall, B, that, in the experiment in question, first a light was paired with a bell many times. Then an animal was conditioned to salivate to the bell. Later when the light was substituted for the bell, the animal salivated to the light. These experimental results cannot be explained by thinking of what the animals learned as stimulus–response sequences because the sequence consisting first of the light and then the salivary reaction never occurred during the training phase of the experiment. But if we were to think of some habits as essentially stimulus–stimulus connections, the occurrence of the salivary reaction in the transfer stage would be understandable. Therefore, it seems plausible to me, at least, to conclude that some habits consist of stimulus–stimulus connections, and specifically in the case at hand the connection of light with bell." In gross standard form, the argument is

(1) *If habits were stimulus–stimulus connections, then transfer of the salivary response to the light as stimulus would occur.*
(2) *Transfer of the salivary response to the light as stimulus does occur.*
(3) *Therefore, some habits are stimulus–stimulus connections.*

Now certainly this argument is not valid; it has a counterexample. But, more than that, it does not even purport to be a deductive argument. The premises support the conclusion in a probabilistic way. But if so, then the argument would be an inductive argument and not a third kind at all. Those who say that abduction is not a unique kind of argument form contend that if it were, then there would be some kind of connection between premises and conclusion other than a necessary one or a probabilistic one. What such a connection might be is difficult to fathom. Rather, so the objection goes, abductive arguments seem to be a special class of inductive arguments—those in which the intention of the arguer is to present his reasons, or at least some of his reasons, for adopting a particular hypothesis or theory.

Finally, we come to the tantalizing philosophical question, raised by the philosopher David Hume, whether inductive arguments do really record a unique and justifiable species of reasoning called inductive inference. We do *seem* to reason inductively, as the examples of inductive arguments presented above show, but that fact, as Hume pointed out, does not prove that it is *correct* to reason in this way. Hume observed that there seems to be no *connection* at all between the premises and conclusion of an inductive argument. If it is always possible for the conclusion of such an argument to be false when the premises are true, Hume asked, then what support do the premises lend to the conclusion? Some have suggested that the question of the justification of induction can be settled by noting that correct inductive inferences have been reliable in the past—that is, inductive inferences from true premises have usually led to true conclusions—but, as Hume pointed out, this seems circular. If the problem of the justification of induction is to show why *any* inductive argument should be accepted, then surely it is unsatisfactory to appeal to the further inductive argument that future inductive arguments will be reliable because past ones have usually been reliable.

Hume often visualized the problem of induction as involving inferences from the past to the future. For example, we argued earlier from *past* cases of people jumping off the bridge to conclusions involving a *future* case. So, Hume wondered, what reason could there be to suppose that the future will resemble the past? But his reason for skepticism about inductive arguments concerning the future makes it clear that his challenge applies equally well to any argument that is not valid. For example, suppose one knows that the vast majority of football players exceed 200 pounds in weight. Then one might make the inference recorded by the following argument:

A (1) *Nearly all football players exceed 200 pounds.*
(2) *Joe Namath is a football player.*
(3) *Therefore, there is a 90 percent probability that Namath weighs more than 200 pounds.*

In this case there is no inference about anything in the future from some statement about the past. Rather, one is inferring something about a member of a certain class, the class of football players, from a fact about other members of that class. But even in this case Hume could ask what support the fact that most football players weigh more than 200 pounds lends to the truth of the claim that Namath weighs more than 200 pounds? Since Namath's weight has nothing to do with the weight of football players, how can the fact that they have a certain weight be relevant to the truth of a claim about his weight?

Some philosophers have thought that Hume's challenge can be met by thinking of inductive arguments as a species of deductive argument. Simply put, they note that the mathematical theory of probability tells us what probability a certain sentence has of being true for certain evidence. If, for example, we know that 90 percent of football players exceed 200 pounds and that Joe Namath is a football player, then we know that there is a 90 percent probability that Joe Namath weighs more than 200 pounds. It is then suggested that the following apparent inductive argument is really valid and hence not really inductive at all:

B (1) *Ninety percent of football players weight more than 200 pounds.*
(2) *Joe Namath is a football player.*
(3) *Therefore, there is a 90 percent probability that Namath weighs more than 200 pounds.*

To construe an inductive argument such as **A** as being genuinely an (incomplete) deductive argument such as **B** seems at first to solve Hume's problem. If **B** is a valid argument, then if it records an inductive inference, that inference must be correct. In other words, there is no problem justifying deductive inference, so if inductive inference were a species of deductive inference, there would be no problem justifying inductive inference either.

There is, however, a major objection to this attempt to solve Hume's problem. It is that we can easily produce another "inductive" argument, which yields a contrary conclusion. Consider:

C (1) *Ninety percent of human beings do not weigh more than 200 pounds.*
(2) *Joe Namath is a human being.*
(3) *Therefore, there is a 90 percent chance that Joe Namath does not weigh more than 200 pounds.*

C has as much claim to being valid as **B**. Now the premises of **B** and **C** are both *true*. **B** and **C** would both be *sound* on the deductivist view, so their conclusions must both be true. But it would have to be the case both that there is a 90 percent chance that Joe Namath weighs over 200 pounds and that there is a 90 percent chance that he does not weigh over 200 pounds. This is impossible. It cannot be that two sound arguments have incompatible conclusions, so it seems that if one is justified in inferring the conclusions of **B** and **C** from their respective premises, then they cannot both be sound. But since the premises in each case are obviously true, **B** and **C** cannot both be valid. There is no reason to think, however, that they can differ with respect to validity, since they have the same form. It must be, then, that any inference from the premises of **B** and **C** to their respective conclusions, if correct in some sense or other, must be justified on some other ground than their being a species of deductive reasoning.

Some philosophers have concluded from this that there really is no such thing as inductive inference, but that arguments such as **B** and **C** reveal the probability of a certain statement on certain evidence. For example, **B** would state that the **relationship** between

(1) *Ninety percent of football players weigh more than 200 pounds.*

together with

(2) *Joe Namath is a football player.*

on the one hand, and

(3) *Joe Namath weighs more than 200 pounds.*

on the other, is that there is a 90 percent chance that (3) is true *relative to* the joint truth of (1) and (2). Similarly, **C** would state that the relationship between its premises and conclusion is that the conclusion has a 90 percent chance of being true relative to the joint truth of its premises. This suggestion avoids the problem poised above, where we seemed forced to conclude that the conclusions of **B** and **C** were both true, for there is no contradiction in saying that the contrary conclusions of **B** and **C** are both supported to the same degree by their diverse premises. Nevertheless, this is quite different from saying that the contrary conclusions of **B** and **C** are both *inferred* from their respective premises, and the problem we began with was to try to justify the *inference* recorded by argument **A**. Thus it seems that the attempt to *justify* induction by showing it to be a species of deduction fails. For on that account, one is left with the conclusion that either arguments such as **A** do not record a unique species of inference at all, or whatever that species of inference is we have no idea how to justify it. So the problem remains: Either **A** records an incorrect deductive inference or it records some other kind of inference that stands in need of justification.

Perhaps the most direct attempt to meet Hume's challenge is that of P. F. Strawson.[1] He points out that Hume's stated reason for thinking that inductive inference stands in need of justification is that the falsity of the conclusion of an inductive argument is always consistent with the truth of the premises. Strawson feels that this is to say no more than that inductive arguments are not deductive arguments and that short of introducing some *other* reason for thinking that inductive arguments stand in need of justification, there is no call for Hume's skepticism. His solution to the problem of the justification of induction then is to reject the question. He seems to think that it is just a fact that there is a form of inference which is nondeductive and that it stands in no need of justification despite the fact that correct inductive inferences from the true premises may sometimes result in false conclusions.

[1] P. F. Strawson, *Introduction to Logical Theory* (London: Methuen & Co. Ltd., 1963).

APPENDIX

Mechanical Evaluation Techniques

The evaluation techniques to be discussed here are mechanical procedures for determining validity or invalidity. To say that the procedures are *mechanical* is to say that a computer could be programmed to accomplish the same task. They utilize the following relationship: An argument is valid if and only if a certain sentence in the official idiom, namely, the *conditional* corresponding to that argument, is logically true. A sentence of the official idiom is *logically true* if and only if it is true under all assignments of appropriate entities to whatever names, predicates, and sentence letters comprise it.

We shall concentrate first on those logical truths that are expressible in the unextended official idiom. We shall show how truth tables can be used to determine whether or not a sentence is logically true. (Unless otherwise stipulated, in this discussion a *sentence* is a sentence in the unextended official idiom.)

1.
TRUTH TABLES

A *truth table* is a graphic association of sentences with an array of truth values, one or more columns of which are *assignment columns* and others, *valuation columns*. Recall two assumptions stated in Chapter 2 (p. 80) and implicit in DTA: First, every sentence letter in the official idiom expresses either a true or a false proposition under every assignment; and second, no sentence letter expresses both under any assignment. For any sentence A of the official idiom, the assignment columns of A's *truth table* encompass *all* possible assignments to all the component sentence letters of A (or to A itself, in case it is a sentence letter). Every assignment is of a true or false proposition, so the assignment columns capture all these possibilities. The truth value of any sentence constructed solely from the component sentence letters in A can be calculated by means of the appropriate clauses of DTA which interpret the propositional connectives contained in the sentence in question. In particular, interest centers on the truth values, so determined, of all the complex sentences comprising A, in order of their complexity. Since the most complex sentence comprising A is A itself, the last valuation column of A's truth table gives the truth value of A under all the various assignments to its constituent sentence letters.

The general form of the truth table for a sentence Γ_m comprised of the sentence letters A_1 to A_n and the complex sentences Γ_1 to Γ_{m-1} built up out of A_1 to A_n in accordance with SOI is as shown in the table on page 223. If the last valuation column, that for Γ_m itself, consists of only T's, then Γ_m is true under all assignments I_1 to I_k, so Γ_m is *logically true*. If the column consists of only F's, then Γ_m is *logically false*, and if there are some T's and some F's, then Γ_m is *contingent* (i.e., its truth value under an assignment I is contingent on the truth values of $A_1 - A_n$ under I).

To illustrate, consider first the trivial case where Γ_m is itself a sentence letter (i.e., $\Gamma_m = 'p'$ is the foregoing schema). There are only two types of possible assignments, of true propositions and of false propositions. Thus the assignment column is

	p
I_1	T
I_2	F

The values for Γ_m under assignments I_1 and I_2 are then calculated from the values of $'p'$ under I_1 and I_2 by means of the appropriate clause of DTA. Thus DTA (1) says that a sentence letter is true under an assignment I if and only if it is assigned a true proposition; otherwise, it is false under I. Thus Γ_m is true under I_1, because $'p'$ is assigned a true proposition under I_1 and Γ_m is false under I_2 because $'p'$ is not assigned a true proposition under I_2. The full truth table for Γ_m then is

Assignment Columns   **Valuation Columns**

	A_1	A_2	$\cdots$	A_{n-2}	A_{n-1}	A_n		Γ_1	Γ_2	Γ_3	$\cdots\cdot\Gamma_{m-1}$	Γ_m
I_1	T	T		T	T	T		T or F	T or F	T or F	T or F	T or F
I_2	T	T		T	T	F		$\cdot$	$\cdot$	$\cdot$	$\cdot$	$\cdot$
I_3	T	T		T	F	T		$\cdot$	$\cdot$	$\cdot$	$\cdot$	$\cdot$
I_4	T	T		T	F	F		$\cdot$	$\cdot$	$\cdot$	$\cdot$	$\cdot$
I_5	T	T		F	T	T		$\cdot$	$\cdot$	$\cdot$	$\cdot$	$\cdot$
$\cdots$												
I_k	F	F		F	F	F		$\cdot$	$\cdot$	$\cdot$	$\cdot$	$\cdot$

	p	$\Gamma_m = p$
I_1	T	T
I_2	F	F

Γ_m, clearly, is not logically true.

Now consider a complex sentence that is logically true. Let Γ_m be '$p \supset (q \supset p)$'. Γ_m contains two sentence letters. So, referring to the general schema above, A_{n-1} will be 'p' and A_n will be 'q', Γ_1 will be '$q \supset p$', and Γ_2 will be '$p \supset (q \supset p)$'. It can be seen from the schema that for two sentence letters there are four types of assignments (in general, for n sentence letters there are 2^n types of assignments):

	p	q
I_1	T	T
I_2	T	F
I_3	F	T
I_4	F	F

The least complex component complex sentence of Γ_m is '$q \supset p$', so the first step is to calculate its truth value under I_1 to I_4 by applying the clause (3d) of DTA to the values of 'q' and 'p' under I_1 to I_4 (the resultant value is entered under the principal connective '$\supset$', which, in this case, is the only connective):

	p	q	$q \supset p$
I_1	T	T	T
I_2	T	F	T
I_3	F	T	F
I_4	F	F	T

The next smallest complex component of Γ_m is Γ_m itself, so its values under each of I_1 to I_4 are similarly calculated by means of DTA:

	p	q	$q \supset p$	$p \supset (q \supset p)$
I_1	T	T	T	T
I_2	T	F	T	T
I_3	F	T	F	T
I_4	F	F	T	T

Γ_m is true under all possible assignments to its constituent sentence letters and thus is logically true.

1.1 Exercises

1. How many *assignment* columns would be required for truth tables for each of the following sentences?
   a. *p*
   b. ~*p*
   c. *p* v *p*
   d. *p* & ~*p*
   ★e. $((p \supset q) \supset r) \equiv ((p \supset r) \vee (q \supset r))$
   f. $((p \, \& \, q) \, \& \, r) \, \& \, s$
   g. $(p \, \& \, q) \, \& \sim(\sim p \equiv \sim q)$
2. Suppose that *A* and *B* are any two logically true sentences in the official idiom and *C* is any contingent sentence in the official idiom. Relative to this assumption, which of the following arguments are valid and which invalid? Defend your answers:

A (1) *A*	**C** (1) *C*	**E** (1) *C* v *B*
(2) ∴*C*	(2) ∴$(A \supset C) \equiv (C \supset A)$	(2) ∴*A*
B (1) *C*	**D** (1) *C* & *A*	**F** (1) *C* v *B*
(2) ∴*B*	(2) ∴*B*	(2) ∴*C*

★3. How many valuation columns would be required for the sentences in Exercise 1? What are the complex components to be evaluated in each column?
★4. How many rows are required for truth tables for the sentences in Exercise 1?
★5. Construct truth tables for the sentences in Exercise 1.
6. Which of the sentences in Exercise 5 are necessarily true, which contingent, and which necessarily false? Defend your answers.

Difficult
7. Suppose that some sentence in the official idiom of the form $A \equiv B$ is logically true and that $B \supset A$ is contingent. What can you conclude about the following argument?
   (1) *A*
   (2) ∴*B*

2.
CORRESPONDING CONDITIONALS

The conditional corresponding to an argument is the conditional sentence in the official idiom whose antecedent consists of the conjunction of the premises of the argument in question and whose consequent is the conclusion. Consider an arbitrary argument **A** with premises $A_1, \ldots, A_{n-1}$ and conclusion A_n.

A   (1) A_1
       (2) A_2

      .

      .

$(n-1)\ A_{n-1}$
   $(n)\ \therefore A_n$

The conditional corresponding to **A** is $(((A_1 \mathbin{\&} A_2) \mathbin{\&} \cdots) \mathbin{\&} A_{n-1}) \supset A_n$.

Argument **A** is valid if and only if its corresponding conditional is true. For those who are interested, we will show that this is so. Suppose that **A** is valid. Then, by the definition of validity, **A**'s conclusion is true under all assignments under which the premises are jointly true. That means that there are no assignments under which the premises are jointly true and the conclusion false. Now, the premises are $A_1, A_2, \ldots, A_{n-1}$ and the conclusion is A_n. So there are no assignments under which $A_1, A_2, \ldots, A_{n-1}$ are all true and A_n is false. By DTA (3c), any assignment that makes $A_1, A_2, \ldots, A_{n-1}$ all true also makes $(((A_1 \mathbin{\&} A_2) \mathbin{\&} \cdots) \mathbin{\&} A_{n-1})$ true; so there are no assignments under which $(((A_1 \mathbin{\&} A_2) \mathbin{\&} \cdots) \mathbin{\&} A_{n-1})$ is true and A_n is false. Then, by DTA (3d), there are no assignments under which $(((A_1 \mathbin{\&} A_2) \mathbin{\&} \cdots \mathbin{\&} A_{n-1}) \supset A_n$ is false. Therefore, it is logically true. But this sentence is the conditional corresponding to **A**. Thus, if **A** is valid, then its corresponding conditional is logically true.

Now suppose that **A**'s corresponding conditional is logically true. Then, by definition of *logical truth*, there are no assignments under which $(((A_1 \mathbin{\&} A_2) \mathbin{\&} \cdots) \mathbin{\&} A_{n-1}) \supset A_n$ is false. By DTA (3d), it follows that there are no assignments under which $(((A_1 \mathbin{\&} A_2) \mathbin{\&} \cdots) \mathbin{\&} A_{n-1})$ is true and A_n is false. Then, by DTA (3c), any assignment that makes $(((A_1 \mathbin{\&} A_2) \mathbin{\&} \cdots) \mathbin{\&} A_{n-1})$ true also makes $A_1, A_2, \ldots, A_{n-1}$ jointly true. Hence there are no assignments under which $A_1, A_2, \ldots, A_{n-1}$ are jointly true and A_n is false. But $A_1, A_2, \ldots, A_{n-1}$ are the premises of **A** and A_n is the conclusion. So there are no assignments under which the premises of **A** are true and the conclusion is false. By the definition of *validity*, then, **A** is valid. Thus, if **A**'s corresponding conditional is logically true, then **A** is valid.

Since DTA, together with truth tables, can be employed to determine whether or not an arbitrary sentence in the official idiom is logically true, it can be employed to determine whether or not the conditional corresponding to an argument is logically true. To illustrate, recall the argument concerning truth in poetry. In official standard form it is represented (on p. 123) as:

(1) $p \supset q$
(2) $\sim p$
(3) $\therefore \sim q$

The corresponding conditional is '$((p \supset q) \mathbin{\&} \sim p) \supset \sim q$', whose truth table, constructed in the manner described above, is as follows:

	p	q	I $\sim p$	II $\sim q$	III $p \supset q$	IV $(p \supset q) \mathbin{\&} \sim p$	V $((p \supset q) \mathbin{\&} \sim p) \supset \sim q$
I_1	T	T	F	F	T	F	T
I_2	T	F	F	T	F	F	T
I_3	F	T	T	F	T	T	F
I_4	F	F	T	T	T	T	T

This conditional is false under I_3, so it is not logically true. Thus the corresponding argument is invalid. [Note that I_3 makes the premises of the argument (in valuation columns I and III) true and the conclusion (in valuation column II) false.]

It is important to recognize that the mere *truth* of the corresponding conditional is not enough to establish the validity of an argument. According to DTA (3d), the conditional corresponding to the argument above, for example, is true if '$((p \supset q) \mathbin{\&} \sim p)$' is false, as under I_1 and I_2, or '$\sim q$' is true, as under I_2 and I_4; but as we know from Chapter 1 that the falsity of one or more premises of an argument or the truth of its conclusion does not suffice for the validity of the argument.

2.1 Exercises

1. Refer to your answers to Exercise 1, Section 10.1 of Chapter 2 (p. 124). Give the conditional corresponding to each of these arguments in official standard form.
2. Suppose that $A \supset B$ is the conditional corresponding to some valid argument and that B is logically false. What can you conclude about the premises?
3. Give the truth tables for the corresponding conditionals to arguments b, c, and d in Exercise 1. Which arguments are valid? Defend your answers.

3.
THE FELL-SWOOP METHOD[1] FOR NONQUANTIFICATIONAL ARGUMENTS

Constructing a truth table can often be an unwieldy way of determining validity. If, for example, we wanted to evaluate an argument containing, say, six distinct sentence letters, a truth table with sixty-four rows would be required. Fortunately, it is not always necessary to construct truth tables because it is possible to prove "at a fell-swoop" whether there is a row in the truth table for the corresponding conditional (or any other sentence) where it is false. A *row* in the truth table for a sentence A is, of course, an assignment I of truth values to the sentence letters in A, together with the calculated values under I of all the complex sentences comprising A, the calculation being performed in accordance with the relevant clauses of DTA. Suppose that A is the conditional to some argument. If there is *no* row in the truth table for A where it is false, it is true under all assignments and hence is a logical truth. So the argument it corresponds to is valid. If there *is* such a row, then A is not logically true and the corresponding argument is invalid. Briefly, the procedure is this: First, we make the supposition that the corresponding conditional, A, is not logically true. If the supposition is correct, then there must be at least one row R containing an assignment I to the sentence letters in A such that A is false under I. We then use the relevant clauses of DTA to determine whether or not there is such an I. We might deduce one of two things: On the one hand, we could discover that it follows from our supposition that A is not logically true that I is itself contradictory—that it assigns both true and false propositions to at least one sentence letter. We know that there is no such assignment I to any sentence letter, so if this follows from the supposition, we know that there is no I under which the corresponding conditional is false. On the other hand, we might discover that it is possible to make an assignment to the sentence letters that is consistent with the supposition that A is false. If so, we have discovered an assignment I to the sentence letters comprising A under which A comes out false.

For the sake of the contrast between the truth table and fell-swoop methods, we illustrate the latter by testing the same corresponding conditional as above: $A = '((p \supset q) \& \sim p) \supset \sim q'$.

First, suppose that the A is not logically true. Then there is at least one row R under which A is false. We record this supposition by placing an F over the main connective:

$$\begin{array}{c} F \\ ((p \supset q) \, \& \, \sim p) \supset \sim q \end{array}$$

Now if A is false in row R, then, by DTA (3d), '$((p \supset q) \& \sim p)$' must be true, whereas '$\sim q$' is false. We record this by putting T's and F's over the next strongest connectives:

$$\begin{array}{ccc} T & F\ F \\ ((p \supset q) \, \& \, \sim p) \supset \sim q \end{array}$$

[1] This felicitous phrase is due to W. V. Quine.

Now, if the antecedent is true, then by DTA (3c), each conjunct is true and if the consequent is false, by DTA (3a), 'q' must be true. So

$$\begin{array}{ccccc} \text{T} & \text{T} & \text{T} & \text{F} & \text{F} \\ ((p \supset q) & \& & \sim p) & \supset & \sim q \\ & & & & \text{T} \end{array}$$

We shall record assignments to sentence letters below the line. Because we have now determined that 'q' is true in the consequent, we must make 'q' true in all its occurrences—again, it is not possible for a sentence to be both true and false in the same context. So

$$\begin{array}{ccccc} \text{T} & \text{T} & \text{T} & \text{F} & \text{F} \\ ((p \supset q) & \& & \sim p) & \supset & \sim q \\ & \text{T} & & & \text{T} \end{array}$$

Since '$\sim p$' is true, 'p' is false in all its occurrences:

$$\begin{array}{ccccc} \text{T} & \text{T} & \text{T} & \text{F} & \text{F} \\ ((p \supset q) & \& & \sim p) & \supset & \sim q \\ \text{F} \quad \text{T} & & \text{F} & & \text{T} \end{array}$$

We have now arrived at an assignment for each of the sentence letters comprising A; there is nothing left to do. Because we were not forced to assign contradictory values to any sentence, it follows that there is an assignment **I** to the sentence letters comprising A under which A is false—that which assigns falsity to 'p' and truth to 'q'. So row R exists. In fact, R is row (iii) in the full truth table for A displayed on p. 198.

In case the corresponding conditional to an argument is found not to be logically true, one of the assignments under which it is false (i.e., some row R in which it is false) is recorded below the sentence as follows:

$$\begin{array}{ccccc} \text{T} & \text{T} & \text{T} & \text{F} & \text{F} \\ ((p \supset q) & \& & \sim p) & \supset & \sim q \\ \text{F} \quad \text{T} & & \text{F} & & \text{T} \end{array}$$

The corresponding conditional is false under the following assignment:

$$\mathbf{I}('p') = \text{F}$$
$$\mathbf{I}('q') = \text{T}$$

Thus the argument is invalid.

Now let us test the corresponding conditional to a valid argument, for example, the irate consumer's argument against Earl Butz's egregious advice. In official standard form, it was represented (on p. 198) as:

(1) $(p \supset q) \supset r$
(2) $\sim r$
(3) $\therefore \sim (p \supset q)$

First, we formulate the corresponding conditional, A:

$$(((p \supset q) \supset r) \ \& \ \sim r) \supset \sim (p \supset q)$$

Suppose that there is some row R in which A is false:

$$\begin{array}{c} \text{F} \\ (((p \supset q) \supset r) \mathbin{\&} \sim r) \supset \sim(p \supset q) \end{array}$$

If A is false in R, then, by DTA (3d):

$$\begin{array}{c} \text{T} \qquad\quad \text{F F} \\ (((p \supset q) \supset r) \mathbin{\&} \quad \sim r) \supset \sim(p \supset q) \end{array}$$

By DTA (3a) and DTA (3c):

$$\begin{array}{c} \text{T} \quad \text{T T} \quad \text{F F} \quad \text{T} \\ (((p \supset q) \supset r) \mathbin{\&} \sim r) \supset \sim(p \supset q) \end{array}$$

By DTA (3d):

$$\begin{array}{c} \text{T} \quad \text{T T} \quad \text{F F} \quad \text{T} \\ (((p \supset q) \supset r) \mathbin{\&} \sim r) \supset \sim(p \supset q) \\ \text{F} \end{array}$$

And, since each occurrence of 'r' must have the same value:

$$\begin{array}{c} \text{T} \quad \text{T T} \quad \text{F F} \quad \text{T} \\ (((p \supset q) \supset r) \mathbin{\&} \sim r) \supset \sim(p \supset q) \\ \text{F} \quad\ \text{F} \end{array}$$

Now we look at the antecedent of the first conjunct of A's antecedent. We have been forced to assign F to 'r' and T to the entire first conjunct on the supposition that row R exists. By DTA (3d), it follows that the antecedent of this conjunct must also be false in row R:

$$\begin{array}{c} \text{F} \quad \text{T} \quad \text{T T} \quad \text{F F} \quad \text{T} \\ (((p \supset q) \supset r) \mathbin{\&} \sim r) \supset \sim(p \supset q) \\ \text{F} \quad\ \text{F} \end{array}$$

It is already clear that A is logically true, since '$p \supset q$' has contradictory values; nevertheless, by definition of *logical truth*, to show A to be logically true, it is necessary to show that there is no assignment **I** to the *sentence letters* contained in A under which it is false. Now, to make '$p \supset q$' false in the antecedent of the first conjunct of A's antecedent, **I** must assign truth to 'p' and falsity to 'q' in R:

$$\begin{array}{c} \text{F} \quad \text{T} \quad \text{T T} \quad \text{F F} \quad \text{T} \\ (((p \supset q) \supset r) \mathbin{\&} \sim r) \supset \sim(p \supset q) \\ \text{T} \quad \text{F} \quad\ \text{F} \quad\ \text{F} \end{array}$$

Consistently assigning these values throughout, we get

$$\begin{array}{c} \text{F} \quad \text{T} \quad \text{T T} \quad \text{F F} \quad \text{T} \\ (((p \supset q) \supset r) \mathbin{\&} \sim r) \supset \sim(p \supset q) \\ \text{T} \quad \text{F} \quad\ \text{F} \quad\ \text{F} \quad\ \text{T} \quad \text{F} \end{array}$$

Now, we see that in A's consequent, 'p' is true and 'q' false, whereas '$p \supset q$' is true. This is impossible according to DTA (3d). For if '$p \supset q$' is true under **I**, then **I** must assign 'p' falsity or 'q' truth. But 'p' is assigned truth and 'q' falsity in row R. Thus, if '$p \supset q$' were true in R, either 'p' or 'q' would have to be both true and false. But this contradicts our assumption that no sentence letter is ever assigned both truth values. We shall circle such an impossible assignment thus:

$$\begin{array}{c} \text{F} \quad\; \text{T} \quad\; \text{T} \quad\; \text{T} \;\; \text{F} \;\; \text{F} \quad\quad \text{T} \\ (((p \supset q) \supset r) \;\&\; {\sim}r) \supset {\sim}(p \supset q) \\ \text{T} \quad\; \text{F} \quad\; \text{F} \quad\quad \text{F} \quad\quad \text{T} \quad\; \text{F} \\ \text{F} \end{array}$$

to indicate that it follows from our supposition that there is a row R in which A is false that the assignment **I** under which A is false is contradictory—in other words, that "a row R in the truth table for A under which it comes out false" is one in which, *per impossible,* **I** assigns both truth and falsity to 'p' or 'q'. Hence there is no such R, and our supposition that A is not logically true is false. Since A is, therefore, logically true, the argument to which it corresponds is valid.

This conclusion is indicated by the circled contradictory assignment. Every fell-swoop must end either with a recorded assignment to the sentence letters comprising the sentence in question under which it is false or a circled contradictory assignment to one of the sentence letters, indicating that there is no row R in which consistent assignments to the sentence letters comprising the sentence in question render it false.[2]

[2] Note that there is only one possibility for falsity in the case of sentences of the forms $\sim A$, $A \supset B$, and $A \lor B$, so a single fell-swoop will suffice for showing whether there is *no* row R under which a sentence, all of whose complex components are of these forms, is false. (If there is only one possibility for falsity of a sentence and the supposition that it is false in a row R leads to contradiction, then clearly there is no row R in which the sentence is false.) But for sentences some of whose complex components are of the forms $A \& B$ or $A \equiv B$, a single fell-swoop *may* not suffice. The supposition that there is a row R under which, say, $A \equiv B$ is false has two subcases, corresponding to the two ways $A \equiv B$ can turn out to be false:

$$\begin{array}{ll} \quad\quad\; \text{F} & \quad\quad\quad\; \text{F} \\ \text{(a)} \quad A \equiv B & \text{(b)} \quad A \equiv B \\ \quad\quad \text{T} \;\; \text{F} & \quad\quad\quad \text{F} \;\; \text{T} \end{array}$$

To show that case (a) leads to contradiction is not to show there is *no* row in which $A \equiv B$ is false, only that the row in which A is assigned truth and B falsity is not such a row. There is still the other possibility to be investigated. There is no row R in which $A \equiv B$ is false if and only if both cases lead to contradiction. Similarly, there are three subcases for sentences of the form $A \& B$:

$$\begin{array}{lll} \quad\quad\; \text{F} & \quad\quad\quad\; \text{F} & \quad\quad\quad\; \text{F} \\ \text{(a)} \quad A \& B & \text{(b)} \quad A \& B & \text{(c)} \quad A \& B \\ \quad\quad \text{T} \;\; \text{F} & \quad\quad\quad \text{F} \;\; \text{T} & \quad\quad\quad \text{F} \;\; \text{F} \end{array}$$

This is not to say that more than one fell-swoop is required in all cases in which a sentence of one of these forms is a component of the sentence being tested, for there might not be more than one way to make the whole false even though there is more than one way to make a component false. Consider, for example, the following sentence:

$$\begin{array}{c} \quad\quad\; \text{F} \quad\; \text{F} \\ A \supset (B \equiv (A \equiv B)) \\ \text{T} \end{array}$$

There is only one way to make the antecedent true, so even though there are two ways to make the biconditionals in the consequent false, there is only one way to make the whole false. Thus, if the supposition that the whole is false leads to contradiction, then the sentence is logically true (as it happens to be).

3.1 Exercises

All of the following questions are based on your answers to the Exercises in Section 10.1 of Chapter 2 (p. 124).

1. Evaluate the arguments for Exercise 1.
★2. Evaluate the arguments for Exercise 2.
★3. Evaluate the arguments for Exercise 3.

4.

EXTENSION OF THE FELL-SWOOP METHOD

To evaluate arguments whose validity depends upon their quantificational structure, we must make use of DTA (2), DTA (4a), and DTA (4b). This does not mean that the method has to be extended to evaluate all arguments *containing* quantified sentences. The following argument, for example, contains quantified sentences, but its validity does not depend upon the inner structure of those sentences:

(1) *If all philosophers are tedious pedants, then if there are philosophers, then there are tedious pedants.*
(2) *All philosophers are tedious pedants.*
(3) *There are philosophers.*
(4) *Therefore, there are tedious pedants.*

To evaluate this argument, we need only to apply the fell-swoop method to its corresponding conditional, which, on the obvious scheme of abbreviation, is

$$\{[\{(x)(Px \supset Tx) \supset [(Ex)(Px) \supset (Ex)(Tx)]\}$$

with the following truth-value assignments shown: T above the main connective; T under $(x)(Px \supset Tx)$; T and F under $(Ex)(Px)$; F under $(Ex)(Tx)$;

$$\& (x)(Px \supset Tx) \& (Ex)(Px)\} \supset (Ex)(Tx)$$

with T over $(x)(Px \supset Tx)$, T over $(Ex)(Px)$, F over $(Ex)(Tx)$; T under the first ampersand and F under the final $(Ex)(Tx)$.

We see that there is no assignment to the constituent sentences under which the corresponding conditional is false; so it is a logical truth and the argument is shown to be valid.

The situation is quite different for a cousin to the foregoing argument:

(1) *All philosophers are tedious pedants.*
(2) *There are philosophers.*
(3) *Therefore, there are tedious pedants.*

In official standard form, using the obvious scheme of abbreviation, the argument is

(1) $(x)(Px \supset Tx)$
(2) $(Ex)Px$
(3) $\therefore (Ex)Tx$

This argument, like any other, is valid if and only if its corresponding conditional is logically true. It is valid. But the fell-swoop method, so far developed, is inadequate for showing this, for it appears possible to find an assignment under which it is false:

$$[(x)(Px \supset Tx) \& (Ex)(Px)] \supset (Ex)(Tx)$$

with T over $(x)(Px \supset Tx)$, F over $(Ex)(Tx)$; T under $(x)(Px \supset Tx)$, T under $(Ex)(Px)$, F under $(Ex)(Tx)$.

The corresponding conditional is false under the following assignment:

$$\mathbf{I}('(x)(Px \supset Tx)') = T$$
$$\mathbf{I}('(Ex)(Px)') = T$$
$$\mathbf{I}('(Ex)(Tx)') = F$$

The difficulty is that the logical truth of the foregoing sentence depends upon the inner structure of the constituent sentences and not merely upon the interpretations of '&' and '⊃'. The interpretations of '&' and '⊃' alone do not guarantee that there is no assignment to the syntactic parts of the sentence under which it comes out false. Thus more of the logical form must be exposed to show that such "assignments" as the above are impossible. This is done by "expanding" the embedded quantified sentences by means of DTA (4a) and DTA (4b).

Consider some arbitrary assignment **I** over a universe **U** of four entities. According to DTA (4a), premise (1) is true under **I** if and only if the result of replacing every free occurrence of 'x' in '$(Px \supset Tx)$' with a name of every e in **U** is true under **I**. Recall our assumption that every e in **U** has a name in the extended official idiom under every assignment. Let us choose 'a', 'b', 'c', and 'd' as names for the four elements in **U**. Now the result of replacing every free occurrence of 'x' in '$(Px \supset Tx)$' with a name of every e in **U** is the following list:

   (i) $Pa \supset Ta$
  (ii) $Pb \supset Tb$
 (iii) $Pc \supset Tc$
  (iv) $Pd \supset Td$

DTA (4a) says that premise (1) is true under **I** if and only if (i) is true under **I**, *and* (ii) is true under **I**, *and* (iii) is true under **I**, *and* (iv) is true under **I**. According to DTA (3c), this situation obtains just in case the following conjunction in the extended official idiom is true under **I**:

   (1') $(((Pa \supset Ta) \,\&\, (Pb \supset Tb)) \,\&\, (Pc \supset Tc)) \,\&\, (Pd \supset Td)$

This conjunction is the "expansion" of premise (1). It is true under **I** if and only if (1) is.

Now let us expand premise (2). By DTA (4b), (2) is true under **I** if and only if the result of replacing every free occurrence of 'x' in 'Px' with a name of some e in **U** is true under **I**. Now the result of replacing every occurrence of 'x' in 'Px' with a name of some e in **U** is the following list:

   (i) Pa
  (ii) Pb
 (iii) Pc
  (iv) Pd

DTA (4b) says that premise (2) is true under **I** if and only if at least (i) is true under **I**, *or* (ii) is true under **I**, *or* (iii) is true under **I**, *or* (iv) is true under **I**. According to DTA (3b), this situation obtains just in case the following alternation in the extended official idiom is true under **I**:

   (2') $((Pa \lor Pb) \lor Pc) \lor Pd$

The conclusion of the argument is expanded in the same way as premise (2), since both are existentially quantified. It is true under **I** just in case

(3′) $((Ta \lor Tb) \lor Tc) \lor Td$

is true under **I**.

Now the argument in question is such that for all assignments having universes with four elements, it is impossible for the premise sentences to be true and the conclusion sentence to be false if and only if the following conditions *cannot* simultaneously be met:

(1) $((((Pa \supset Ta) \& (Pb \supset Tb)) \& (Pc \supset Tc)) \& (Pd \supset Td))$ is true under **I**.
(2) $(((Pa \lor Pb) \lor Pc) \lor Pd)$ is true under **I**.
(3) $(((Ta \lor Tb) \lor Tc) \lor Td)$ is not true under **I**.

These conditions, in turn, cannot be met if and only if the following is a logical truth:

$$\{[(((((Pa \supset Ta) \& (Pb \supset Tb)) \& (Pc \supset Tc)) \& (Pd \supset Td))] \&$$
$$[(((Pa \lor Pb) \lor Pc) \lor Pd)]\} \supset (((Ta \lor Tb) \lor Tc) \lor Td)$$

This is the real conditional corresponding to the argument we are considering. To show it to be a logical truth, we have only to apply the fell-swoop method as before:

$$
\begin{array}{}
& T & T & T & T & T & T & T & T & T \\
\{[(((((Pa & \supset Ta) & \& (Pb & \supset Tb)) & \& (Pc & \supset Tc)) & \& (Pd & \supset Td))] & \& [(((Pa & \lor Pb) \\
& F & F & F & F & F & F & F & F & \boxed{\begin{array}{c}T\\F\end{array}} \quad F
\end{array}
$$

$$
\begin{array}{}
& T & T & F & F & F & F \\
& \lor Pc) & \lor Pd)]\} & \supset (((Ta & \lor Tb) & \lor Tc) & \lor Td) \\
& F & F & F & F & F & F
\end{array}
$$

Thus the corresponding conditional is logically true. It can be shown that if the corresponding conditional is logically true when the premises are expanded over domains of size 2^k, where k is the number of monadic (or one-place) predicate letters, then the argument is *valid*. This argument contains only two monadic predicate letters, so the fell-swoop above shows it to be valid.

The necessity for stipulating that the universe must be of size 2^k can be conveyed in the following way. Consider

(1) $(Ex)Fx$
(2) ∴$(x)Fx$

If we were to limit **U** to one element, we would discover that there are no assignments with universes of that size in which (1) is true and (2) false because all the expansions of these sentences over such universes have the form of

(1) Fa
(2) ∴Fa

Clearly, there are no assignments under which '*Fa*' is true and '*Fa*' false. But were we to consider a universe of two elements, we would easily find such an assignment:

(1) Fa v *Fb*
(2) *Fa* & *Fb*

Let **I** ('*Fa*') = T
　　I ('*Fb*') = F

Thus the argument is invalid.

To recapitulate: To determine whether a quantificational argument (containing only one-place predicates) is valid or invalid, it is sufficient to prove that its corresponding conditional is logically true upon the expansion of its constituent quantified sentences for a universe of 2^k entities. Thus to evaluate a quantificational argument containing k distinct one-place predicates, expand the universally quantified sentences it contains to 2^k conjuncts and expand the existentially quantified sentences it contains to 2^k alternations, then evaluate the corresponding conditional, so expanded, for logical truth by means of the fell-swoop method.

The evaluation method thus described provides a *decision procedure*; that is, it is a way of telling in a finite number of steps whether or not a quantified argument (containing only one-place predicates) is valid. There are, however, limitations to this decision procedure; it works only for quantificational arguments containing nothing but one-place predicates. We have not chosen a limited decision procedure when a more powerful one is available—it has been shown by Alonzo Church that there is no decision procedure for the entire class of quantificational arguments.[3] This does not mean, of course, that we shall never be able to tell whether or not an argument containing predicates of more than one place or names is valid. It means, rather, that there is no *mechanical* procedure which will tell with respect to any conceivable argument whether or not it is valid. To evaluate arguments for which there is no decision procedure, the informal method of Chapter 3 must be used. (In more advanced logic, formal techniques of an entirely different kind are developed in order to demonstrate the validity of such arguments. We have said nothing about these techniques in this text because that would have obscured the principal lesson of the text: For the purposes of clarifying reasoning, determination of the logical form of an argument is of vastly greater importance than determination of its validity or invalidity. Indeed, the advanced techniques also depend upon the correct characterization of the logical forms of arguments.)

4.1 Exercises

The following exercises are based on your answers to the Exercises in Section 15.1 of Chapter 2.

1. Evaluate the arguments for Exercise 1. Expand the quantifiers over a universe of two entities.

[3] Alonzo Church, *Introduction to Mathematical Logic* (Princeton, N.J.: Princeton University Press, 1954).

★2. Evaluate the arguments for Exercise 2. Expand the quantifiers over a universe of two entities.

★3. Evaluate the arguments for Exercise 3. Expand the quantifiers over a universe of two entities.

  4. Evaluate the arguments for Exercise 4. Expand the quantifiers over a universe of two entities.

★5. Evaluate the arguments for Exercise 5. Expand the quantifiers over a universe of two entities.

5.
SUMMARY OF IMPORTANT DEFINITIONS IN APPENDIX II

Where A is any sentence of the official idiom:

1. A is *logically true* if and only if A is true under all assignments **I**.
2. A is *logically false* if and only if A is false under all **I**.
3. A is *contingent* if and only if A is true under some **I** and A is false under some **I**.
4. The *conditional corresponding to* (an argument) **A** is the conditional sentence in the official idiom whose antecedent is the conjunction of **A**'s premises and whose consequent is **A**'s conclusion.
5. A *decision procedure* is a procedure for telling in a finite number of steps whether or not some thing has a given property (e.g., whether or not an argument is valid).

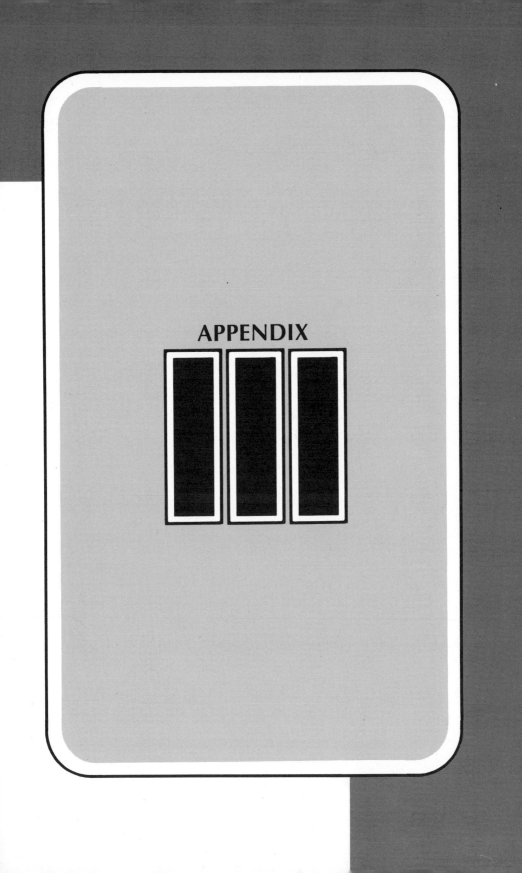
APPENDIX

Answers to Selected Exercises

CHAPTER 1
SECTION 1.1

3. No. Propositions do not belong to language at all. They are abstract things that are expressed by declarative sentences in various languages. Because the French speaker asserted the *same thing* as the English speaker, the proposition expressed by 'Le monde est rond' is the same as that expressed by 'The world is round.' The fact that these sentences belong to different languages is irrelevant.

6. The *simple* sentences 'Tom is tall' and 'Dick is short' express the same propositions in (a) and (b), but (a) and (b) *as wholes* express different propositions because the propositions expressed by 'Tom is tall' and 'Dick is short' are differently related. In particular, the proposition expressed by (a) will be false if it happens that Tom is tall but Dick is *not* short, whereas the proposition expressed by (b) may very well be true in that case. Since no proposition can be both true and false in the same circumstances, (a) expresses a different proposition than (b).

SECTION 2.1

5b. One cannot conclude anything about the validity or invalidity of **B** merely on the basis of this information; **B** is valid if and only if it *has a* valid form. Although the form it shares with **A** is not valid, it may or may not have some *other* valid form. If, however, **A** and **B** have in common the logical form that results from replacing *every* nonlogical phrase in their argument description(s) with an appropriate uppercase letter, '*A*', '*B*', and so on, then one *can* correctly conclude that **B** is invalid from the information that **A** is invalid.

6c. *A:* 'More fertilizer is produced from crude oil.'
B: 'The Green Revolution will succeed the Third World.'
C: 'We will cut back on petroleum from consumption in other forms.'
D: 'More fertilizer will be produced from crude oil.'

Argument Form:
(1) If *A*, then *B*.
(2) Either *C* or it is not the case that *D*.
(3) It is not the case that *C*.
(4) Therefore, it is not the case that *B*.

7c. Make the following replacements of sentences in argument description **C** on p. 21 in accordance with the form displayed in the above answer:

For 'More fertilizer is produced from crude oil' (i.e., *A*), put 'Steel floats'.

For 'The Green Revolution will succeed in the Third World' (i.e., *B*), put 'Wood floats'.

For 'We will cut back on petroleum consumption in other forms' (i.e., *C*), put 'Ostriches fly'.

For 'More fertilizer will be produced from crude oil' (i.e., *D*), put 'Ostriches fly'.

The result is

C' (1) If steel floats, then wood floats.
    (2) Either ostriches fly or it is not the case that ostriches fly.
    (3) It is not the case that ostriches fly.
    (4) Therefore, it is not the case that wood floats.

Because the argument expressed by this argument description, **C'**, has the same form as the original but also has true premises and a false conclusion, it is a counterexample to the original. Notice that whereas the original argument may *seem* valid because it *seems* that the right sort of "connection" holds between premises and conclusion, the counterexample makes it obvious that there is no such "connection."

8. If the argument in question is invalid, then, by definition of *validity* (p. 16), *there is* some (possibly unknown) replacement of the nonlogical phrases in its argument description with (perhaps different) nonlogical phrases such that the resultant argument description expresses an argument with true premises and a false conclusion. This latter argument has the same form as the original because it is the result of replacing the nonlogical phrases in the original argument description with (perhaps different) nonlogical phrases. By definition of *counterexample,* this is a counterexample to the original argument because it has the same form as the original and also has true premises and false conclusion. Thus, if one knows that an argument is invalid, then he knows, by definition of *validity, logical form,* and *counterexample,* that it has a counterexample even if no one is able to *produce* one.

SECTION 3.1

3. Circular arguments are always valid. It is not possible to replace all the nonlogical phrases in the argument description of a circular argument in such a way that results in another argument description with true premises and a false conclusion. Consider any replacement of the nonlogical phrases in the conclusion sentence, resulting in a false sentence. Then the very *same* replacement will have to be made for that same sentence when it appears among the premise sentences. Since this replacement makes the sentence in question false, it does not make all the premise sentences true. So, no replacement of nonlogical phrases in the argument description both makes the premise sentences true and the conclusion sentence false. A sound argument is a valid argument with true premises. Circular arguments are always valid. Therefore, any circular argument with true premises is sound.

4. If an argument is invalid, it does not make any difference what fallacy, formal or informal, is committed. If an argument is valid, it does not matter that it may also commit some informal "fallacy."

SECTION 4.1

1. This argument description probably does not represent an *actual* inference because in all likelihood, no one ever inferred what (3) expresses from what (1) and (2) express. Nevertheless, it represents a *possible* inference because it is possible for some one to make such an inference. It does not, in all probability, record an inference just because there is no actual inference for it to record. *If* some one made such an inference and if someone wrote down the argument description with the intention of representing that piece of reasoning, then the argument description *would* record the inference.

2. This is a perfectly good use of the word 'imply', but it is not the technical use of that word employed in the text. In the text, implication is a relation between propositions (or sets of propositions and propositions), whereas in this sentence 'imply' expresses a relation between a *person* and a proposition. In this use of the word, one probably has in mind something like the following: "That President Brewman *said* a certain thing is strong evidence that *he believes* a certain different thing or wants us to believe it." Notice that the *proposition* that no one presently employed by the University is engaged in classified research does not imply the proposition that some former employes of the university may have been so engaged.

SECTION 5.1

4d. False. If Jones's inference from A to B justifies a belief in B, then

(1) A implies B,

and

(2) Jones is justified in believing A.

If B is false, it follows from (1) that A is false. This, however, is consistent with Jones being justified in believing A, since we know that one can be justified in believing false propositions. Now Jones cannot be justified in simultaneously believing and disbelieving A. Since, by (2), he is justified in believing A, it is false that he is justified in disbelieving A.

SECTION 6.1

4. Yes. Someone might believe the conclusion of an argument merely on the basis of being sufficiently impressed with the presentation of the argument or because he trusted the person giving the argument always to give sound arguments. Yes, an argument could be used to test a hypothesis or explain something without also recording an inference. Recall the case involving the scientist's testing of the hypothesis that light has mass. He did not have to infer the conclusion of the argument; it would have sufficed for him to determine that *it would be correct* to infer the conclusion from the premises. Then if, for example, it turned out that Alpha Centauri was not observed to be in the appropriate position, he would know that his hypothesis was false.

CHAPTER 2
SECTION 1.1

1d.   This is not an argument in gross standard form because the conclusion is not numbered.

SECTION 2.1

2.   If it is "part of his argument" that living fetuses are experimented upon, this proposition is one of the premises or the conclusion. If it is a *relevant* contextual feature, then it helps one decide what the premises or conclusion are. Roberti's conclusion seems to be that experimentation on fetuses is wrong, but this admits of two interpretations. On the one hand, we could take him to be declaring only that it would be wrong to experiment on fetuses if it happened to occur to somebody to do it, or on the other hand that someone is now doing something wrong, namely experimenting on fetuses. To help decide which is Roberti's conclusion, we may note one contextual factor that clearly does seem to be at work. That is that the argument is given in a letter to the editor. This seems to indicate at least that Roberti *believes* that fetuses are being experimented upon; one does not normally write letters to the newspaper denouncing activities that would be immoral, without giving any thought to those persons, if there are any, who engage in them. The suggestion here is that very likely there is some practical point to Roberti's argument. That fetuses are experimented upon does, then, seem to be a *relevant* contextual feature, because it, together with the assumption that Roberti's writing to the newspaper shows that he is aware of this fact, helps us to decide between two possible conclusions that he might be arguing for. Further, these two contextual factors indicate that he *also* takes the proposition that fetuses are experimented upon as a premise of his argument. Note that although contextual features themselves are not premises or conclusions of arguments, there is no reason why statements reporting the presence of such factors should not be part of an argument.

One final point. Although Roberti does not explicitly say that experimentation on living fetuses is *wrong,* his argument would be absurd if he were not taken to endorse the additional premise that if something violates the Judeo-Christian ethic, then it is wrong. His remark that this ethic has "served our civilization well" is some evidence that he does endorse the needed premise. Roberti's argument is probably best represented in gross standard form as:

(1) Experimentation on living fetuses is a violation of the Judeo-Christian ethic.
(2) If something violates the Judeo-Christian ethic, then that is wrong.
(3) Someone is experimenting on living fetuses.
(4) Therefore, someone is doing something wrong in experimenting on living fetuses.

5.   b. (1) No one in his right mind would admire Hitler.
       (2) Wallace admires Hitler.
       (3) Therefore, Wallace is not in his right mind.
    e. (1) If you take the final, then you pass Professor Black's course.
       (2) If you pass his course, then you must take his final.

     (3) So, taking the final is both necessary and sufficient for passing his course.

h. (1) If number were an idea, then arithmetic would be psychology.

   (2) Arithmetic is psychology if and only if astronomy is psychology.

   (3) If astronomy is psychology, then astronomy is concerned with the ideas of the planets.

   (4) Astronomy is not concerned with the ideas of the planets.

   (5) Hence number is not an idea.

r. (1) A woman on welfare who has two illegitimate children can choose between going off welfare and having as many babies as she wants or staying on welfare and being sterilized.

   (2) If she can choose between these alternatives, then she has a free choice.

   (3) If she has a free choice, then if she chooses to stay on welfare, it is no imposition on her freedom to sterilize her.

   (4) Therefore, if she chooses to stay on welfare, it is no imposition on her freedom to sterilize her.

SECTION 3.1

3.   *Correct* paraphrases preserve logical form. In particular, any correct paraphrase of an argument into the official idiom will display as much of the logical form of that argument as the expressive power of the official idiom permits. Since the official idiom is more expressive, in this respect, than natural languages, paraphrase into the official idiom has the capacity to expose more of the logical form of arguments in a natural language that is apparent from their formulation in that natural language. The relationship between paraphrase and truth conditions is this: Any paraphrase of an English sentence into the official idiom preserving its truth conditions is *adequate*. A correct paraphrase is adequate, but the converse is not necessariy true.

SECTION 4.1

3.   c. Yes. 'p' and 'q' are sentences in the official idiom, by clause (1) of SOI (the definition of 'sentence in the official idiom'). '$(p \ \& \ q)$' is the result of applying clause (4b) to 'p' and 'q'; so it is a sentence in the official idiom.

   h. No. 'q' and 'p' are sentences in the official idiom, by clause (1) of SOI, but 'pq' is not the result of applying any of the clauses of SOI to 'q' and 'p'; hence, by the clause (6) of SOI, it is not a sentence in the official idiom.

   k. 'A' is not a sentence in the official idiom; so by clause (6) of SOI (k) is not a sentence in the official idiom. Recall that 'A' is a meta-variable—it *stands for* sentences in the official idiom.

SECTION 5.1

5.   'It is not the case that Tom is tall' has the same truth value as '$\sim p$' just in case 'Tom is tall' has the same truth value as 'p'. The truth *conditions* of a sentence differ from its truth *value* in the following way: The truth condi-

tions of a sentence are given by an association of all the possible combinations of truth values of the simple sentences it contains and the truth value of the whole sentence for each such combination.

SECTION 6.1

3. The truth conditions for (a), (b), and (c) are shown by the following truth table:

p	q	$p \& q$	(a) $\sim(p \& q)$	$\sim p$	$\sim q$	(b) $p \vee \sim q$	(c) $\sim p \& q$
T	T	T	F	F	F	T	F
T	F	F	T	F	T	T	F
F	T	F	T	T	F	F	T
F	F	F	T	T	T	T	F

Now '(It is not the case that San Francisco is in California) and San Francisco is in Nevada' is true if and only if both conjuncts are true. And the first conjunct is true just in case 'San Francisco is in California' is false. Thus the sentence is true just in case 'San Francisco is in California' is false and 'San Francisco is in Nevada' is true and it is false otherwise. These are the truth conditions for (c), so this is an adequate paraphrase for the English sentence as a whole. It seems to be a *correct* paraphrase also because the English sentence also has the form of the conjunction of a simple sentence and the negation of a simple sentence. (a) and (b) have the same truth conditions, so one is an *adequate* paraphrase if and only if the other is. In fact, both are inadequate because their truth conditions do not match those of the sentence in question.

4e. $(\sim q \& s) \supset (p \supset \sim r)$

SECTION 7.1

4.3. $\sim p$ (p: 'You should take logic'.)
4.6. p (p: 'Norman Mailer is illiterate'.)
4.25. $p \supset q$ (p: 'John is over 35'.; q: 'John can run for President'.)

SECTION 8.1

4.5. $p \supset q$ (p: 'You give us more funds'.; q: 'We'll improve the library'.)
6.6. A propositional connective is any phrase which, when attached to one or more sentences, creates another sentence. Thus 'Bismark said that . . .', 'Johnson thought . . .', and '. . . but ____' are propositional connectives. For example, When 'Bismark said that . . .' is attached to 'one can have guns or butter', the result is 'Bismark said that one could have guns or butter'.'____ but . . .' in this context clearly joins the two sentences about Bismark and Johnson; the sentence is a stylistic variant of one having the form $A \& B$. Now '. . . or ____' and '. . . and ____' and even 'It is possi-

ble that . . .' (for 'can') are also propositional connectives, but the internal structure of the two main conjuncts cannot be represented in the official idiom because 'Bismark said that . . .' and 'Johnson thought . . .' are non-truth-functional. The truth value of a sentence of the form 'Bismark said that A' is not determined solely by the truth value of A. Probably Bismark said some true things and some false things and failed to say some true and some false things. In other words, any truth value for 'Bismark said that A' is compatible with any truth value for A, so the connective is non-truth-functional. Since this is so, the entire sentence 'Bismark said that one could have guns or butter' has to be paraphrased as a sentence letter even though '. . . or ____' is functioning as a truth-functional sentence connective (i.e., 'one can have guns or one can have butter but not both'). Similar considerations apply for the second conjunct. Thus the sentence is paraphrased as 'p & q' (on the obvious scheme of paraphrase).

6.9. The connective is 'if . . . then ____' but the truth value of (9) is not determined solely by the falsity of the antecedent—that Gerald Ford is William Douglas. Rather the truth of this sentence, if indeed it is true, depends on the fact that William Douglas had nothing but contempt for Gerald Ford's attempt to impeach him.

SECTION 9.1

2. Where **A** and **B** are arguments in gross standard form, **A** is the same as **B** if and only if they have the same paraphrase into the official idiom (on the same scheme of abbreviation).

SECTION 10.1

2a. (1) $(p \vee q) \vee \sim r$
(2) $\therefore (\sim q \ \& \ r) \supset p$

  p: 'You fish early in the morning.'
  q: 'You fish in the evening'.
  r: 'You catch bass in August'.

3. e. (1) $p \supset q$
(2) $p \supset p$
(3) $\therefore (p \supset q) \ \& \ (q \supset p)$

  p: 'You take the final'.
  q: 'You pass Professor Black's course'.

  h. (1) $p \supset q$
(2) $q \equiv r$
(3) $r \supset s$
(4) $\sim s$
(5) $\therefore \sim p$

  p: 'Number is an idea'.
  q: 'Arithmetic is psychology'.
  r: 'Astronomy is psychology'.
  s: 'Astronomy is concerned with ideas of planets'.

SECTION 11.1

4. According to English grammar, 'men' in 'Men are mortal' is the grammatical subject, but the word corresponds to a predicate letter in the official idiom. The difference between the two treatments of the phrase is this: To treat 'men' as a predicate, as does the official idiom, makes clear what contribution it makes to the truth value of the sentence 'Men are mortal', whereas the treatment of this phrase as a grammatical subject, if anything, obscures this.

6. d. Yes. 'x' and 'y' are variables, 'F^2__' is a two-place predicate letter, so 'F^2xy' is a sentence in the official idiom, by SOI (1). Hence, by SOI (5b), '$(Ex)F^2xy$' is a sentence in the official idiom. Hence, by SOI (5b), '$(Ey)(Ex)F^2xy$' is also a sentence in the official idiom.

    h. 'F^3xy' is not a sentence in the official idiom, because it is not the result of applying any clause of SOI [in particular, SOI (1)] to 'F^3__', 'x', and 'y'. So, by SOI (6), (h) is not a sentence in the official idiom either.

    k. No. 'F' and 'G' are not sentences in the official idiom, so '$F \lor G$' is not the result of an application of any clause of SOI. Consequently, by SOI (6), (k) is not a sentence in the official idiom.

SECTION 12.1

2a. The truth conditions for (a) are as follows: (a) is true with respect to any universe **U** just in case some entity e in **U** is both a number and is even. Relative to **U'**, (a) is true because **U'** contains 2 and 4, which are even numbers. Relative to **U''**, (a) is also true because **U''** contains 4.

5g. (g) is true if and only if at least one alternate is true, that is, if '$(Ex)Fx$' is true relative to **U** or '$(x)x$' is true relative to **U**. Now, $(Ex)Fx$ is true relative to **U** if and only if there is some e in **U** such that the result of replacing 'x' in 'Fx' by the name of e is a true sentence. The Hudson is in **U** and the result of replacing 'x' in 'Fx' with a name of the Hudson, (namely, 'b') is the true sentence 'Fb'. Thus the first alternate is true and this, in turn, makes (g) true.

SECTION 13.1

4.6. $(Ex)(Fx \ \& \ \sim Gx)$
4.13. $(Ex)(Gx \ \& \ F^2ax)$
5.8. $(x)(Fx \lor Gx) \supset (F_1x \ \& \ G_1x)$ (F__: '. . . knows Mabel', G__: '. . . knows George', F_1__: '. . . admires Mabel', G_1__: '. . . hates George')
8.2. $(x)(\sim I^2xa \supset Fx)$ (I^2__: '. . . is identical to ____', a: 'John', F__:'. . . can have a drink')

SECTION 14.1

1.5. $(x)((Fx \lor Gx) \supset Hx)$ (F__: '. . . is a woman', G__: '. . . is a child', H__: '. . . will be rescued first')
1.17. $(x)((Fx \supset Gx) \ \& \ (Hx \supset G_1x))$($F$__: '. . . is an American', G__: '. . . likes beer', H__: '. . . is French', G_1__: '. . . drinks wine')
1.27. $\sim(Ex)(y)((Fx \ \& \ Fy) \ \& \ Gxy)$ (F__: '. . . is a number', G^2__: '. . . succeeds ____')

SECTION 15.1

2c.   (1) $(x)(Fx \supset (Gx \lor Hx))$
     (2) $(Ex)(Fx \,\&\, {\sim}Gx)$
     (3) $\therefore (Ex)(Fx \,\&\, Hx)$

     $F\_\_$: '. . . is an athlete'.
     $G\_\_$: '. . . is dumb'.
     $H\_\_$: '. . . is rich'.

3c.   (1) $(x)(Fx \supset Gx)$
     (2) Ga
     (3) $\therefore Fa$

     $F\_\_$: '. . . causes cancer'.
     $G\_\_$: '. . . is a public health menace'.
       a: 'smoking'
     (Note that 'smoking' is here taken as a *subject term* or *name* of the activity of habitual smoking. Why was 'smoking' not abbreviated as the predicate $H\_\_$: '. . . is an instance of smoking'?)

5b.   (1) $(x)(Fx \supset {\sim}Gx)$
     (2) Ga
     (3) $\therefore Fa$

     $F\_\_$: '. . . is in his right mind'.
     $G\_\_$: '. . . admires Hitler'.
       a: 'Wallace'

CHAPTER 3
SECTION 1.1

1.   No. Argument **C** is not a counterexample to **A,** although they share form **B** because **C** does not represent a way of assigning propositions to the sentence letters in **A**'s more detailed paraphrase in official standard form, namely,
     (1) $p \supset q$
     (2) p
     (3) $\therefore q$

     according to which the resulting argument would have true premises and a false conclusion.

SECTION 2.1

4.   No. The universe of an assignment contains only *existent* entities, and neither Sherlock Holmes nor his brother exists (or ever existed).

5e. $\langle 2, 1, 4 \rangle$, $\langle 4, 2, 6 \rangle$, $\langle 4, 1, 6 \rangle$

6g.   vii

SECTION 3.1

2d.   '$p \equiv {\sim}p$' is false under all three assignments.

3vi.   '$(x)(Ey)H^2xy$' (intuitively, 'Every number is larger than some number') is false under **I** (intuitively, because 1 is not larger than any number in **U**). This can be seen as follows: '$(x)(Ey)H^2xy$' is true under **I** if and only if '$(Ey)H^2a_1y$' and '$(Ey)H^2a_2y$' and '$(Ey)H^2a_3y$' and '$(Ey)H^2a_4y$' are all true under **I**, by DTA (4a). Now consider the first of these sentences, namely, '$(Ey)H^2a_1y$'. This sentence is true under **I** if and only if '$H^2a_1a_1$' or '$H^2a_1a_2$' or '$H^2a_1a_3$' or '$H^2a_1a_4$' is true under **I**, by DTA (4b). But *none* of these sentences is true under **I** because none of the ordered pairs $\langle 1, 1 \rangle$, $\langle 1, 2 \rangle$, $\langle 1, 3 \rangle$, or $\langle 1, 4 \rangle$ belongs to the set $\{\langle x, y \rangle : x, y \text{ belong to } \mathbf{U} \text{ and } x \rangle y\}$. Thus '$(Ey)H^2ay$' is false under **I**. But then not all of the preceding existentially quantified sentences that result from replacing 'x' in '$(Ey)H^2xy$' by a name of some e in **U** are true. But then, by DTA (4a), '$(x)(Ey)H^2xy$' must be false under **I**.

SECTION 4.1

2a. (1) $(p \lor q) \lor {\sim}r$
     (2) $\therefore ({\sim}q \ \& \ r) \supset p$

STEP (1). Suppose that there is an assignment **I** under which

(a) '$(p \lor q) \lor {\sim}r$' is true, and
(b) '$({\sim}q \ \& \ r) \supset p$' is false.

(Assumption for indirect evaluation)

STEP (2). Then

(a) '${\sim}q \ \& \ r$' is true under **I**, and
(b) 'p' is false under **I**.

[from step (1b) by DTA (3c)]

STEP (3). So

(a) '${\sim}q$' is true under **I**, and
(b) 'r' is true under **I**.

[from step (1) by DTA (3c)]

STEP (4). But then 'q' is false under **I**.

[from step (3a) by DTA (3a)]

STEP (5). '$p \lor q$' is false under **I**.

[from steps (2b) and (4) by DTA (3b)]

STEP (6). '${\sim}r$' is false under **I**.

[from step (3b) by DTA (3a)]

STEP (7). So '$(p \lor q) \lor {\sim}r$' is false under **I**.

[from steps (5) and (6) by DTA (3b)]

STEP (8). Step (6) contradicts step (1a), so the argument is valid.

3e. (1) $p \supset q$
     (2) $q \supset p$
     (3) $\therefore (p \supset q) \ \& \ (q \supset p)$

STEP (1).   There is an assignment **I** such that
    (a) '$p \supset q$' is true under **I**.
    (b) '$q \supset p$' is true under **I**.
    (c) '$(p \supset q)$ & $(q \supset p)$; is false under **I**.
                                   (Assumption for indirect evaluation)

STEP (2).   '$(p \supset q)$ & $(q \supset p)$' is true under **I**.

               [steps (1a) and (1b) by DTA (3c)]

STEP (3).   Step (2) contradicts the assumption for indirect evaluation [namely, step (1c)], so the argument is valid.

3h.   (1) $p \supset q$
       (2) $q \equiv r$
       (3) $r \supset s$
       (4) $\sim s$
       (5) $\therefore \sim p$

STEP (1).   There is an assignment **I** such that
    (a) '$p \supset q$' is true under **I**.
    (b) '$q \equiv r$' is true under **I**.
    (c) '$r \supset s$' is true under **I**.
    (d) '$\sim s$' is true under **I**.
    (e) '$\sim p$' is false under **I**.

STEP (2).   's' is false under **I**.

               [from step (1d) by DTA (3a)]

STEP (3).   'r' is false under **I**.

               [from steps (1c) and (2) by DTA (3d)]

STEP (4).   'q' is false under **I**.

               [from steps (1b) and (3) by DTA (3e)]

STEP (5).   'p' is false under **I**.

               [from steps (1a) and (4) by DTA (3d)]

STEP (6).   'p' is true under **I**.

               [from step (1e) by DTA (3a)]

STEP (7).   Steps (5) and (6) are contradictory, so the argument is valid.

SECTION 5.1

2c.   (1) $(x)(Fx \supset (Gx \lor Hx))$
       (2) $(Ex)(Fx$ & $\sim Gx)$
       (3) $\therefore (Ex)(Fx$ & $Hx)$

STEP (1). There is an assignment **I** (with universe **U**) such that
   (a) '$(x)(Fx \supset (Gx \vee Hx))$' is true under **I**.
   (b) '$(Ex)(Fx \And \sim Gx)$' is true under **I**.
   (c) '$(Ex)(Fx \And Hx)$' is false under **I**.

STEP (2).   '$Ft \supset (Gt \vee Ht)$' is true under **I** for all t.

   [from step (1a) by DTA (4a) and (C)]

STEP (3).   '$Ft_1 \And \sim Gt_1$' is true under **I** for some t_1.

   [from step (1b) by DTA (4a) and (C)]

STEP (4).   '$Ft_2 \And Ht_2$' is false under **I** for some t_2.

   [from step (1c) by DTA (4a) and (C)]

3c.   (1) $(x)(Fx \supset Gx)$
       (2) Ga
       (3) $\therefore Fa$

STEP (1).   There is an assignment **I** (with universe **U**) such that
   (a) '$(x)(Fx \supset Gx)$' is true under **I**.
   (b) 'Ga' is true under **I**.
   (c) 'Fa' is false under **I**.

STEP (2).   '$Ft \supset Gt$' is true under **I** for all t.

   [from (1a) by C]

STEP (3).   Counterexample:

   Let **U** = $\{1, 2, 3\}$.
   Let **I** assign 1 to every subject letter [e.g., **I**('a') = 1].

   I('$F\_\_$') = $\{2, 3\}$
   I('$G\_\_$') = $\{1\}$

Notice that 'Fa' is false under **I**, by DTA (2), for the entity e in **U** that **I** assigns to 'a' (namely, 1) does not belong to the set **I** assigns to '$F\_\_$' (namely, $\{2, 3\}$). 'Ga' is true under **I** because **I**('a') = 1 and 1 belongs to **I**('$G\_\_$'), or $\{1\}$. Finally, $(x)(Fx \supset Gx)$' is true under **I** because 'Ft' is false for every subject letter t. Hence '$Ft \supset Gt$' is true for every subject letter t and, by DTA (4a), '$(x)(Fx \supset Gx)$' is true under **I**.

5b.   (1) $(x)(Fx \supset \sim Gx)$
       (2) Ga
       (3) $\therefore \sim Fa$

STEP (1).   There is an assignment **I** such that
   (a) '$(x)(Fx \supset \sim Gx)$' is true under **I**.

(b) *'Ga'* is true under **I**.
(c) *'~Fa'* is false under **I**.

STEP (2).   *'Fa'* is true under **I**.

[from step (1c) by DTA (3a)]

STEP (3).   *'Ft ⊃ ~Gt'* is true under **I** for all *t*.

[from step (1a) by DTA (4a) and (C)]

STEP (4).   *'~Ga'* is true under **I**.

[from steps (2) and (3) by DTA (3d)]

Notice that one of the subject letters *t* mentioned in step (3) is *'a'*.

STEP (5).   *'Ga'* is false under **I**.

[from step (4) by DTA (3a)]

STEP (6).   Step (5) contradicts step (1b), so the argument is valid.

APPENDIX II
SECTION 1.1

1e.   This sentence contains three distinct sentence letters, so three assignment columns are required (one for each sentence letter).

3e.   Valuation columns are required for the following complex components of (4e):   *'p ⊃ q'*,   *'(p ⊃ r'*,   *'p ⊃ r'*,   *'q ⊃ r'*,   *'(p ⊃ r) v (q ⊃ r)*,   *'((p ⊃ q) ⊃ r) ≡ ((p ⊃ r) v (q ⊃ r))'* (i.e., six columns in all).

4e.   Since (4e) contains three distinct sentence letters, $2^3 = 8$ rows are required.

5e.

p	*q*	*r*	*p ⊃ q*	*(p ⊃ q) ⊃ r*	*p ⊃ r*	*q ⊃ r*	*(p ⊃ q)* v (q ⊃ r)	*((p ⊃ q) ⊃ r)* ≡ ((p ⊃ r) v (q ⊃ r))
T	T	T	T	T	T	T	T	T
T	T	F	T	F	F	F	F	T
T	F	T	F	T	T	T	T	T
T	F	F	F	T	F	T	T	T
F	T	T	T	T	T	T	T	T
F	T	F	T	F	T	F	T	T
F	F	T	T	T	T	T	T	T
F	F	F	T	F	T	T	T	T

SECTION 3.1

2a.   (1) *(p v q) v ~r*
(2) ∴*(~q & r) ⊃ p*

Corresponding conditional: '$((p \lor q) \lor {\sim}r) \supset (({\sim}q \& r) \supset p)$'
Evaluation:

$$
\begin{array}{ccccc}
\text{T} & \text{T} & \text{F} & \text{T} & \text{F} \\
 & \text{F} & & \text{T} & \\
\end{array}
$$

$$((p \lor q) \lor {\sim}r) \supset (({\sim}q \& r) \supset p)$$

$$
\begin{array}{ccccccc}
\text{F} & \text{F} & \text{T} & & \text{F} & \text{T} & \text{F} \\
 & \text{T} & & & & & \\
\end{array}
$$

3e. (1) $p \supset q$
      (2) $q \supset p$
      (3) $\therefore (p \supset q) \& (q \supset p)$

Corresponding conditional: '$((p \supset q) \& (q \supset p)) \supset ((p \supset q) \& (q \supset p))$'
Evaluation:

$$
\begin{array}{ccccccc}
 & \text{T} & \text{T} & \text{T} & \text{F} & \text{T} & \text{F} & \text{F} \\
\end{array}
$$
Case (1): $((p \supset q) \& (q \supset p)) \supset ((p \supset q) \& (q \supset p))$
$$
\begin{array}{ccc}
\text{T} & \text{F} & \text{T} \quad \text{F} \\
\text{F} & & \\
\end{array}
$$

$$
\begin{array}{ccccccc}
\text{T} & \text{T} & \text{T} & \text{F} & \text{F} & \text{F} & \text{T} \\
\end{array}
$$
Case (2): $((p \supset q) \& (q \supset p)) \supset ((p \supset q) \& (q \supset p))$
$$
\begin{array}{cc}
\text{T} \quad \text{F} & \text{T} \quad \text{F} \\
\text{T} & \\
\end{array}
$$

$$
\begin{array}{ccccc}
\text{T} & & \text{F} & \text{F} & \text{F} \quad \text{F} \\
\end{array}
$$
Case (3): $((p \supset q) \& (q \supset p)) \supset ((p \supset q) \& (q \supset p))$
$$
\begin{array}{ccc}
\text{T} \quad \text{F} & \text{T} \quad \text{F} & \text{T} \quad \text{F} \\
\text{T} & & \\
\end{array}
$$

3h. (1) $p \supset q$
      (2) $q \equiv r$
      (3) $r \supset s$
      (4) ${\sim}s$
      (5) $\therefore {\sim}p$

Corresponding conditional: $((((p \supset q) \& (q \equiv r)) \& (r \supset s)) \& {\sim}s) \supset {\sim}p$
Evaluation:

$$
\begin{array}{cccccccc}
\text{T} & \text{T} & \text{T} & \text{T} & \text{T} & \text{T} & & \text{F} \\
 & & & & & \text{T} & & \text{F} \\
\end{array}
$$

$$((((p \supset q) \& (q \equiv r)) \& (r \supset s)) \& {\sim}s) \supset {\sim}p$$

$$
\begin{array}{cccccccc}
\text{T} & \text{F} & \text{F} & \text{F} & \text{F} & \text{F} & \text{F} & \text{T} \\
\text{F} & & & & & & & \\
\end{array}
$$

SECTION 4.1

2c. $(((Fa \supset (Ga \lor Ha)) \& (Fb \supset (Gb \lor Hv))) \& ((Fa \& Ga) \lor (Fb \& Gb))) \supset$
$$((Fa \& Ha) \lor (Fb \& Hb))$$

Note that there are nine ways the consequent can be made false. Since there are no fewer ways the antecedent can be made true, nine fell-swoops are required. This may seem inconvenient, but note that if a full truth table were used, $2^6 = 128$ rows would be required. The consequent has the form $(A \& B) \lor (C \& D)$. For this to be false both alternates must be false. Each alternate can be made false in three ways, and each way of making one false is independent of the various ways of falsifying the other. Hence there are $3 \times 3 = 9$ ways the sentence can be falsified. In fact, this argument is valid. For illustrative purposes we give one of the nine fell swoops:

$$
\begin{array}{}
\quad\ T \qquad\qquad\quad T \quad\ T \qquad\qquad\quad T \\
(((Fa\ \supset\ (Ga\ \lor\ Ha))\ \&\ (Fb\ \supset\ (Gb\ \lor\ Hb)))\ \&\ ((Fa\ \&\ Ga) \\
\quad\ F \qquad\qquad F \qquad F \qquad\qquad\quad\ F \qquad\quad F
\end{array}
$$

$$
\begin{array}{}
\qquad\qquad\qquad T \qquad\qquad\ F \quad\ F \quad\ F \quad\ F \\
\lor\ (Fb\ \&\ Gb)))\ \supset\ ((Fa\ \&\ Ha)\ \lor\ (Fb\ \&\ Hb)) \\
\qquad\qquad\qquad (F) \qquad\qquad\ F \quad\ F \quad\ F \quad\ F \\
\qquad\qquad\qquad (T)
\end{array}
$$

3c.

$$
\begin{array}{}
\qquad\ T \quad\ T \quad\ T \quad\ T \quad\ F \\
(((Fa\ \supset\ Ga)\ \&\ (Fb\ \supset\ Gb))\ \&\ Ga)\ \supset\ Fa \\
\qquad F \quad\ T \quad\ T \quad\ T \quad\ T \quad\ F
\end{array}
$$

Counterexample: $\mathbf{I}('Fa') = F$
                   $\mathbf{I}('Ga') = T$
                   $\mathbf{I}('Fb') = T$
                   $\mathbf{I}('Gb') = T$

5b.

$$
\begin{array}{}
\qquad\ T \quad\quad\ T \qquad\qquad\quad T \quad\ F \\
\qquad\ F \qquad\qquad\qquad\qquad\qquad\qquad F \\
(((Fa\ \supset\ {\sim}Ga)\ \&\ (Fb\ \supset\ {\sim}Gb))\ \&\ Ga)\ \supset\ {\sim}Fa \\
(T) \qquad\quad T \qquad\qquad\qquad\qquad\ T \quad\ T \\
(F)
\end{array}
$$

Index